T0301058

DO YOUR BEST

how to be a SCOUT

DO YOUR BEST

how to be a SCOUT

by BEAR GRYLLS

HODDER &
STOUGHTON

First published in Great Britain in 2023 by Hodder & Stoughton
An Hachette UK Company

4

A CIP catalogue record for this title is available from the British Library

Hardback ISBN 978 1 399 80987 0
ebook ISBN 978 1 399 80988 7

Design and Art Direction: Nicky Barneby, BARNEBY *design & art direction*
Text illustration: Rachel Akerman
Cover illustration: Eleanor Crow
Editing: Jo Stockdale and Jessica Lacey

Printed and bound in Italy by L.E.G.O Spa

Hodder & Stoughton policy is to use papers that are natural, renewable and recyclable products and made from wood grown in sustainable forests. The logging and manufacturing processes are expected to conform to the environmental regulations of the country of origin.

Hodder & Stoughton Ltd
Carmelite House
50 Victoria Embankment
London EC4Y 0DZ

www.hodder.co.uk
www.scout.org
www.scouts.org.uk
www.beargrylls.com

About Me

My name ....

My Scout group ....

My Patrol/team ....

My superpower ....

My pet(s) ....

My favourite snack ....

My ideal adventure ....

My big dream ....

THIS IS ME

TO THE SCOUT IN ALL OF US.

May that Scouting spirit and
those enduring friendships never die.

Contents

PART THREE

How to be **YOU**

USEFUL STUFF THAT JUST MIGHT COME IN HANDY

Welcome

This isn't my book, it's your book.

It's a book to be read in a tent during a rainstorm, on a minibus on the way to the mountains, or on a raft drifting down a river. Or just to keep at your bedside. It's not like an ordinary book. If it gets a little torn, bashed about a bit and smells slightly of woodsmoke, then that's OK. It's doing its job.

In these pages you'll find some incredible stories of adventure, courage and survival. You'll find some amazing people to look up to. One day, people will look up to you too.

Think of this book as a friend who has walked the path ahead of you, and will guide you along the way. Keep it with you on your journey. There'll be incredible moments when you feel you can do anything. There'll also be tough times when you won't know what to do.

This is where this book can help you out.

It's stuffed full of practical advice (just like a rucksack bursting at the seams). You'll find out how to make a shelter, how to lead a team, how to dig a snow hole, make a fire and create a distress signal. It's everything you need all in one place. Just like that pack on your back when you're heading off into the hills with the sun shining on your face.

This is your book, so you should read it your way. You can start at the beginning, the middle or the end. It's totally up to you. I've divided things up into three main sections: How to be a Scout, How to be an Adventurer and How to be You. I might also signpost you back to some useful things in a different part of the book. You can skip ahead to the camping section if you want to, and save other bits for later (I won't tell anyone), or you can read a chapter when you need it – like How to be a camp cook or How to find your way.

Because it's a book you might keep for many years (or even forever), you might want to save some chapters for when you're older. Or you can gobble it all up in one go. Like homemade banana ice cream. But above all, read it your way.

So who are the Scouts? Well, first, we're a family. In fact, we're one of the biggest families the world has ever seen. There are 57 million of us around the world, all learning skills, exploring the outdoors and helping others. Scouts are friends to all and have courage in all difficulties.

You might be a Scout already, or perhaps you're just thinking about becoming one. Scouts isn't something you do, it's something you are. It's about always looking ahead, doing your best and, of course, being prepared. Scouts like to look on the bright side. We don't call rain, rain. We call it Scouting sunshine! We know that every day is what we make of it.

By reading this book, you're already part of the Scouts family. (Welcome!) We're open to everyone, no matter what you believe in or what your gender or background is. We're all different and that's what makes us strong. It's what makes us interesting. It's what makes us Scouts.

Scouts is a home for all, a place to find your feet and your place in the world. Life is a great adventure, and you're the only person who'll decide which way it will go. This book will give you the courage to grab those opportunities and to shine brightly.

There'll be tough times, when you feel like you're on your own. That might be one of the times to look at these pages and feel better about things. It's OK not to feel OK sometimes. It's OK to struggle, and sometimes to fall down – it's about picking yourself up again that counts, in the longer game of life.

This is a book for anyone who is a Scout, was a Scout or wants to be a Scout. Everyone's welcome around our campfire. Here's to your journey. Remember, if you lose your way, it all comes down to three things (just like the three fingers in our Scout salute): courage (when it matters), kindness (in everything) and developing and strengthening that 'never give up' spirit inside us all.

Your friend,

Bear Grylls
Chief Ambassador of World Scouting

You Only Get One Shot at Life. Make it Count.

Get out in the sunshine. Get out in the rain. Learn the names of things. Know the trees, the stars and the people in your street. Learn to say thank you in ten languages.

Learn how to start a fire and put it out. Make things. Share things. Find out where you fit in and feel happiest. Do what you love. Make other people happy but make time for yourself too. Brew tea on a mountainside. Drink soup in the rain. Fall asleep smelling of woodsmoke.

Find people you like. Find people nothing like you (we learn the most from them). Dream big and ask for little. If someone shows you how to do something, listen. Practise. Get good. Then pass it on. Remember to say thank you. Write them a card.

Swim in the ocean. Feel the salt on your skin and the wind in your hair. Look up at the stars but keep your feet on the ground. Fall off bicycles and dance on beaches. Sleep on a hillside in a bivvy bag and a woolly hat. Watch the sun rise over the sea.

Close gates. Open doors. Be kind to animals and give away your change. Help other people. Build them up (it always makes you shine brighter).

Eat fruit but save room for the occasional marshmallow (and remember they taste better nearly burnt). Chop enough wood. Give yourself some slack. Learn to do things properly. How we do anything, is how we do everything.

Don't be afraid to make a fool of yourself. Be good. Be kind. Eat plums. Have fun. Stop shopping and start living. Never pass up good advice. Remember what goes around comes around.

Stand up for what you believe in but remember to listen more than you speak. Keep an open mind. Never be afraid to admit you're wrong (people will respect you more for it). Be there when someone needs you and they'll never forget it. Never be afraid to ask for help. Keep learning, keep smiling and keep looking to the horizon. That's where the future begins.

Most of all, don't count the days. Make the days count. In Scouts, this is what we do. We keep learning. We look after each other. We show courage in the big moments. And the small ones. We know the power of a kind deed. It's why we love to help other people.

We have fun. We don't just do badges, we do memories. We do adventures.

After all, adventure is a state of mind.

PART ONE

How to be a

SCOUT

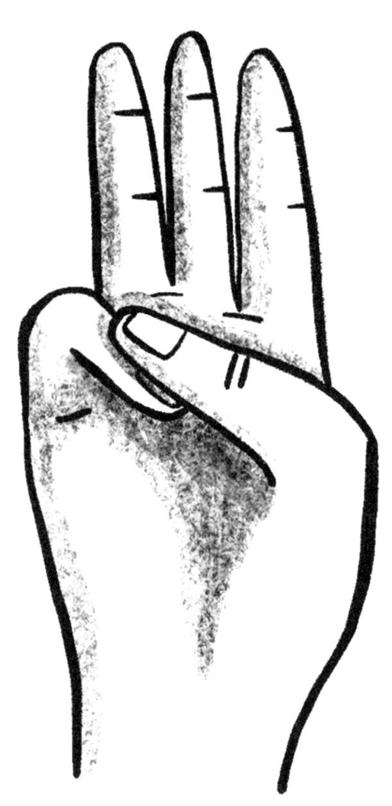

How to be

PART OF OUR WORLDWIDE FAMILY

THERE ARE MILLIONS OF SCOUTS across the globe. All of us are different, but we're united by our promise. Like any family, we look out for each other. We're there in the good times and the tough times too. Scouts are all ages, but our spirit of kindness and courage never gets old. We like to say: 'Once a Scout, always a Scout.'

What Is a Scout?

That's a big question, isn't it? Well, luckily, there's a short answer. It's a person who does their best and helps other people.

Take away the badges, the neckerchief, uniform, special belts, decorations, woggles, hats and medals and you're still a Scout. In prisoner-of-war camps during the Second World War, Scouts and former Scouts got together and formed secret Scout troops. They made badges out of bottle tops and bits of sackcloth. They whispered their promise so the guards couldn't hear them.

As long as you have courage and kindness, that spirit of adventure and a spark of mischief, you're a Scout. It's a fire inside that no one can put out, no matter how hard they try.

Scouts are quick to smile and slow to complain. We like to do things well, learn new skills and take pride in everything we do. We share our skills with others. When things don't go well, we start again. We know that cheerfulness counts for a lot, especially if it's cold and we can't get the fire going.

It's probably fair to say we love the outdoors more than most (rarely indoors since 1907, if you want to put a date on it). We know that a night under the stars beats a night inside any day of the week. Even if it rains.

Scouts are curious too. We always want to know what's around the next bend, over the next hill or beyond the next horizon. It's that curiosity that drives us on. We can trek for miles, scoff a pan of grub and then collapse happily into a tent at the end of the day.

We love the smell of woodsmoke. We eat more marshmallows than is maybe good for us. But we earn our treats. We work hard and do good things.

We love the natural world, but we know we're responsible for it too. We take care not to harm it, reusing and recycling. We lobby world leaders to make the right calls for our planet, and we do our bit too. When we camp, we leave nothing behind but our thanks, and we take nothing away except memories.

When people are in distress or need our help, we're there for them. We're proud to say that over a century of Scouting, we've supported refugees, run immunisation programmes and delivered aid to disaster zones. We've fundraised, hiked the distance to the moon (and back) and raced round the world, all to help other people.

Scouts are strong on our own, but together we're invincible. We'll build you a bridge out of old crates and a tower out of wooden poles. We know almost every knot ever invented, and a few more besides. (And if we don't know our knots, we know to do lots!) We have badges and plenty of tricks up our sleeves. We know how to light a fire with a block of ice and how to cook an egg in an orange (not kidding!).

Above all, never underestimate a Scout.

A Scout is a friend to all. We make people feel welcome. If there's a party, everyone gets invited. If there's a campfire, everyone gets a treat. We're kind to animals and look after our possessions. We're good at fixing things.

Remember, when you make your promise to do your best, you become a member of a worldwide family of Scouts. When one Scout meets another anywhere in the world, they greet them like a brother or sister. And probably swap a badge or two.

But here's the thing: you never unmake your promise. No matter how old you grow, or far you travel, that Scout inside you will always be there. That bright-eyed young person who nervously raised their hand to make the Scout promise all those years ago is still there. Scouts is not something you do, it's something you are.

Being a Scout brings out the best in us. When we get together with Scouts across the world, we dream of a better future for our planet, and peace between the peoples.

What Do Scouts Do?

We bring people and communities together. It's about friendships first. That might seem old-fashioned, but it never goes out of fashion. Those friendships reach across cultures, faiths, races, beliefs and gender. It's all rooted in respect for yourself and respect for others.

Scouting is also a character factory. It teaches young people that there's more to life than having the latest trainers or jacket. It encourages the idea that we'll only really be happy if we work together, push our limits and do our best to help other people.

Good character is not formed in a week or a month. It's created little by little, day by day. This is exactly how we work in Scouting – offering activities on a weekly basis that make us think, develop and grow.

We teach young people to dig deep and go the extra mile. Life is really very simple: what we put in is what we get out. And nowhere is that more true than in Scouting.

Scouting is also there to inspire us to get into the outdoors. Nature is a language that can be learnt. Once you identify a beech tree, tie a clove hitch or cook a simple meal over a fire that you've built yourself, you'll never forget it. There's nothing quite like setting up your tent (even in the rain), getting a fire going and – most importantly of all – starting to cook. It's scientifically proven that sausages taste better when cooked outside at camp.

The Scout Promise

All 57 million Scouts around the world make a promise. This is a commitment to do your best and do your duty. You make it when you're invested in Scouting. This is the day you get your World Membership Badge and neckerchief and officially become a Scout. At the same time, Scouts make the Scout sign, holding up three fingers of their right hand, each finger representing a different part of the promise. The words change a little from country to country, but the three key things are about doing your best, doing your duty and helping other people.

At World Scout Jamborees, tens of thousands of Scouts make their promise at the same time, all using their own words, in their own languages. It's an amazing feeling being part of this, and it reminds us we're all part of one family.

We take an oath to be kind and helpful – simple values, but values that endure, and that's how, together, we change the world. Every child has the right to an adventure. Life is about grabbing opportunities. The prizes don't always go to the biggest, the best and the strongest – they go to those who persevere. These are simple life lessons that Scouting teaches.

The Scout Motto

BE PREPARED

This famous motto was invented by the founder of the Scouts, Robert Baden-Powell (based on his initials). It's about being ready for anything that life might throw at you. Learn skills like teamwork, leadership, resilience, problem-solving and initiative and you'll be prepared to face the world. The good news is that you learn all of these things in Scouts, without even noticing. Write it on your pencil case.

The Scout Neckerchief

The cloth Scouts wear around their neck isn't just for decoration. It tells people we're part of a worldwide family of Scouts. While there are many different colours, patterns and designs, the neckerchief shows we belong to one family of Scouts. But in an emergency, it can also double up as a bandage, a sling or even a belt.

Now admittedly, some of us call it a scarf, or necker, while some call it a neckerchief. In Scotland, they call it a neckie. In Brazil, it's called a *lenço*. In fact, it doesn't matter what we call it. It's a symbol of togetherness and it's the way Scouts are recognised everywhere they go.

While the neckerchief has been around from the very beginning, the famous 'woggle' (used to keep your neckerchief in place) has only been with us since the 1920s. Some say that the woggle was invented at Gilwell Park, the home of Scouting, in Epping Forest, southeast England. Bill Shankley, one of the leaders at Gilwell, is said to have used the word 'woggle' in the same way we use the word 'widget', to describe a gadget that doesn't have a name yet.

How to Roll Your Neckerchief: Method 1

1. Lay your neckerchief out flat on a table, with the wide end nearest to you, and the point furthest away from you.
2. Smooth out any bumps or folds.
3. Now start to roll the scarf from the wide end towards the point. Flatten any part of the scarf that isn't smooth with your hands.
4. Try and keep the roll as tight as possible.
5. Keep going until you have a triangle left over that is around the width of your handspan.
6. Carefully, gather up the neckerchief and hang it around your neck, with the small triangle behind you, with the two long parts dangling in front of you.
7. Tidy up the ends so the pattern is even on both sides.
8. Secure with a woggle, or tie a friendship knot.

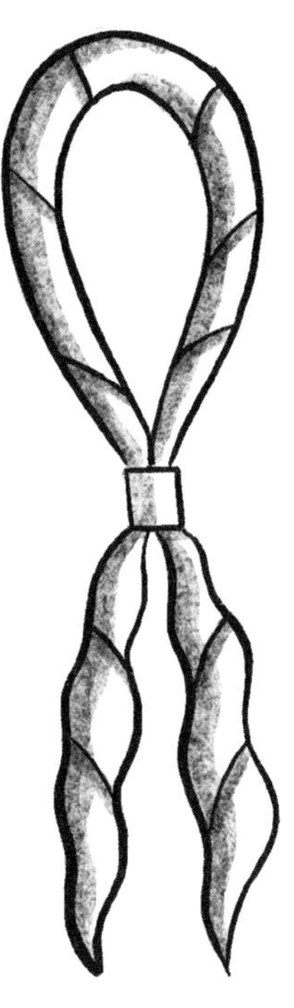

How to Roll Your Neckerchief: Method 2

1. Hold your unfolded neckerchief out in front of you with the point facing downwards.
2. Grip the two points at the wide end in your fingertips and pull outwards so it's tight. This should resemble an upside-down triangle.
3. Now flick the point forwards over the top several times, keeping the two wide ends stretched out at either side.
4. The neckerchief should now be rolled, with just a small triangle left over.
5. Tidy up the two sides so the pattern is even.
6. Put on your neckerchief and keep it in place with a woggle or friendship knot.

How to Use Your Neckerchief in an Emergency

We know that Scouts are a resourceful lot. This means they can adapt and use what they have to make the things they need. The humble neckerchief can be put to an amazing number of different uses – and it has the added bonus of being around your neck. Here are sixteen different things you can make with your neckerchief.

HEADSCARF

Drape the wide end of the neckerchief over the top of your head, letting it rest on your brow, then knot behind your head.

HEADBAND

Fold your neckerchief into a long strip, wrap it around your head above your ears, then knot it securely behind your head.

FACE MASK

Place the wide end of your neckerchief over your nose and mouth, then knot tightly behind your head (making sure you can still breathe!).

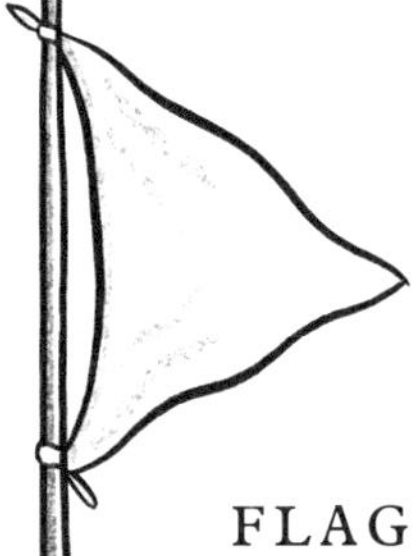

FLAG

Tie the two points of the wide end of your unfolded neckerchief to the end of a long stick to make your flag.

BELT

Roll your neckerchief into a long, thin strip, then thread it through your belt loops to make an emergency belt.

BAG

Put your possessions in the centre of the unfolded neckerchief, then tie the loose ends to the end of a stick, which you can carry on your shoulder.

LASHING

You can use one or two neckerchiefs as a lashing to bind two sticks together to make a longer stick. Make sure the lashings are at wide intervals to keep the sticks secure.

FLANNEL

Use your neckerchief to wash your face (then wash your neckerchief).

RESCUE LINE

Knot several rolled neckerchiefs together to form an emergency rescue rope.

HEAD BANDAGE

Use your neckerchief as a head bandage, by creating a tight headscarf, following the instructions on page 15.

HAND BANDAGE

Lay the neckerchief out flat. Now place the hand in the centre of the wide end. Fold in the three corners, wrapping the hand like a parcel, securely tying the ends at the wrist.

ELBOW OR KNEE BANDAGE

Place the joint in the wide end of the neckerchief, then wrap tightly before tying the ends.

ARM SLING

Lay the scarf out diagonally across the chest, with one end loosely draped over the shoulder, the other dangling under the elbow. Bring the elbow end of the scarf up and over the elbow and forearm, round the back of the neck and knot it to the other loose end.

How the Scouts Began

Scouting began, like most successful things, with a good idea.

A man called Robert Baden-Powell (1857–1941), a senior officer in the British Army, noticed the incredible inventiveness and courage of many of the youngest soldiers under his command.

As a young army officer, B-P, as he was often known, had specialised in scouting, map-making and reconnaissance, and he trained soldiers in what were essential skills for any military person of the time.

B-P's methods were, at times, out of the ordinary. He set up small units or patrols, under a single leader, and made sure there was special recognition for those who did well. (The proficiency badges he awarded then were a preview of the Scout badges that are so loved and admired around the world today.)

B-P knew that this 'outdoor skills' concept could apply to those outside the military. He understood that all young people seemed to be at their best when they were working together in small teams in the outdoors. That was where they seemed to make friends most easily, learnt new skills and were at their happiest.

So, as his army career was drawing to a close, B-P decided to go to work on a much bigger idea.

What if you could bring children together from all backgrounds to camp together, eat together and learn from each other? They could dress in a simple, practical uniform, suitable for the outdoors, follow a common set of rules and be a team, help others and improve their own skills.

He'd already seen how well this had worked when training soldiers in the army. He knew that it could work just as well, if not better, for much younger people.

The First Experimental Scout Camp

To test out his idea, Baden-Powell decided to hold a camp on Brownsea Island, in Poole, Dorset, in the south of England, for a group of boys from all walks of life. Despite only being a mile or so from the mainland, he chose it as his own magical 'treasure island'. He had sailed there as a boy and knew it would feel special and different.

So on 29 July 1907, twenty boys from all different backgrounds landed on the island to begin the camp. Canvas tents were pitched and a flag was flying proudly in the centre of the camp. The next eight days would be packed with adventure, from stargazing and fire lighting to life-saving, cooking, tracking, sailing and games. Together, this programme would create the model for a worldwide movement.

The twenty boys were from different backgrounds: ten from public schools and ten from the local Poole and Bournemouth Boys' Brigade. It was radical thinking for the time, bringing people from different classes together like this. No barriers. Only bonds.

The boys were divided into four small teams, called Scout Patrols: Wolves, Bulls, Curlews and Ravens. To this day, Scouts still meet in Patrols, each one with its own name. Baden-Powell wore a fleur de lis badge on his hat. He had used this symbol with his army scouts, and a version would later become known as the Scout badge. It's extraordinary how much of what we recognise as Scouting today was there from day one.

From the start, the camp was about learning useful skills and developing good values, such as courage and kindness. There weren't many lie-ins. There was a strong focus on practical, outdoor skills including tent pitching, backwoods cooking, finding your way, raft and bridge building; all things Scouts still learn today. At the end of each day, the boys and their leaders would gather round the campfire while Baden-Powell shared stories of his adventures in the flickering light.

By 9 August, the camp was over and the great Scouting experiment declared a success. Baden-Powell now set himself the task of getting his idea out to the world.

How Scouting Spread

Following the camp, Baden-Powell began to put his concept down on paper.

Just a few months later, in January 1908, the first part of Baden-Powell's book, *Scouting for Boys*, was published. The book was published in six fortnightly parts, each at a pocket-money price. They were hungrily snapped up by young people who started forming themselves into Patrols.

Astonished at the interest shown in his scheme, by the end of January, Baden-Powell announced there would be a separate Scouts organisation. By 1910, there were over 100,000 Scouts in the UK, including at least 6,000 girls.

Over the next few years Scouts expanded its programme and reach, with Sea Scouts, new badges and, in early 1914, the creation of a new trial section, the Wolf Cubs for eight to eleven-year-olds, which officially began in 1916.

Scouts quickly spread across the globe, inspiring millions to get into the outdoors with their friends and do their best. In 1929, Baden-Powell was honoured by the movement for his achievement, and declared Chief Scout of the World.

TEN GOOD THINGS *to Know About Scouts*

1. Eleven of the twelve people who walked on the moon were Scouts (we don't know how James Irwin, the twelfth one, got there!).
2. Scouts have stood on the summit of Everest and at the North and South Pole.
3. Scouts offers over 200 activities, from abseiling and coding to drama and water-zorbing.
4. Scouts is open to all – and today there are millions of girls and women in Scouts across the world.
5. An estimated 500 million people have been Scouts since it began.
6. One person began Scouts in 1907. Today, there are 57 million around the world.
7. John Lennon and Paul McCartney, from The Beatles, were both Scouts (and wrote songs that have been sung around millions of campfires since!).
8. Scouts takes place in over 200 countries and territories around the world.
9. Scouts have been presidents and prime ministers.
10. In 2018, 500 Scouts broke the record for making themselves into the world's largest human fleur-de-lis (the Scout badge).

WHEN I WAS A SCOUT

The best thing about my early years in smoky London was that I got to join the Scouts, and I loved it. I remember my first day, walking in and seeing all these towering Scouts with neatly pressed shirts, covered in awards and badges. I was a skinny, shy boy, and I felt even smaller than I looked.

But as soon as I heard the Scout leader challenge us to cook a sausage with just one match, out on the pavement, I was hooked. How would we ever achieve that?

One match, one sausage ... hmm, but it will never burn long enough, I thought. Then I was shown how first to use the match to light a fire, then to cook the sausage. It was a eureka moment for me.

If anyone present during those Scout evenings had told me that one day I would hold the post of Chief Scout, I would have probably died of laughter. But what I lacked in stature and confidence I always made up for with guts and determination, and those qualities are what really matter in both the game of life and in Scouting.

I found great release in Scouting and great camaraderie as well. It was like a family, and it didn't matter what your background was. If you were a Scout, you were a Scout, and that was what mattered. I liked that and my confidence grew.

I've been on a truly incredible journey since, in my role as UK Chief Scout and Chief Ambassador of World Scouting. From mountaintops to jungles. From UN headquarters to presidential offices. Across oceans, into slums and refugee camps. From the Olympics to the biggest Jamborees on earth (a Jamboree is a huge Scout camp, as you'll find out soon!).

One of the reasons I became a Scout was to spend more time with friends in the outdoors. It's among the greatest experiences in life and should be accessible to everyone, no matter where they live, what they look like or how they grew up.

When I travel around the world, I often get to meet many inspirational people, from Hollywood actors to global politicians, and often they will say to me, 'You know, Bear, I was once an Eagle Scout,' or 'I was a Queen's Scout' or 'I was a King's Scout' (I always remind them that they still are!).

That tells me something about those people: they've got character. That they've learnt some cool life skills and lived some adventures.

But above all, it tells me that they never gave up. (Remember, most people tend to give up when the storms of life hit, but not Scouts.)

This is what sets the great people in life apart. They have often done something extraordinary, but time and again it starts from humble beginnings. And this is where Scouts comes in. We help people, from wherever they come from, to be extraordinary and to do the extraordinary. We help young people to soar.

AS A SCOUT TRY TO ...

Be kind (every day).
Be brave (in every way).
Be grateful (for what you have).
Be accepting (about what you don't have).
Be determined (in all you do).
Be yourself (there's only one you).
Be cheerful (when things look grim).
Be a friend (through thick and thin).
Be a sharer (break things in two).
Be prepared (no matter what life throws at you).

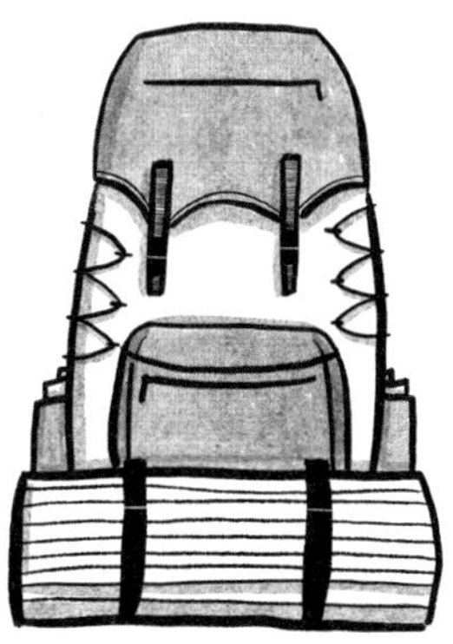

The Seven Ways to Be a Great Scout

There are seven Scouting principles that make us stand out, and these have been passed down through generations. You can remember them with a simple mnemonic: Ten Long, Fine Fingers Caught The Rat! Which stands for Trust, Loyalty, Friends, Family, Courage, Time, Respect.

1. **BE TRUSTWORTHY**

   The T is for Trustworthy. What does that really mean? It means you're the sort of person who keeps their promises. If you say you're going to do something, then you do it. Words are power, and people come to know us by the words we speak and the actions that follow them. So be a Scout who is trustworthy and keeps their word.

   Don't deal in lies. Instead, be someone people can rely on. Look at the other words that link to trustworthy: loyal, faithful, honourable and true. These are all part of Scouting, and things that we can develop in ourselves. Remember, your character is made up of all the everyday decisions you make. So take this first principle and pin it to your chest. It will serve you well in life.

2. **BE LOYAL**

   The L stands for Loyalty. We live in a world where, if we don't like something, there's great pressure just to bin it and replace it. We see this applied to so many things, from gadgets to friendships. But the more we seek perfection, the less satisfaction we find.

   Loyalty seems quite old-fashioned, but the truth is that loyalty is more relevant than ever. Who's ever been let down by a friend? Or has ever had a friend stick up for you in a difficult moment? Life is about relationships, and relationships thrive when we show loyalty. How we act in big moments defines us, and how we behave when important things are on the line is how we are remembered and valued. So let's be the sort of person that shows loyalty.

3 BE A FRIEND TO ALL

The F stands for Friends – being friendly and considerate. As Scouts, we're beacons that people all around the world look up to. People admire Scouts because of what we do and how we act – and our day-to-day attitudes determine whether people come away from meeting us with a good or bad feeling. Make people feel great about themselves and it can last a lifetime – and it's the same the other way. Being friendly and considerate means listening to people properly; it means looking them in the eye and saying our pleases and thank yous. A smile lights up your face and has been medically proven to make you feel better. So let's wear that smile and be the best ambassadors we can for our movement.

4 BE PART OF A GLOBAL FAMILY

The second F stands for Family. As Scouts, we're part of a worldwide family of 57 million people, united by a common purpose of adventure, service and friendship. What a family to belong to. In this busy world, there isn't always a sense of strong community. That's why being part of this special Scouting family counts for so much. Don't underestimate the power of family, and the power that a sense of belonging can give to people. Families look after their own in times of need. They protect, encourage, share and support. That's us.

5 BE COURAGEOUS

The C is for Courage. A Scout is courageous. And courage is a big one.

Courage has always been at the very heart of Scouting. Scouts all over the world helped their countries in the two World Wars. They brought in the harvest, acted as coastguards and messengers, and even guided fire engines to bomb sites.

Courage is often about how we react to overwhelming odds. And it is impossible to be courageous if at first you aren't also afraid. Courage means facing our fears, and walking through them – and despite them. And one thing I have learnt in the wild is that the answer to fear is not to run but to face it. When we run from our fears, they tend to grow. But when we walk towards them, they often fade away. That is courage.

Courage is not about being gung-ho or a show-off. In fact, courage is the opposite. It is quiet strength in the face of great adversity. It could be a young Scout battling a life-threatening illness, yet always with a smile, determination and the kindest of hearts. For sure, they are scared, yet every day, they make a choice to tackle life head-on with courage and optimism. That's real courage.

One final thought: the most courageous people are also often the most unlikely. So whoever you are, take heart, as underneath you're probably braver and more courageous than you think.

6 BE CAREFUL WITH YOUR TIME AND POSSESSIONS

The T is for Time, and the sixth Scouting principle is this: 'A Scout makes good use of time and is careful of possessions and property.' The one thing that we all have, in equal amounts, is time. When we all reach the end of our life and look back, those who've used their time wisely will reap the rewards – you'll have so many great memories and friendships. But if we spend too much time on our phones, TVs and consoles, we aren't going to have much to look back on with pride. All our lives are products of all the many daily small decisions we make – so use your twenty-four hours – or 1,440 minutes – wisely!

The second part of this principle is about being careful with our possessions and property. We live in a consumer-driven world, where, if something breaks, we throw it out. That's going to cost both you and the environment. Nothing lasts forever, but sometimes things can last way longer if we learn how to fix them. That's a great quality and skill.

Throughout history, and especially during war and other times of crisis, people were encouraged to 'make do and mend'. Or as Scouts say: 'Improvise, adapt, overcome.'

On the Apollo 17 mission to the moon in 1972, the astronaut Gene Cernan accidentally ripped a piece of the mudguard off the Lunar Rover, the moon buggy they used to travel around. While this doesn't sound very serious, it meant that every time they drove the buggy, they were getting covered in moon dust and were dangerously overheating.

Naturally, the first thing they thought of was duct tape. With a little help from the bright sparks at mission control, they made a new mud-guard out of a map and tape (no one knows how he managed to find the end of the tape with his giant space gloves – it's hard enough on earth).

Problem solved. Resourcefulness always wins the day.

The moral of the story is: be grateful for what you have. Look after your things. And if something breaks, there's usually a way to fix it – especially if you use a little imagination.

7 BE RESPECTFUL

The final Scouting principle for us to live by, the R, is Respect: respect for ourselves and others. And it's a great one to end on. If you give someone respect then they'll respect you back – it's how the world works. People tend to want to hang out with those people who listen to them and value what they have to offer. That comes down to one thing: giving people respect. It means listening, being grateful and considering others' feelings.

Live like that and you'll be loved by many.

Respect for ourselves can take a lifetime to learn, but it matters. Be gentle and look after yourself.

THE SCOUT BUCKET LIST: *Eighteen Things Every Scout Should Do*

Accomplish all of these and you can call yourself a true Scout. It might take a few years, but if you keep going, then you'll tick off every one in the end. And if you've done all eighteen, then maybe do them all over again with a new friend! None of this stuff ever gets old.

1 SLEEP OUT UNDER THE STARS
Find a patch of grass and stare up at the Milky Way. Feeling the cold night air on your skin is a great way to find your place in the universe. A bivvy bag is ideal for this: a waterproof covering that you and your sleeping bag will fit snugly inside, while leaving your face exposed. Count comets and shooting stars until you drop off.

2 GO TO A WORLD SCOUT JAMBOREE (OR AT LEAST AN INTERNATIONAL CAMP)
World Scout Jamborees happen every four years, and in a different country each time. Tens of thousands of Scouts attend from all over the Scouting world for a festival of peace and friendship. They've been happening since the first one in London in 1920 and there's really nothing like them on earth. It's where you'll learn how to say your promise in Spanish, how to cook a Hungarian goulash and swap badges with a New Zealander. And if you don't manage to get a place at a World Scout Jamboree, then don't worry. There are plenty of international camps that happen all over the world. Find one near you. You'll never forget it.

3 PASS ON A SKILL TO ANOTHER SCOUT

You've only truly mastered a skill when you know it well enough to teach someone else. If you feel like you can tie the highwayman's hitch (see page 231) with your eyes closed, then now's the time to pass that skill on.

4 VOLUNTEER (AND GIVE YOURSELF A CHEER)

Becoming a volunteer will make you shine brighter. Helping other people does great things for your soul and brings out the best in you. Whether you do some shopping for an elderly neighbour or help run the Cub pack, this'll help you be the best version of you. Because when we give, we always receive.

5 TIE SOMEONE'S FRIENDSHIP KNOT

You know you've truly made a friend in Scouts when they ask you to tie a friendship knot in their neckerchief (see page 268). In fact, if you can tie a friendship knot, you'll find you have lots of friends. This skill is in high demand.

6 TAKE PART IN A CAMPFIRE

Campfires are not just for keeping warm. They're places for Scouts to get together, sing badly and glug hot chocolate. Be brave and lead your fellow Scouts in a song or a sketch. Show them a magic trick or tell a tall tale. Don't worry about making a fool of yourself – that's the whole point! People will love you all the more for your sense of adventure and fun.

7 GET OUT OF YOUR COMFORT ZONE

Remember, you only start learning when you reach the edge of your comfort zone, so don't be afraid to stick a toe over the edge. Talk to someone new, get onto that stage or put that scuba diving mask on and go diving! You won't look back.

8 REMAKE YOUR PROMISE IN AN UNUSUAL PLACE

Whether it's in a kayak in the middle of a lake, standing at the top of a hill at dawn or on the end of a surfboard, remind yourself of how important the Scout promise is by making it again in a place you'll never forget.

9 CLIMB A MOUNTAIN

Whether it's a real mountain or a metaphorical mountain, go attempt the impossible. Fail and try again. Push yourself. Aim big. Never give up.

I got to be part of a military team to climb Mount Everest, the highest peak on earth, when I was twenty-three – and it changed my life. It reminded me that all of life is a challenge. And the bigger we dare to dream, the bigger the adventures ahead will be.

There are all sorts of different 'mountains' we can climb. It could just as easily be a particular challenge you've been thinking about for a long time, like writing a book, learning a new skill, making a new friend, or breaking a negative habit. Remember, growing as a person doesn't happen by chance. It happens with change. And change always starts with a decision. And climbing our own 'Everest' starts with that first small step . . .

10 GO ON A LONG JOURNEY

People once travelled great distances to discover new lands and meet new friends. Without cars or planes, these journeys once took weeks, months or even years (Marco Polo once travelled for nearly twenty-five years before returning home – see page 248). Pick a spot on a map and travel the slow way – by bike or on foot. As they say: life is the journey, not the destination.

11 MAKE THE WORLD'S BEST HOT CHOCOLATE

Every now and again, treat yourself. You deserve it. Pile the mini-marshmallows high. Squirt on the cream until it looks like Mount Everest. Stick in some crumbly chocolate flakes. Now savour every moment. Go on, you've earned it.

12 BE A LEADER

You might not know it, but you're already a leader. If you have any influence on others, it means you're already leading. That might simply be in your family, or sports team, or your Scout group. If people watch what you do, in any way, then you're a leader. So be a good one. Be proud of how you behave, and lead with kindness and integrity. Then people will follow you anywhere.

Next time you see a chance to step up, why not take it? When all eyes are on you, you'll be surprised at what you can do. It's your time to shine. Go for it!

13 COOK A THREE-COURSE DINNER IN THE OUTDOORS

The greatest dinner parties are those held in 5-billion-star hotels. That's right: the ones that have no roofs, just the night sky above. So get the fire going, wrap up your potatoes in tin foil and prepare for a feast. Everything tastes better outdoors!

14 EARN YOUR TOP AWARD

Whether it's becoming a King's Scout, an Eagle Scout or getting the Chief Scout's Silver Award, there'll be an award that's the highest possible for you and your friends. Plan how you'll achieve it, then go for it. Don't stop until you've tied off the last stitch as you sew it onto your shirt.

15 GO ON A NIGHT HIKE

Watch the moonlight as it peeps through the trees, listen for the hoot of an owl or wave your torch around like a lightsaber. These are just a few of the rituals of the night hike. Remember to stay safe on roads, wear hi-vis jackets and pack spare batteries for your torch – especially if you're doing impressions of Luke Skywalker. Tasty snacks are compulsory.

16 BE A FRIEND (WHEN SOMEONE NEEDS YOU MOST)

Everyone goes through a rough patch, but not everyone tells you about it. Watch out for people who are quieter than usual, or who are on their own or looking sad. You could be the friend that makes all the difference. A friend in need is a friend indeed. And a true friend walks in when the rest of the world walks out.

17 PLANT A TREE

One of the most hopeful things you can do is plant a tree. It'll help keep our air clean and our earth green. And it could still be growing after we are long gone. I've come across some truly amazing trees in my life. Some of them over 1,000 years old. (And I thought Scouting was ancient!)

18 MAKE YOURSELF PROUD

This could be doing some little act of kindness: holding open a door, giving someone a smile or giving up your place in a queue. Whatever you do, make yourself proud by making someone else's day.

Honouring Our Queen's and King's Scouts At Windsor Castle

The highest accolade a Scout can achieve in the United Kingdom (and in many other countries around the world too) is the King's Scout Award. This has a long and proud history, going back to 1909, when King Edward VII agreed to award the 'King's Scout Badge' as the highest achievement for Scouts, on the recommendation of Robert Baden-Powell, the movement's founder.

I've had the honour to attend the Day of Celebration and Achievement every year since I became Chief Scout, and each time I'm bowled over by the courage, selflessness and determination of these young people. In 2023, I was honoured to give the address during the service in St George's Chapel, Windsor.

This is what I said that day:

Being part of this Scout celebration here at Windsor is always special. But it's special because of you. All of you here: you're our bravest, our brightest and our best. You're the dreamers, the doers and the change-makers. And you're the reason I'm so proud to be your Chief Scout.

To be here today, whether as a Queen's Scout, a King's Scout, a Gallantry Award recipient or a volunteer hero, takes effort and hard work. It takes something extraordinary and often a moment of huge courage.

And courage is in our DNA as Scouts. But courage isn't just about the past – what we've done – courage is also about the future – how we choose to live our lives.

When I first joined the Cubs, I was the shyest kid in the room. I just wanted to vanish. In fact, I still do sometimes . . . like about two minutes ago!

But the bravest thing we can sometimes do in life is to consciously choose to tackle the difficult, to fully embrace the challenges of life head on, to be a sticker, a stander-upper. A never-give-upper!

Because the truth about this King's Scout parade – and this whole day – is that it isn't the end of your journey. It's really the beginning.

The world needs leaders like you like never before. There's conflict and hardships almost wherever we look. There's disunity and often fear. Yet there's also such huge potential for good.

When I went to Ukraine to meet with President Zelensky a few months ago, I saw a man coping with the biggest challenges and obstacles you can imagine. Yet his face was bright. Full of hope. Because challenges unite us. And they ignite us. They bring out the best in us. We are designed for challenge. And Scouts embody that.

The world needs Scouts like you now more than ever. To show a kinder way in how we live, a more dynamic and inspiring way to tackle life. To embody that Scouting purpose and resilience. Just look how far we have all come already. All across the world, Scouting is giving memories and skills that can, and often do, last a lifetime.

Since 2009, when I first stood as Chief Scout in this chapel, Scouts in the UK alone have helped more than 2 million young people to experience that friendship and adventure that is found in Scouting. We've opened more groups in the country's most challenging areas than ever before, changing young lives and giving them opportunities.

We've listened, we've adapted and we've grown. There's a reason we're called a movement and not an organisation. We move with the times.

But together we can still do so much more.

I gave you each a scroll at the beginning. What's inside represents you. I'm going to ask you to stand up one at a time and open it.

Because when I look around this chapel, this is what I see. This is what Scouting does best. We give potential. We equip, we prepare, we encourage, then we watch as young people soar.

Potential. This place is electric with it.

Scouting has given all of you the fuel: the skills, the opportunities. But you must be the ones that now run and use it. So go out there and change the world for the better. Change your community for the better. Change your life for the better. You can do that!

Because one thing I know for sure, and I've learnt this first-hand over the most incredible years as Chief Scout, is that Scouts can do anything!

How to

NEVER GIVE UP

THERE'LL BE A thousand times in your life when things will feel too tough. When things don't go your way or you have to deal with something that just seems impossible. In these moments, there's a simple message to remember, and it's this: courage, kindness . . . and never give up.

All of us will hit bumps in the road. We'll maybe have a fall-out with one of our friends, we'll find ourselves on the losing end of a game and some of our well-made plans will come to nothing. Maybe there won't be a single reason – but still you just feel down.

At these times, life doesn't feel fair. It feels like the world is against us (while others seem to be effortlessly succeeding). It's in these moments we need to remember that everyone goes through these sort of battles. The storms. But the storms never last forever, and they always make us stronger.

So hold on, reach out to a close friend or Scout buddy for some help or just for a chat. But above all, take heart and keep going. And remember 'NGU': never give up.

This ability to keep going is the most precious skill of all. Because resilience conquers all.

It's all too easy to pack up and go home when times get tough. It's often easier to close the door. To say goodbye to the dream. But where does that leave us? Back where we started. People live their lives filled with regret for the things they never did, the places they never went, but most of all for not picking themselves up and trying again.

All the good stuff is on the other side of failure, persistence and fear.

So when life gets tough, don't say: 'Why me?' Say: 'Try me.'

We need to challenge ourselves if we are to grow. As the saying goes: 'Smooth seas do not make skilful sailors.' So many successful people have become the people they are today simply by never giving up. So write it on your heart and make never quitting part of your DNA. As the world's greatest Sherpa climber, Nims Purja, once said: 'Giving up isn't in my blood!' He is right. And as a Scout, it's not in yours either!

FROM THE SIDELINES TO SUPERSTARDOM

Michael Jordan, the legendary basketball player, was dropped by his high school team. That only made him practise twice as hard. That extra effort paid off. It got him into the Tar Heels, the team at the University of North Carolina, and eventually the Chicago Bulls. He went from being the kid on the sidelines to one of the greatest players of all time. That's the never give up spirit.

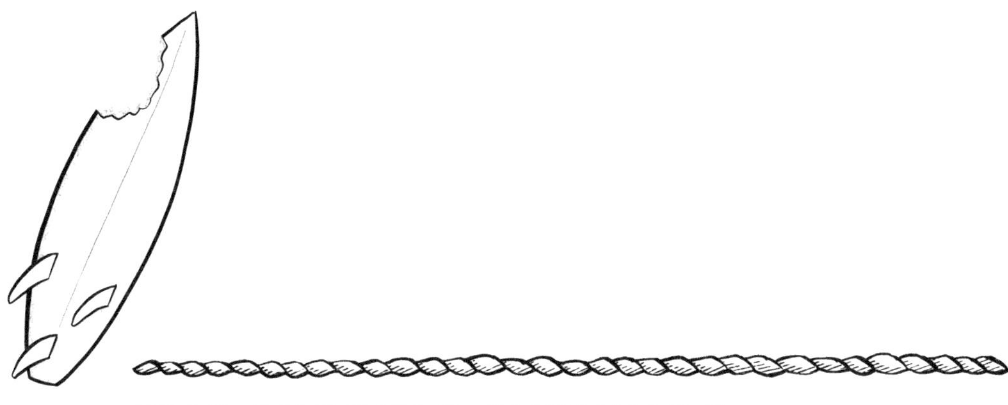

THE SURFING SURVIVOR

Bethany Hamilton was born in Hawaii and learnt to surf at the age of just three. When she was thirteen, she was surfing with friends when she was attacked by a four-metre tiger shark, which bit off her left arm, just below the shoulder. Her friends got her to shore and she was rushed to hospital. Incredibly, only twenty-six days later, she was back surfing again. Having taught herself to surf with one arm, she entered professional competitions the following year. Bethany has since gone on to win many awards, write books and inspire others to find their confidence again.

Helping Others

As Scouts, we must always help people when they are going through a storm in their life. It is our Scouting superpower: we help others when they are struggling. And we know that we are always stronger together.

There's no limit to the good we can do when we are there for people in a crisis.

I once heard a Scouting saying that goes like this:

When someone falls down, we help them *stand.*
When someone feels tired, we encourage them to *endure.*
When someone is struggling, we *stand right there beside them.*

The Can-Do Formula

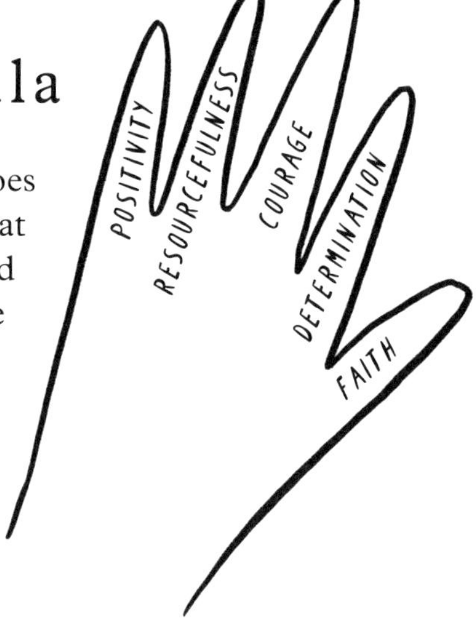

POSITIVITY
RESOURCEFULNESS
COURAGE
DETERMINATION
FAITH

It's easy to say 'never give up'. But how does this really help you when you're in that tough place and you're trying to respond to that crisis or get over that setback? One great thing is to remember the can-do formula – using five superpowers everyone has (probably without realising).

1 POSITIVITY is power. It's looking on the bright side. And there's always a bright side, no matter how bleak things seem. When polar explorers are frozen, tired and still hundreds of miles from home, there's still those few energy bars left in their rations, that blue sky above them and the prospect of a hot shower and warm hug from family sometime in the future. Focus on the good things in life, and the miles ahead pass twice as quickly. Positivity is a choice. And the best reason for choosing it is to think about the alternative. And being negative never leads anywhere good.

2 RESOURCEFULNESS is a Scouting speciality. It's about using what you have, not what you wish you had. It's about thinking smart and working out what you can do, rather than complaining about what you can't. If you're stuck in the mountains and only have a single length of rope, a knife and an empty bottle, then this is what you'll have to work with. People have survived on much less. Remember, pack the right skills and the right attitude and you won't need much else. Adaptability, resourcefulness and ingenuity. It conquers so much. As they say in survival: one person's trash is another person's treasure.

3 COURAGE is at the heart of so much in life. It's what pulls us through. It's the courage to go for things. To try and not be afraid to fail. But remember it's OK to feel fear. That's normal. Being brave isn't the absence of fear. Being brave is having that fear but finding a way through it. Author Zig Ziglar says that fear

has two meanings: 'Forget everything and run, or face everything and rise.' As Scouts, we choose the second option.

4 **DETERMINATION** is grit. It's about digging deep and finding the strength to carry on. Why? Because you know it will be worth it in the end. We all have reservoirs – actually, oceans – of strength inside us that we haven't discovered yet. It's there inside, waiting to be tapped. Dig deep and use it. As Baden-Powell, the founder of Scouting, said: 'Never say die till you're dead!' That's power.

5 **FAITH** is possibly the most important of all. It's about having faith in your own abilities and having faith in others. As Scouts, we are a force for good. And as Scouts, we are unafraid to have faith in something bigger than ourselves, if that's what we choose to believe. Everyone is able to go on their own spiritual journey, and Scouts is open to those of faith and no faith alike. For me, I find faith in the Almighty. And I use that strength every day. All faith has power. When you believe you can succeed, and others believe in you too, you're already halfway there. Just a gram of faith is enough to move a mountain.

When Things Go Wrong

The first thing to do is stay calm. Others around you may be starting to panic, and panic is contagious. But so is calm. So do your best to choose to be calm in the crisis. It is a characteristic of all true Scouts. We think calmly and clearly, and that allows us to act decisively, wisely and fast.

'If you can keep your head while all about you / Are losing theirs' (to quote 'If', that famous poem by Rudyard Kipling), then you've got a good chance of succeeding. Be that calm person in the room and others will look to you for leadership. Calmly reassure them. Give them purpose and a task, and together you'll get to the other side.

And remember, it's not really an adventure until something happens! It's how you deal with that 'adventure' that counts. And that's when we'll learn the most.

Ask for Help

Sometimes the bravest thing to do is ask for help. No one has to go through tough times alone. As people, we're all vulnerable; we experience doubts, we get scared and we lose faith in ourselves. That's natural. And the most reassuring thing is that everyone feels that way at some point.

Have the Courage to Fail

Nothing great was ever achieved without failure. Those who succeeded are the ones who fell down nine times and picked themselves up ten times.

It's only when we fall down that we see what we're made of. It's easy to be positive when everything is going well, but at the heart of all great endeavours is the ability to stagger back up and keep moving forwards, however grim it gets. That's the test of a true Scout and champion. We get back up, we never give up and we know the power of failure. Failure is a stepping stone to success. A doorway we must go through in order to succeed.

Remember this too: don't let success go to your head and don't let failures go to your heart. Or as Winston Churchill once said: 'Success is not final, failure is not fatal: it is the courage to continue that counts.'

Keep Trying

The most important muscle to train isn't your outer muscles (even though as Scouts we should always do all we can to be as physically fit and strong as possible). The most important muscle in our life is our inner 'effort muscle' – the muscle that represents the Scouting attitude that says nothing can beat us. We will overcome. We will try again. We will determine to keep going. Whatever.

This inner 'effort muscle' is just like all other muscles: it needs to be trained. And the more we use it, the stronger it gets. So know the power of doing your best. Because every time we do our best, that 'effort muscle' gets stronger!

Never Be Afraid to Dream Big

Dreams are what drive us on. To achieve something, whether that's the summit of Everest, writing a book, winning a race or getting to the moon. Every dream is different, and we all have our own Everest. Everest is a state of mind. Keep trying and there's always hope. Give up and that hope vanishes in an instant.

The only way to achieve your dreams is through humility, kindness, courage and resilience. The rest is detail. So dream big. And don't listen to the dream-stealers.

TEN TOP TIPS to Get You Through Tough Times

1 ASK FOR HELP
There's always someone to talk to. Asking for help is a sign of strength not weakness.

2 ACCEPT THERE ARE SOME THINGS YOU CAN'T CHANGE
Don't waste energy complaining about the rain. It won't stop a single drop. Remember, the storms make us stronger.

3 REMEMBER THAT THIS WILL PASS
At some point, you'll be on the other side of this problem. Think how good you'll feel when this is all over and you can be proud that you prevailed and endured.

4 FOCUS ON THE GOOD THINGS, NOT THE BAD
If life isn't going your way, then think about what good things you have. Watch a favourite film, read a book or talk to a friend. When life hands a Scout some lemons, we make lemonade!

5 SLEEP

Good regular sleep (eight hours is ideal) will make you feel better about everything. Don't look at the bright screen on your phone before going to bed, and say sorry to someone if you've upset them. There is no pillow as soft as a clear conscience!

6 MOVE

It's amazing how your cares float away when you go for a walk, swim or jog. It makes you feel like you've literally outrun your problems and left them behind. So get outside, get fresh air, get moving. Get sun on your face and earth under your bare feet as much as you can (I do this every day). Be a person who thrives in the outdoors.

7 SPEND TIME WITH POSITIVE PEOPLE

Negative people will drain your energy at the best of times, let alone when things are tough. Avoid the dream-stealers – those who dismiss your goals or aspirations. Life is full of dream-stealers. Ignore them! Instead, hang out with those who make you feel better about life. People tend either to be a radiator or a drain. 'Radiators' light and warm up a conversation or situation. 'Drains' sap the energy and positivity from you. We all probably know some of both types of person. Hang out with 'radiators' – and choose to be one yourself!

8 THINK ABOUT HOW THIS EXPERIENCE WILL HELP YOU GROW

Every tough experience is also a lesson in life. You'll be better equipped next time you face a crisis. So don't look at a failure as just a failure. Instead, consider it a great lesson. This has helped me many times, and trust me, I have failed often!

9 EAT WELL

When you're feeling down, it's all too easy to reach for chips and doughnuts. Comfort food. But comfort food is a cheap hit and a temporary answer. In fact, it answers nothing, but tends to leave us weaker, lower and unhappier. Instead, pick natural foods, whole foods; the stuff you'd find in nature. These are the foods that as humans we have evolved over hundreds of thousands of years to thrive on. Food is fuel. Put the good stuff in and you'll get good results out.

10 NEVER GIVE UP

No matter how hard things get, if you just keep going, you'll get to the other side. Never give up has a strength all of its own. Use it and depend on it. Make having an NGU spirit your superpower.

FACING THE BATTLES OF LIFE

I have met so many incredible young Scouts who have had to display all of these qualities in spades when battling some of the toughest things in life.

If you're going through some tough times right now, please know that all of us in the wider Scouting family are right beside you, cheering you on as you keep going. Remember, it's how we act in the big moments that defines us all. So hang on in there. You're amazing, your Scouting strength is shining through, and we love and admire you so much. You've got this!

If I'm speaking to young Scouts who are struggling in their expedition or challenge, the message is also simple: keep going, be kind, be courageous, be doggedly determined. You'll get there!

To all of you Scouts in the heat of your challenge right now – in the hurt locker as they say – remember that the pain and fatigue won't last forever, but the pride in a job well done will do. So rally round each other, form a plan, dig deep, work smart, work together, be positive, be kind, be courageous and never give up.

If you do all that, despite the hardships, despite the feelings and deprivations, you will finish this and do it so well, showing yourself and the world what you are made of. Do me proud.

Failure, struggle, setbacks and pain all nourish courage.

You simply can't be strong or brave if you've only had perfect things happen to you. So embrace the day, seize it, whatever it holds – it's our chance to make progress towards the good stuff. The dawn will always come, and as Scouts we always chase the light!

How to be a

TEAM PLAYER

GREAT TEAMWORK makes almost anything possible. One person might have an idea to change the world, but if they want to make it happen, they're going to need a team around them.

'On our own we can achieve so little', said Helen Keller, 'but together we can do so much'. When we join forces and pool our talents, then we're unstoppable. 'Individually,' as the saying goes, 'we are one drop, but together we're an ocean.'

Teamwork isn't just about everyone mucking in (although that definitely helps). There can't be passengers or spectators when it comes to great teams. Great teams are well organised, plan carefully and follow some key principles on their journey to success.

SIX THINGS *Every Good Team Needs*

1 A LEADER

A leader is there to show others the way. But this doesn't mean they have to have all the answers, the loudest voice or the biggest personality. Instead, a leader is someone who'll explain the vision – where the team needs to get to – and then empowers you to do your best. Their main task is to inspire, encourage and support you to get there together and get there successfully. It's their job to make sure everyone feels valued and able to contribute their own talents and skills towards the collective result.

2 CLEAR OBJECTIVES

What's your team setting out to do? Reach the summit of a mountain? Before you take a single step, you need to plan ahead and agree what success looks like. When do you want to reach the top? How long should it take? What will you do if you fall behind? Discuss potential difficult scenarios and agree on successful outcomes. Make sure everyone shares that same goal and is happy with the objective. There is power to unity, and Scouts should always aim to be united.

3 CLEAR ROLES

While everyone needs to play their part, everyone should play *different* parts. One person might be great at coming up with ideas. Another might like the planning and detail. Someone else might be great at encouraging others, or have a particular skill like navigation, first aid or money management. Think carefully about your roles, and make sure everyone knows what their specific job is before you begin. If you find someone struggling with their role, try to help them find one more suited to them. Try to play to people's strengths.

4 PEOPLE WHO CAN WORK TOGETHER

Getting together, swapping ideas and talking things through are what good teams do. Share your ideas and get others to challenge them. Don't be afraid to change your mind or admit you're wrong. Remember, this isn't about you, it's about the team! No idea is too crazy. Be prepared to discuss it all, the good, the bad, the outrageous. Then pick the best and smartest – and commit to it.

5 GOOD COMMUNICATION
It's so important that you can all talk honestly about challenges you're facing and the journeys ahead. If you don't, then problems don't get resolved and you can't offer each other the help you need. Remember, a problem shared is a problem halved. Make time to listen to each other and keep an open mind. And all great Scout leaders always listen more than they speak. Remember, we have two ears and one mouth. Use them in proportion!

6 TRUST
This is the most important one of all. You've got to trust each other if you're going to succeed. Park your ego and make sure you've got each other's backs. Stick together when the going gets tough and celebrate together when things go well. Great teams get really close and often stay friends for life. That's the magic.

SOME GREAT TEAMS

The Apollo 11 moon landing

In July 1969, only three people went to the moon (and only two walked on it). However, behind them (238,855 miles behind them, to be precise) there was a team of 400,000 others who did everything from design the rocket and do the maths, to clean the launch tower and make the tea. And that teamwork paid off in style. If the sky's the limit, how did we get to the moon? Think *big*! Scouts always do.

The All Blacks (New Zealand's national rugby team)

Although they come from a small country of just over 5 million people, this team has dominated the sport of rugby for decades. How? Because they believe that everyone is equal and everyone has an equally important part to play. They think of themselves as a single unit, rather than fifteen players and a coach.

The Ferrari Formula 1 pit crew

This is one of the best drilled and most impressive teams in the world. In just a few seconds, they can replace the tyres, refuel, clean the driver's visor and jump out of the way just in time for the car to rejoin the race and still be in the lead. How? Because everyone knows their specific role and they practise until it becomes second nature. They don't need to speak while doing their job and they rehearse endlessly to make sure no one gets in each other's way. Finally, they have a 'lollipop person' who only waves a flag when they're happy that everything has been done perfectly.

Scout Teams

One of the reasons Scouts works so well is that everyone is part of a small team. These are called Sixes, Patrols and so on. These groups are small enough to get on with something quickly, but big enough so that there's enough brain power and willing hands to get the job done.

This is how Scouts learn to be great team players. Who knows what teams you might end up with in the future? Perhaps one day you'll help launch a mission to Mars!

A Team's Journey: The Five Stages

When a new team comes together, not everything falls into place all at once. It takes time for people to get to know each other, work out each other's strengths and then focus on the challenge ahead. Here are the key stages, based on a theory by an American psychologist.

1 FORMING
This is the 'getting to know you' stage. It's when we work out what we're trying to achieve, who's good at what and how we'll use our different talents to achieve our goal.

2 STORMING
This is the trickiest part, as conflicts emerge. Perhaps a few people are getting on each other's nerves. You might need to bite your tongue and agree to disagree on some things. But if you get through this stage, you can get to the good stuff.

3 NORMING

Things are starting to settle down now. The team has got to know its strengths and different ways of working.

4 PERFORMING

Now the teething issues are sorted, the team is really starting to fly. You're well on your way to your goal, encouraging and supporting each other all the way to the top.

5 ADJOURNING

All good things must come to an end. You've achieved your goal and now the team members are heading off to do other things. But before you do, make sure you celebrate. Reflect on what went well and what you could do better. This'll help you when you're in your next team.

TEN TOP TIPS *for Great Teams*

1. There's no limit to what you can achieve if you empower and build others up.
2. Don't let success go to your head.
3. Don't let failures go to your heart.
4. Remember the can-do formula (see page 38): positivity, resourcefulness, courage, determination and faith.
5. Come back alive, come back as friends and come back successful – in that order!
6. Together stronger: lift others up.
7. Share the load.
8. Shoulder more than others.
9. Share your fears and share your kindnesses.
10. Never give up (obviously!).

How to Be a Great Team Player

There are so many things you can do to be a better team player. Of course, you can always work harder and practise your skills more, but that's only half the battle. Great teams are made up of great people who listen to and respect each other.

Make time to really talk and listen to others about how they feel and what they want as team members. If you understand them better, and help them get what they need, they'll spend more time helping you too. This is also how you move from being teammates to being friends.

Using empathy – the ability to see and understand things from someone else's perspective (and 'stand in their shoes') – is so powerful. Imagine how the other person is feeling and you'll suddenly see the team (and yourself) from a different point of view. The result is that everyone's happier and feels more supported and the team achieves its goal more quickly.

Above all, teamwork is about being a friend when it matters.

How to

LEAD

TEAMS WORK BEST when they have a strong leader. That's a person to help and guide them, to remind them where they're heading and how they're going to get there. But how do you know if you're a good leader, and can leadership be learnt? Let's find out.

A leader is someone (as author John C. Maxwell said) who 'knows the way, goes the way and shows the way'. But he wasn't just talking about leading a team through the mountains. It could equally be a team that needs to build a raft, sail across the Atlantic or even go to space.

You hear a lot about 'born leaders' and 'natural leaders' but actually, leadership is a skill that can be learnt, like any other. We can all be leaders if we set our heart and mind to it. Even if in many tasks we might feel like a more natural 'follower', there will almost always be ways in our lives, in Scouting or in our chosen career that we can, and should, show leadership. It is in us all to lead and to guide in some way or another.

A good leader is rarely the noisiest person in the room, the toughest, the strongest or even the smartest. It's usually the person who cares the most. Surprised?

A good Scout leader is someone who helps everyone in the team to be their best, and someone who encourages and looks after people. They'll be someone who lifts people up when they're feeling down, and ultimately, they'll be the person responsible for achieving what the team has set out to achieve.

What Leadership Is (and What It Isn't)

Let's get one thing straight: leadership isn't about telling people what to do or how to do it. Anyone can do that.

Great leadership is about *bringing people with you*. The true gift is persuading people to *want* to follow you. You can't be a leader unless people follow. You can bark at people all you like, but unless they believe in you, and want to help and follow you, you'll never be a true leader.

The knack is making people listen, allowing them genuinely to believe in you, and most of all, to believe in themselves. That's the key part. Great leaders build people up and help them to excel. They make you believe you can do more together than alone.

When you think about the positive leaders you've looked up to, you'll notice they all shared the qualities of courage, kindness and empathy – the ability to understand how others feel. They make you know that they care for you. Because no one cares how much you know until they know how much you care. That's the heart of a great leader: care for those in their charge. Care, above themselves.

For some, leadership's a calling. Others surprise themselves. Sometimes the quietest people show the steeliest resolve and the greatest leadership in tough times. And you often don't see it until the time comes. There's a great saying: 'A good leader is like a tea bag. You don't know how strong it is until it gets into hot water.' And remember this too: a good sense of humour is as vital to a leader as resilience and resolve.

Great leadership is having grace under pressure – that certain calm poise or stillness when things are at their worst. It's so rare, but you find it in a true leader.

Why Scouts Starts Leadership Early

In Scouts, we pride ourselves on developing leadership from the earliest age. Since the Scout movement began, we've given hundreds of thousands of young people the chance to step up, take charge and feel what it's like when all eyes are on you. As a Sixer in Cub Scouts, you start to develop those skills of supporting those who fall behind and learning the power of a friendly word of encouragement.

One of the most inspiring and successful things UK Scouts run is their Young Leaders' Scheme. These are incredible fourteen to eighteen-year-olds who support younger Scouts planning their games and activities. These are the new generation of volunteers. They're also the future CEOs, astronauts and Olympians. Think about people like Michelle Obama (First Lady to US president Barack Obama), Neil Armstrong (first man on the moon), Richard Branson (adventurer and entrepreneur), Ellie Simmonds (Paralympian gold medal winner), Tim Peake (British astronaut) or Steven Spielberg (Oscar-winning movie director). They all got their start in Scouts.

One thing you'll notice is that people never forget a great leader. Even after Tim Peake spent 186 days in space, he made time to go back and thank his Scout leaders who inspired and believed in him all those years before. That's humble, kind, effective leadership.

Think too about Dwayne Fields, another Scout, and the first Black Briton to reach the North Pole. It was his Scout leader who believed in him and inspired him to forge his own path in life. He broke away from the streets and went from being the victim of knife and gun crime to achieve astonishing feats. Now he inspires others to believe in themselves and find their dreams too, for example, by taking them on expeditions to the Antarctic and up some of our tallest mountains.

We're lucky to have people like these. Their courage, integrity and optimism guides the next generation of leaders (like you).

So if you find yourself leading a team, think about what will make the difference. It's about giving that reassuring smile when someone loses their nerve. It's about showing that courage and calmness even if you're not sure of yourself. It's about putting your faith in others and in something bigger than yourself, like the mission.

And remember, sometimes the bravest thing you can do as a leader is ask for help. It's OK to let people know that you have feelings too. That you sometimes find things tough. That you don't always have the answers. This just shows you're human, and people will respond to your integrity and humility. As leaders, we don't always get it right. But if people know we will always stand up for them and do what's right, then we'll succeed in the end.

Remember these words from former US president, John Quincy Adams: 'If your actions inspire others to dream more, learn more, do more and become more, you are a leader.' There's a leader inside all of us, capable of so much more than we think.

Great Leaders in History

Let's look at some of the great leaders in history: South Africa's legendary president Nelson Mandela, Kenyan environmentalist Wangari Maathai, who won the Nobel Peace Prize, former US president Barack Obama, Antarctic explorer Ernest Shackleton and the Indian leader Mahatma Gandhi. What do they have in common?

Determination? Sure.

Courage? Plenty.

Energy? Of course.

But the most important thing was belief. Belief in their cause, belief in themselves and belief in those around them. They were determined to do the right thing. They believed it so passionately it shone through them and out of them to others. It beamed so brightly that others could almost feel the glow. This made them easy to follow. They also expressed themselves in a way that convinced others to follow. Honestly, openly, with zest, heart and passion.

FROZEN OUT: Leadership When Everything Goes Wrong

The explorer Ernest Shackleton wasn't the first to the South Pole, or even the second. He didn't succeed in his dream to cross Antarctica. His ship, the *Endurance*, was crushed in the ice and his crew was stranded at the bottom of the world. So why do we still remember him?

Perhaps because he so truly showed those qualities we understand as leadership on his 1914–17 expedition. First, he had a relentless optimism. Even in the darkest times, Shackleton had the ability to lift spirits with games and singing. It was no coincidence that while they abandoned almost everything from their ship before it sank to the bottom of the Weddell Sea, he insisted that meteorologist Leonard Hussey took his banjo with him. Lose morale and you've lost everything. (Later, at least some of the crew members grew a little tired of his 'six known tunes', but that's understandable considering they had to wait 127 days to be rescued!)

The second big thing is that Shackleton inspired people with his vision. He explained to his crew exactly what they were going to do, and most importantly, how they could achieve it together. He made time to talk with everyone from the cook to his second-in-command. Crossing Antarctica wasn't his goal, it was *their* goal. He fostered that great spirit of unity.

Next, he wasn't too proud to change his plan. When things went wrong (and they went very wrong), he made a new plan. All of that encouragement and time he'd invested in his team now paid off. They were prepared to follow him even when things looked hopeless. And because he never gave up, they never gave up.

He made his daring voyage to South Georgia to seek help, and then made three separate attempts to go back for his crew marooned on Elephant Island. Each time, he was beaten back by the elements. But finally, he succeeded in rescuing every one of them. Above all, he never left anyone behind. This is so key for any Scout leader. Write it on your heart: we never leave anyone behind.

THE BRAVEST LEADER OF ALL: *Prisoner 46664*

In the 1960s, Nelson Mandela knew that racial discrimination in South Africa was wrong. As did millions of others. Like them, he believed he was right to challenge the apartheid system, and he believed that one day all South Africans would be free and enjoy the same rights.

What made him different was that he believed he could change the system.

He suffered every setback you can imagine. He was imprisoned for twenty-seven years in three separate prisons, including one on an island where he was forced to do hard labour. Why imprison him there under such harsh conditions? The authorities were afraid of what he could do.

While he was on Robben Island, Mandela was given the prisoner number 46664 – a way to dehumanise him; they treated him as a number instead of a man. And they worked him from dawn to dusk, breaking rocks and having no communication with anyone else.

Can you imagine? Day after day of toil and loneliness. Would it make you angry? Would it make you feel hopeless?

It only made Mandela more convinced that he needed to do the right thing and stop the hatred and discrimination. After many, many years, his bravery and patience eventually paid off. He won the attention of the world with his quiet, determined leadership against the struggle. The apartheid system was dismantled, and he became the first black president of South Africa. As president, he did not seek revenge on those who imprisoned him. He sought peace and reconciliation so his country could rebuild itself in a spirit of partnership and togetherness.

TEN TOP TIPS *for Being a Great Leader*

1 LEAD BY EXAMPLE

Those in your team are always watching you. They want to see how you behave and react to things. If you're calm in a crisis, they're more likely to be calm. If you work hard, they're more likely to work hard. If you do your share of the dull or tedious stuff, they're less likely to complain. A group or organisation always reflects its leader, so think carefully about your words and actions, because your team will mirror them. But remember, it's not a team if only one person does all the work. Nelson Mandela famously said, 'Lead from the back – and let others believe they are in front.' Or as former US president Harry S. Truman once said: 'It is amazing what you can accomplish if you do not care who gets the credit.'

2 LET PEOPLE KNOW WHERE THEY'RE HEADING (AND WHAT THEY NEED TO DO)

People need direction. They need to know where they're heading and how they're going to get there. But even more importantly, they need to know why. If you can explain why it's vital you build that raft or reach that fundraising target, they'll be so much more willing to give their all. People who *want* to do something will work twice as hard as the person who is told they *have* to do something.

There's one more thing too: a great team should be filled with talented people, but they shouldn't all have the same talents. Make sure you give people a clear role or task in the team that matches their particular skills and interests.

3 BE POSITIVE

Things will go wrong. Plans will fall apart and you'll lose your way. You'll hear others complain and it'll be so temping to join in. Resist the temptation. If you can stay positive and upbeat, determined to get things back on track, this will give your team the lift they need to do the same. There were plenty of serious setbacks before people finally landed on the moon, particularly the loss of the three crew of *Apollo I* in a fire in January 1967. But they eventually succeeded thanks to the positive vision of the leaders and their determination not to give up. So anticipate some failures along the way, some setbacks. These are simply reminders that you're on the right path!

4 LISTEN (AND BE PREPARED TO CHANGE)

Being the leader doesn't automatically mean you're the person who always has the best idea. That idea could just as well come from the quietest person in your team. Your role as a leader is to give them the opportunity to speak, make sure their voice is heard, to listen to what they have to say, and then make a decision.

And here's the biggest challenge of all: you shouldn't be afraid to change your mind based on what you've heard. Admitting you were wrong, or that someone has a better idea than you, is one of the biggest and bravest things you can do as a leader. And remember, no decision is almost always worse than a wrong decision! As a leader, you need to be able to make decisions, to amend them if needed and then to follow them through.

5 BE APPROACHABLE

People will only share things with you if you're open and approachable. That's why a lot of great leaders have an 'open door policy', showing that they're happy for anyone to share a story or idea. However, lots of people still don't walk through the open door because they're intimidated and afraid they'll be made to look foolish. A good leader will always be thinking about others, and how people feel, and they'll make a special effort to talk to people and get to know them, so they feel they can always talk openly with them.

6 DON'T BE AFRAID TO SHOW YOU'RE VULNERABLE

Just because you're the leader doesn't mean you have to be a superhero. As a leader, you don't have to be perfect. You just need to be honest. Leaders are human too. They have weaknesses and get grumpy and tired like the rest of us. But the best leaders admit this at times and are respected more because of their honesty. Remember, vulnerability is the door to connection with others.

7 KEEP YOUR EYES ON THE HORIZON

Sometimes the solution to a problem isn't something you know yet. That's why leaders always need to have their ear to the ground and their eyes on the horizon. Technology develops at lightning-quick speed. Just think, twenty years ago no one had heard of social media, and 150 years ago, no one had heard of motor cars. Champion new ideas and see how they can help you and your team. No one knows what's just around the next corner. But good leaders will be the first to find out. Good leaders have vision. And that means being willing to embrace new ideas and concepts – even if they don't always work out perfectly!

8 BE RESILIENT

Get used to this idea: you'll have more setbacks than you'll have successes. That's why you need to develop an inner core of strength to draw on in tough times. Sometimes you'll feel very lonely – mostly when things are going wrong.

But if you can come back with another idea and smile through the rain, then you have the makings of a great leader. The secret to that is building your resilience; your determination to pick yourself up and keep going.

There'll come a time when we face something so hard, so draining and difficult, that we feel that this time it's impossible to find a solution. This will be your true test. When you face your own 'Everest'. The trick is to know there's always a way, and that at some point, you'll be on the other side, smiling again. Just make a decision to keep going, despite the feelings of fear or failure. Keep going and you will endure.

9 KEEP YOUR PROMISES

The most precious thing a leader can earn isn't money; it's trust. And the best way to earn this is to keep the promises you make. Once people understand that you're reliable, and that you keep your word and do what you say, then they will trust you. Once we can depend on a leader, to know that they'll always try to do the right thing, then we feel safe to follow them anywhere. But this won't happen overnight. People want to see that you do this time and again.

10 KEEP LEARNING AND DEVELOPING

It's important to understand your strengths and weaknesses. For example, if you know that you talk more than you listen, make a real effort to let others speak. If you know that you're backward when it comes to forward planning, make time to do more of this. Bad leaders never admit their weaknesses, even to themselves, and that's why they never get better as a result. Humility in everything is so fundamental to great leadership. This is never more important than with our own many failings. Be human. Be real. And people will follow you.

As a leader, things will go wrong, but you should never stop trying. There's no short cut to your goals that somehow magically avoids failure. Failure is just a doorway. We must pass through a few, maybe many, of them in order to succeed.

As they say: 'A light can only shine through cracked vessels.' We should never try to hide our struggles or failings, but instead know that they are part of what make us. And when we acknowledge them openly and honestly, then the light shines through those cracks and people will warm to you. But no cracks, no light!

FIVE TOP TIPS to Be a Better Leader

1. Leadership isn't about being in charge, it's about taking care of those in your charge.
2. A leader should always have integrity; be trustworthy and avoid the easy route.
3. Serve others and put them first.
4. Build others up and empower them.
5. Lead by example: walk towards and through the difficult stuff.

EATING CRACKERS WITH THE PRESIDENT

I once had the honour of having an adventure in the wilds of Alaska with former US president Barack Obama. Undeniably, he has many of those great leadership qualities of strength, stillness and wisdom, but he also has a great sense of humour. When I cooked him some wild salmon on an open fire, he said it would've been nice to have a cracker to go with it. We talked about our responsibilities and our concerns for the world around us. Spending time with him, I really understood why people wanted to follow him. He listens and makes you feel valued, but he lets you know he's just a person like you and me too – who happens to like the occasional cracker!

How to

camp cookbook
survival guide
BIRDS
scouting
EPIC ADVENTURES
HOW TO BE A SCOUT
WILDLIFE
KNOTS
SAILING
MAPS
POLAR BEARS
ARCTIC ADVENTURES
FORAGING
GREAT ADVENTURES
MOUNTAINS
Ghost stories
TRACKING
camping
PLANTS
JOURNIES

MAKE A DIFFERENCE

WE ALL KNOW it feels good to help people. But why? Well, partly because it's a natural human instinct; your mind and body somehow know it's the right thing to do. But helping others goes far beyond just ourselves.

Helping others is what makes civilisations work: cooperating and looking after each other means that we can create safe places to live where people can be happy, healthy and live longer. And who doesn't want that?

And when it comes to making a difference in this world, so much comes down to one word: kindness. The word itself comes from the old German word *kundi* (meaning 'natural' or 'native'), from other words like *kunjam* and *kin* which mean 'family'. Kindness is what a family naturally shows each other. And if a society acts like a family, looking after its most vulnerable, then that's a society that's working well.

Margaret Mead, an anthropologist (someone who studies humans), said that a healed femur (thigh bone) is the earliest sign of true civilisation. This seems a strange thing to say, but it actually makes a huge amount of sense when you study it.

In ancient times, someone who broke their leg and wasn't able to hunt or forage would have stood next to no chance of surviving – unless someone was there to look after them. This person, who fed them, allowed them to rest and heal, was one of the first truly civilised people – because they were helping someone other than themselves.

They were being kind.

And when lots of people start acting in this way, then you're well on your way to a fair and just society.

Why Kindness Matters

Helping others helps us forget about some of our own troubles. When we're helping someone who's less fortunate than us, it helps us appreciate how much we have and it helps put things in perspective.

But there's something scientific going on too. When you help someone, your brain releases a hormone called oxytocin, which creates a feeling of connection and empathy. This is the same feeling you get when you're with your family and friends.

Imagine a world where we all helped others. It would be a much kinder, nicer place to live.

Ultimately, helping others allows us to do something that is bigger and better than just ourselves. It elevates us to a place that is greater than anything we can make on our own.

As the inspirational speaker Zig Ziglar once said: 'You can get anything you want in life, if you help enough other people get what they want.' He was right. It is how the world works, even though it feels topsy turvy. But life is topsy turvy. And when we give things away, we actually receive more in return.

And that leads us onto volunteering . . .

Why Volunteering Matters

There are over a billion volunteers in the world. That's one in eight of all the people on earth. These are the people who freely give their time to help others, making their communities better places and improving the lives of those around them. These are the people who keep our society going – it's their kindness and generosity that binds us together.

Whether they give their time regularly or just occasionally, they're doing something great. But they get something even greater in return: that feeling that they're part of something bigger than themselves. Remember, when we give, we receive. It's one of the fundamental laws of the universe. Like: to win a friend, be a friend.

Baden-Powell, the founder of Scouting, said it perfectly: 'The real way to get happiness is by giving out happiness to other people.'

That's it.

Share Your Sunshine

Everyone has their own store of energy. Sometimes it's easier to just stay in and watch a TV series or scroll on your social media. But after a while, you'll start to feel restless. Why? Because you're not really connecting with people and you're giving nothing away. Human beings are sociable and cooperative. We're at our best when we're with others, sharing our talents and skills. There's no one quite like you, and there's no one who's got the same things to offer. So why not put some of that good energy to use? Go help others.

As Baden-Powell also said: 'Leave this world a little better than you found it.'

Volunteering

Giving your time is perhaps the most powerful thing you can do. There are hundreds of thousands of charities that need your time. From helping in a local charity shop, supporting a running club or taking part in a reading or befriending scheme, to supporting vulnerable people, it's best to start by simply finding something you're passionate about. What do *you* care most about? What issues are affecting *you* and *your* family?

And as a young volunteer, your energy is your advantage! Use it to serve others and you will build a solid foundation of happiness for your own life.

Benefits of Volunteering

- Great skills and experience for your CV, or when applying for college.
- A bigger circle of friends in your local area. You'll meet new and different people. Most importantly, you'll meet kind and sparky people (the best kind).
- Better mental well-being.
- That 'warm glow' you get inside when you help someone.
- Volunteering brings people together from many different walks of life, which in turn helps create stronger bonds between us – reminding us that we have more in common than we think.

How to Be a Great Volunteer

1. FIND A CAUSE YOU'RE PASSIONATE ABOUT
   Whether that's being a young leader in Scouts, helping younger children get opportunities to get outdoors or supporting a charity that's tackling an issue that affects you or a family member, you'll give more if you're fired up about it.
2. BE RELIABLE
   Although you're not being paid, people will still be relying on you. Keep your promises, turn up on time and do your best. If you do that, you'll end up with even more interesting opportunities opening up, and you'll be valued and appreciated by many.

3 DON'T BE TOO PROUD

Remember there are all sorts of things that need doing – not all of them glamorous! So don't turn your nose up to opportunities. Be prepared to muck in. If you do some of the mundane things, more challenging things are bound to turn up. Cleaning loos or peeling spuds? Count us in. Just not at the same time!

4 KEEP AN OPEN MIND

Welcome new experiences and different ways of looking at the world. They'll help you develop as a person as well as a volunteer. There's nothing more interesting than finding out how others live their lives.

5 PUT YOURSELF IN OTHER PEOPLE'S SHOES

Empathy is one of the greatest qualities a volunteer can have – the ability to understand what someone else is feeling. It allows you to understand why people do things, and it will help you to be able to best support them.

6 LISTEN

This is one of the greatest skills a volunteer can have. Not simply giving people the support we think they need, but asking them, and then giving them the support they really need. There are lots of ways to be a great listener. The most important is not to speak until the other person has finished.

7 LEARN FROM OTHERS

You're bound to meet volunteers who've been helping longer than you. Ask them questions. Find out what they like doing best and try to get to know them as a person. They're sure to have some really useful tips that will make your volunteering life easier (even if that's just how to find the coffee machine!).

8 BE RESPECTFUL

One of the great things about volunteering is that you'll meet and work with people who are different to you. They might come from a completely different background and culture. If you're not sure how to act, or if you're afraid of offending someone, then ask the person to guide you. Most will only be too happy to help you learn more about them.

9 **BE A TEAM PLAYER**
Remember you're not on your own. As a volunteer, you'll be part of a team and you should have someone there to guide and help you along the way. Don't be afraid to ask for help. That can be the bravest thing to do of all.

10 **BE KIND**
You'll meet all sorts of people as a volunteer. You might not like or get on with all of them. But they could be going through all sorts of things you don't know about. So whatever you do, try to do the kind thing.

There's an eleventh rule too – which is **Have fun**! Volunteering and helping other people is an amazing thing. So wear that smile with pride, even if what you're doing is tough. The greatest gift you can give someone is happiness, and as someone once said, most smiles are started by another smile.

Take On a Fundraising Challenge

To help make a difference, some people take on a challenge to raise money for a great cause. This could be anything from climbing a mountain to paddling a river.

UK Scouts took on the challenge of hiking to the moon together to raise money for local communities during the Covid-19 pandemic. By walking a mile in their gardens and local parks, they collectively hiked the 500,000 miles to the moon and back! Not content with that, they then raced round the world, with teams of Cubs, Beavers, Scouts and Explorers competing against each other. Young people were sponsored to travel a mile or more in their local areas, then they contributed their distance to their team total. The Cubs were first to get all the way around the world! Between these two great challenges, UK Scouts raised over £1 million.

ALONE WE CAN DO SO LITTLE, TOGETHER WE CAN DO SO MUCH

I've developed such huge respect for volunteers: they're a core part of making our world a better place. I have never met a volunteer who resents giving up their time to help and inspire others. In fact, the opposite is generally true. They've learnt something that is often forgotten: that volunteering works both ways. It's not just the recipient who benefits in the obvious ways; the truth is that the volunteer always gains the most.

Volunteering helps take your mind off your own worries and gives you a renewed sense of purpose and perspective. And there's overwhelming evidence that volunteering helps battle stress and anxiety, which so many of us can be prone to.

On top of that, we learn new skills and interests that we can take into the workplace.

I have witnessed first-hand how volunteering can bring together people of all races, ages and backgrounds, and change communities all over the world for the better. This is a vitally important mission for us to be part of.

Raise Awareness of a Great Cause

Maybe you or a member of your family has a condition or illness that's not widely recognised or understood. What could you do to raise awareness of this condition? Maybe you could make a short film, or write a blog or article?

Perhaps you could even contact a charity and offer to be a spokesperson or ambassador, like Nicole, a Scout from Northern Ireland. Nicole has a condition called FND. Due to this, she became a target of online bullying when other young people shared videos of her having seizures. Instead of letting this bring her down, she turned it into a story of resilience. This has helped others come forward and they now have a support network in place. She's now an ambassador, speaking at medical events and summits on what it means to be a teenager with the condition, and was made one of the UK Chief Scout's Unsung Heroes.

Random Acts of Kindness

One brilliant thing you can do is look for ways to be kind in your everyday life. Is there someone standing on their own who looks like they need a friend? Is someone struggling to reach something in the supermarket? Be that person who reaches up and helps them out. That smile you'll receive in return is a great reward!

Take Part in a Big Clear Up

We should all respect and look after the places we live. One Scout decided to take on the challenge of picking up litter in her local area while racing around on her skateboard. What a great idea!

NEO'S STORY – TREATS FOR KIDS

Neo was an eight-year-old Cub Scout from the UK when he set up Treats For Kids. It was 2020, during the Covid-19 pandemic, and he realised there were so many children going through a tough time due to the pandemic and other reasons beyond their control. 'I wanted to do something to help,' he says, 'to put a smile on their faces. I love treats and believe that *all* children deserve treats no matter what they're going through.

'Through my Treats For Kids appeals and fundraising I have donated over 12,901 treats to children via fifteen different charities and organisations, including food banks, hospitals and hospices. Treats have included advent calendars and Easter eggs.'

As a reward for his amazing work helping others, Neo was proudly named as one of the UK Chief Scout's Unsung Heroes.

How to

PROTECT OUR PLANET

THE EARTH IS the only home we have (unless you happen to live on the International Space Station). There is no planet B. That's why it makes sense that we look after our world and do everything we can to protect it.

As Scouts, we love the outdoors. It's where we learn, play and are at our best. But if we use and enjoy the outdoors, then we also have a duty to protect it too. We're not masters of the earth but its stewards, or caretakers. That means it's our job to look after it well, to make sure we hand on a healthy planet to those who come after us.

A key part of looking after our earth is committing to sustainability. That's a word you hear a lot these days. But what does it actually mean? It's about using the resources we need today while making sure future generations have what they need too. That means replanting forests where we've cut down trees. It means not polluting our oceans with plastics and chemicals, and not using and burning cheap fossil fuels without considering the lasting impact on our planet.

But sustainability isn't just about careful use of our natural resources and planning for the future of our planet. It's also about making sure the world economy is in balance so people across the world have what they need to live happy and fulfilled lives. There's a social aspect too – making sure that human rights are respected so that families and communities all over the world can be safe and healthy.

Why We Need to Act Now

It's clear that climate change is happening at an alarming rate. Our planet is rapidly warming as a result of human activities, especially burning fossil fuels, increasing the release of greenhouse gases like carbon dioxide into the atmosphere. We're seeing extreme weather events like floods and droughts almost every day on the news and in every country in the world. That's why we need to take action today, not tomorrow.

It's all too easy to think that stopping climate change is someone else's problem. That it's too big for any of us to solve. Or that it's an issue that can only be tackled by world leaders. The reality is that we can only make the change we need if we all take personal and collective responsibility, acting together and doing our bit. A lot of small actions add up to one big difference.

Bringing Global Warming Under Control

The world is slowly waking up to the reality of climate change. But we still have so far to go. World leaders have declared that the rise in global temperatures must be limited to 2°C by the end of this century if the world is to remain stable and continue to sustain life as we know it.

However, most people believe that we actually need to limit this to 1.5°C if we are to give the earth a fighting chance. The difference between 2°C and 1.5°C doesn't sound much, but it will mean 2 million square metres of permafrost at the poles will be saved and 10 million fewer people losing their homes to rising sea levels. Put it like that and it makes a lot more sense.

If we need a reminder about how serious things have got, just take a look at some of these facts and figures:

- As a result of global warming, 150 billion tons of ice are vanishing from Antarctica every year.
- Every year, 12 million hectares of land are lost to drought; fertile ground for growing crops is becoming desert.
- In just two years (2018–20), 30 million acres of land were lost to forest fires.
- Three hundred thousand people a year are dying from heatwaves, more than a 50 per cent increase over the last twenty years.
- Half of the coral from the Great Barrier Reef has been lost in the last thirty years due to warming oceans.
- Each year, 13 million tons of plastic find their way into our oceans.
- As ocean levels rise due to melting ice, the homes of 200 million people will be lost.

No matter where we live in the world, we can see the effects of climate change all around us. Even in your local supermarket, you'll sometimes see empty shelves where fruit and vegetables should be. Unseasonable floods, snow and hail mean farmers are facing huge challenges, and crops are becoming more unreliable.

TEN THINGS We Can All Do to Stop Climate Change

All this means we need to focus on practical things we can do that will help stop climate change. If we all make some simple changes in our everyday lives, we'll have a better chance of handing on a healthy planet to our children and grandchildren.

1 REDUCE

Simply reducing the amount we buy and use makes a dramatic difference. While there are still millions in the world who do not have enough, there are millions more who have too much. Fast fashion, consumer culture and slick advertising persuade us to buy things we don't need. Yet some of the happiest people I have met are those who often have little, or who have maybe made a decision to remove excess clutter from their lives.

Instead of buying something new, let's repair the things we have. Rather than buying single-use items like plastic straws and bottles, let's invest in reusable ones. Let's hang washing on the line rather than use the tumble dryer.

2 REUSE

Once you're finished with something, whether it's a book, a toy, some clothing or a gadget, pass it on. There's a thriving second-hand market, and you might be able to make some valuable spare change by selling your unwanted things. If you're a Scout and no longer use a uniform you wore when you were younger, give it back to the group. There's bound to be a Scouting family grateful for it. Let's not spend money on buying new things unless we have to.

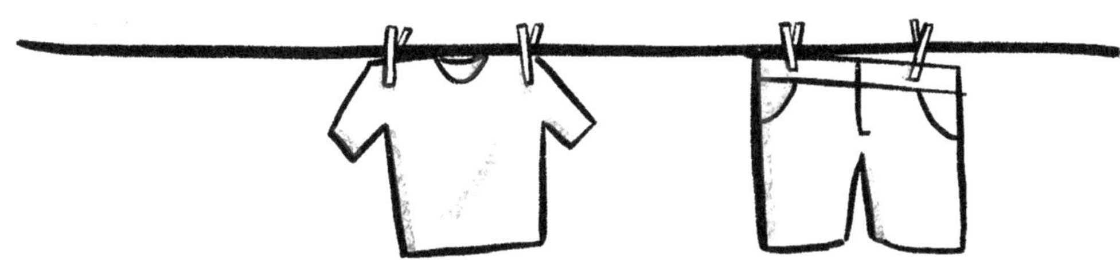

3 RECYCLE

Things can be made from the things we no longer want. New paper is made from old paper; new plastic is made in the same way. Make sure you sort your rubbish so materials that can be recycled, like glass and cardboard, go to the right places. Unless we take the time to do this, so much of what could be recycled ends up in landfill (it's just buried in the ground). By 2050, the world will be producing 3.4 billion metric tons of waste. Despite this, only 20 per cent of waste is recycled. That needs to change.

4 SWITCH OFF YOUR VAMPIRE DEVICES

Many of the gadgets and devices we own have what's called a standby feature. Our smart speakers, TVs, computers, printers and games consoles have a button you press that gives you the impression you've switched them off. The screen goes dark, they go silent or a light goes out. In fact, they continue to drain power, cost you money and harm the environment. That's why some people call these vampire devices – they carry on silently feeding, often at night when we're asleep.

5 THINK BEFORE YOU TRAVEL (AND GO BY BIKE)

Walking and cycling are not only the greenest ways to travel, they can be the most fun too (it's hard to smell the wildflowers at the side of the road when you're flying past them at 70 mph). People are switching more and more to public transport, using cars only when they have to. Working from home has reduced traffic on our roads, yet trucks and cars are still responsible for over 70 per cent of greenhouse gas emissions in Europe, compared with only 0.4 per cent from railways.

6 EAT SUSTAINABLY AND FROM REGENERATIVE SOURCES

Just like any of our planet's resources, our food needs to be sustainable too. This means thinking carefully about where it comes from and what methods are used to produce it. Is our meat produced in farms where animals are treated poorly or farmed too intensively? Are harmful chemicals used to grow the crops to make our bread and pasta? It's important that we ask these questions if we are to preserve the soil and healthy livestock for future generations.

Eating sustainably means choosing food that's been ethically produced, that won't harm our planet, leaving less waste, allowing natural sources to regenerate themselves.

Cutting out waste is also an important factor. Very simply, if we ate all the food we buy, we wouldn't need to produce as much of it. Other simple ways to make our diet more sustainable are to eat seasonal products which are in plentiful supply.

Think about the people producing the food too. If you buy Fair Trade products, for example, you'll know the farmers have received a fair price for their produce.

7 SHOP GREENER

As consumers (people who buy stuff), we have huge power to stop companies that harm our planet: we can simply stop buying from them. But sometimes it can be hard to tell who is and who isn't on the side of our planet. Many businesses will say that they're green and sustainable without doing much to prove it. So do some research into the companies you and your family buy from. Look online to find out if they have a sustainability policy, how they're reducing their environmental impact and what their plans are for the future. You can then make an informed decision about whether to continue shopping from them. This can sometimes be a tough decision. You might find out that a company that isn't doing much to help the environment is also the cheapest, tastiest or most convenient option. You might love their hamburgers, chocolate bars or free delivery service, but if we want to make change, we have to make sacrifices. Be smart and use your power to buy and influence for good.

8 SHOP SMARTER

We all feel guilty sometimes when a tiny product we've bought online arrives in a giant box with masses of plastic. While this is far from ideal, in fact, the packaging amounts for only a small amount of the damage to the environment. The greater affect is to do with the delivery. We can help reduce this by committing to shop locally. We can also make sure we opt to have multiple items delivered at the same time, in a single box, by a single van. It might mean waiting a day or two longer to get your stuff, but just think of the carbon you're saving. You're in charge, remember.

9 USE PICK-UP POINTS

The extra miles the delivery van has to travel to get to your front door adds up. That's why some choose to have their deliveries sent to a pick-up point. You then collect all your deliveries at the same time.

10 BUY LOCAL

By buying local, we can ensure the food we eat and the products we use have not travelled far to get to us. If they haven't been flown halfway across the planet, the carbon footprint is much reduced. If tomatoes are grown locally (or even better, in your garden, allotment or window box), then there's no need to buy a tomato that's spent the last week flying at 40,000 ft across the ocean. Chances are, that tomato has travelled more than many people have in their entire lives! Local tomatoes will also be fresher and juicier than those that have been vacuum packed on the other side of the world. Shopping local also means keeping money in the local economy, which means it could help make your area more prosperous, with better facilities.

Remember, we can't do it all on our own but we can all do our bit. We can't just rely on politicians and business leaders to make big and brave decisions to protect the planet (although we must continue to demand that they do). If we all make small changes to the way we live our lives and spend our money, we can make a big difference too.

So what's the one simple thing you can do to protect our planet? Well, the truth is there is no 'fix-all' answer. There are instead many answers, all of which give us hope. We can work together across generations, understanding that a better future depends on our ability to work together. We need to make changes in the way we live our lives, while also demanding action from our leaders and politicians.

WHY A BETTER FUTURE MATTERS

Sustainability matters. A greener, cleaner world *really* matters. None of us would disagree with that. But words alone aren't enough. That's why this also has to be a time for positive action and real change.

I've spent my life in the outdoors. Climbing mountains, crossing oceans, living eye to eye with incredible creatures in jungles and deserts. The miracle of planet earth never ceases to amaze me. Let's never forget, it's only that thin atmosphere – that fragile halo around the earth – that keeps us alive. I'm concerned not just as a father but as a citizen of the world. As someone who simply wants to protect our world for future generations. Someone who's fearful of how far we might go before it's too late.

Everybody knows the threats our world is facing. Climate change has led to flooding, drought and instability. Our actions and our addiction to fossil fuels have led to an unpredictable and dangerous world. I'm so proud of all the actions our Scouts take. At COP26 back in 2021 in Glasgow, our leaders gathered to take action. Our young people, as active citizens, made their voices heard. I was there with the Scouts, as Chief Ambassador of World Scouting, representing 57 million members around the world as they made a promise to the planet. Every one of them made a pledge to recover, reuse, rethink and recycle.

And if there's one thing that amazes me even more than nature and the outdoors, it's young people. This is their world more than ours. We've been the caretakers, and let's be honest, we haven't made a great job of it. But here's the thing: we never give up hope; we never give up believing things can be better; and we must never give up making change happen.

People talk about a fuel crisis. But do you know what is the most powerful fuel of all? Not nuclear. Not gas. Not even wind. It's education. It's giving young people the skills they need for a changing world. Equipping them for the future.

And it's about putting the outdoors at the heart of growing up. It's only when we stand on hilltops, looking out at the horizon, that we can see why this world is worth fighting for. Only when we feel the wind on our faces, that we can be truly connected to the world around us. We learn to tune into nature; feel its power. Learn to work with it; not to defy it.

Leave No Trace

Growing up on the Isle of Wight, my father would often take me on adventures climbing the cliffs around the coast. I have so many great memories of those beautiful places and I still take my children there. Unfortunately, I can also remember the litter some people would leave behind – which turned into a game for us, scrambling around to see who could pick up the most in five minutes!

For as long as I can remember, my father always taught us to be respectful, whether it's to your friends, family and peers, or to the environment. Being respectful and mindful when it comes to littering is just a small change, but it is one that can make a huge difference to the environment around us.

I meet so many Scouts worldwide who are always keen to get involved with clean-ups, and it is inspiring to see. Plastic pollution is a huge issue that not enough people know about or know how to help, but it really is as simple as being mindful of the space around you. We have such beautiful outdoors spaces across the world for everyone to enjoy, but which can be ruined so easily by litter. If everyone can do their bit and pick up a little each time, we can really make a change.

Scouts are always ahead of the curve on this challenge. They've been out there on our streets, by our canals and in our local communities tackling the problem for as long as I've known. It's in our values as Scouts to be respectful and considerate, which is why the Scouts have already made so much fantastic progress – but more needs to be done.

Sceptics

People sometimes question climate change, and whether the effects of fossil fuels or humans are really significant or not. As Scouts though, a simple reply might be this: if you love something, you do all you can to protect it and respect it. So let's do all we can not to pollute, damage or destroy the beautiful world around us. Let's commit together to protect, restore, reuse, recycle, regrow, regenerate as much as we can – in order to help mother nature thrive, and not to choke her.

Make a Seed Bomb and Plant a Wildflower Garden

One of the most hopeful and inspiring things you can do for our planet is to plant a garden. In the words of the late actress Audrey Hepburn: 'To plant a garden is to believe in tomorrow.' Here's a fun activity you can do with some friends to make this happen.

1. Find an area to plant your seeds. Make sure you get permission from the landowner first.
2. Mix together one cup of wildflower seeds with five cups of peat-free compost and two or three cups of clay powder.
3. Slowly add water until everything sticks together.
4. Roll the mixture into firm balls, about the size of golf balls.
5. Place the balls on newspaper and leave them to dry in a warm place.
6. On the count of three, throw your seed bombs into your designated area.
7. Wait for a thousand flowers to bloom.

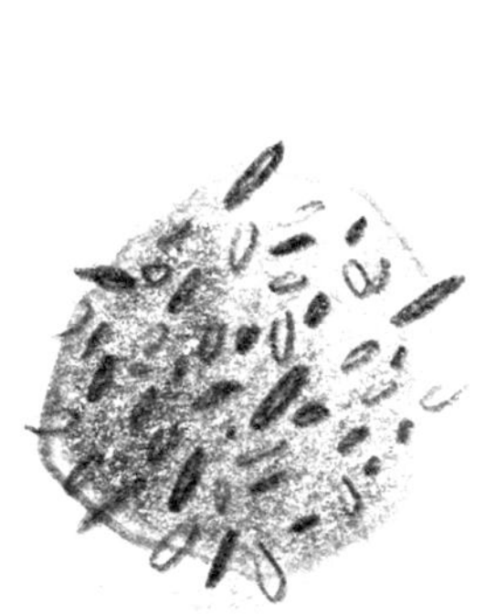

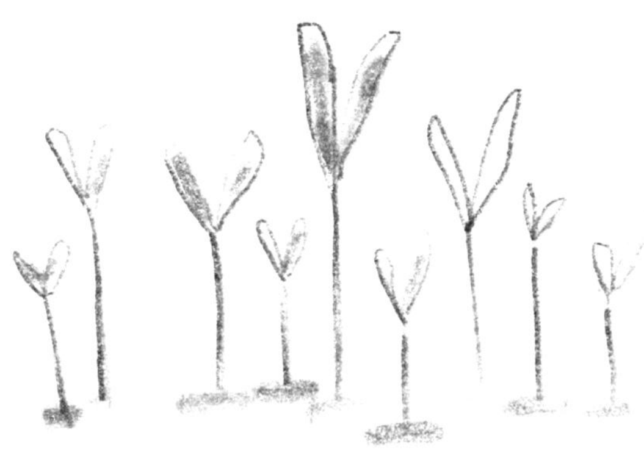

PART TWO

How to be an

ADVENTURER

How to

SURVIVE

ONE THING THAT will never change is that the world is full of dangers. As Scouts, and in order to stay safe, we must always be alert and vigilant. Prepared for those dangers. There might be a time, maybe when out hiking or camping, when you find yourself in trouble, alone and in danger. That's why every adventurer needs some basic survival techniques to keep you (and others) safe until help arrives or the danger passes. Scouts call this 'being prepared'.

A simple trip can suddenly go wrong for all sorts of reasons. You could find you've lost your way and have no phone signal. The weather may have turned – strong winds and driving rain high up on a mountainside can quickly become dangerous. A huge snowfall can make a landscape look completely different, obscuring features that might help you navigate. Avalanches, flash floods, lightning or getting injured. All these factors can change a situation from being an adventure into a disaster.

What's your greatest tool in terms of survival? A knife? A GPS? Well, here's the thing, survival isn't about having a huge bag full of tools, gadgets or the latest windproof technology. Yes, some of that could come in handy (and a basic first aid kit is essential) but there's something much more important. That's your *attitude*. This means how you tackle a situation. Your thoughts, beliefs and what you focus on.

Your attitude is not something you can buy in an outdoor shop. It's something deep inside you that determines how you approach a situation. For example, do you see a problem or do you see a challenge? Because how you think and see things can make the critical difference in terms of staying alive. Attitude is everything. And a great attitude will keep you going when things seem at their worst and help you make the right decisions.

Pack the right skills and the right attitude and you are three-quarters of the way to safety. Survival is not about being fearless. It's about feeling that fear but committing to give your best and give your all, to make it out in one piece. It's about making a decision to live. Our fate is determined by how far we are prepared to push ourselves to stay alive – the decisions we make to survive. Are we able to do whatever it takes to endure and make it home?

Survival Essentials – That You Can't See!

Positivity

Don't waste energy on negative thoughts. Complaining never saved anyone. If you allow your spirit to sag, your body will soon follow. Choose to be positive, even when you might not feel it. Wear positivity like a T-shirt. Put it on every day. Because by keeping a positive mind-set, you're letting your body know that the fight's not over. It's never over. You're in charge and you can decide!

Courage

Take a deep breath. Grit your teeth. You're braver than you think and stronger than you know. Keep moving forward, against the odds, against your fears and against the problems and challenges. That's courage. Doing the difficult, despite the giants that loom over us and threaten us.

Determination

Remember, human beings have an inbuilt survival instinct. Somewhere inside us is a steely core of determination that will give us the strength to pull through the hardest and most terrifying of times. It is always there if you look for it. Be bold, be determined, and develop, train and use that never-give-up spirit. It is nature's gift to you – use it.

Kindness

Survival situations are stressful. People can act in all sorts of strange ways when they're under pressure – and not always in good ways. Be forgiving of people when they are scared and they act irrationally, and choose to act with kindness yourself in those moments. Remember, every action and thought can be your choice. Choose well, choose kindly. Just a few kind and reassuring words can make all the difference to someone in a tough moment.

Resourcefulness

Don't think about all the things you haven't got (and wished you'd brought with you). It's too late for that now. Look at what you do have and think how you can use that instead. Think laterally. Improvise, adapt, overcome. Always. Be smart. One person's trash is another person's treasure.

Faith

Believing that you'll get through this is perhaps most important of all. Keep the faith that at some point you'll be on the other side. Faith, belief, trust, hope. Small words with big consequences. They can change a situation from dire to higher.

Sometimes when we are down on our knees struggling, and we look up for help, we can find ourselves standing taller than ever before. Faith empowers people and gives incredible strength. Scouts follow many faiths, and some have no faith and are on their own spiritual journey. For me, my Christian faith has often been light to a dark path and strength to a failing body.

Finding a faith isn't necessarily about going to church or another religious place. It's quiet and personal and it is rooted in asking for help from something bigger than us. Some call that praying. Some call it meditating. Whatever word you call it, try it. You've nothing to lose and everything to gain.

Remember to Stop

When you're in danger, before you do anything, STOP. A hundred things will be running through your head. Your heart will be thumping and your mind will be racing. You might feel like you need to take action straight away. But this also means you're more likely to make the wrong call.

So the most important thing to do first is STOP. Don't let blind panic make a bad situation even worse. Take a brief moment.

STOP stands for:

- **S**top. Resist the panic.
- **T**ake a moment. Breathe. Allow your pulse to slow and your mind to clear.
- **O**bserve. Take a look at what's around you. Maybe help or some protection from the danger is in sight and you just haven't noticed it yet.
- **P**lan. Now's the time to work out the most important next steps. Prioritise calmly and with consideration.

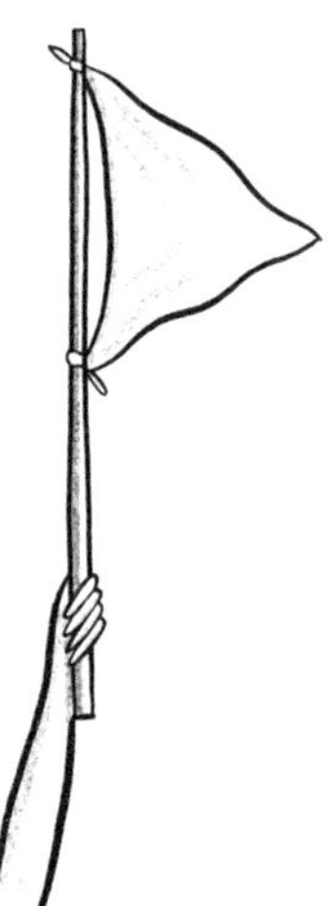

Your Survival Priorities

You now need to think about the four survival priorities: Please Remember What's First. PRWF. Which stands for Protection, Rescue, Water and Food.

Protection

The first, and most important, priority is protection. What is the main and immediate danger? Maybe it is other cars on the road after a pile-up on a motorway. Maybe it is the freezing wind and rain when you have nothing on except a thin shirt. Maybe it is a rising tide or a kitchen fire.

Weather can kill you so fast. The first priority of survival is getting protection from the extreme weather. In the wild, or if you are lost, that protection might take the form of an emergency shelter. Especially in a cold and exposed location. One of the biggest dangers in winter or in the mountains is hypothermia, when your body's core temperature drops below the critical point of 35°C. Look around for a cave, or dig a simple snow hole, or seek out a natural shelter created by rocks or fallen trees. Look at what materials you have. Could you rig up a shelter using a tarpaulin? Just keeping the wind and rain off you will dramatically increase your chances of survival.

Alternatively, in a hot desert, the greatest danger is the heat and the power of the sun. Seek shade, from trees, bushes or a sand dune. You can also make shade by digging a shallow trench into the sand.

A big part of wilderness protection is fire. Fire will keep you warm at night (it's not just the mountains that get cold, it is also the desert, where temperatures drop dramatically after dark). Fire is also vital as it can purify your water, cook food and ward off dangerous animals.

THREE WAYS to Make an Emergency Shelter

1. HOW TO MAKE A SHELTER WITH A TARPAULIN

1. Find two strong trees at least two metres apart. Try lying down lengthways between the trees to check it's long enough for you.
2. Tie a rope to each tree with a clove hitch (see page 233) and connect in the middle, making sure it's tight and reasonably low. If there's snow, attach the rope slightly higher as this will make steeper walls, and prevent snow gathering on your emergency tent.
3. Now drape a tarpaulin over the rope, making sure both sides reach the ground.
4. Secure the tarpaulin to the ground with lengths of extra rope, using small sharpened sticks for improvised pegs. If you have no more rope, you can use stones or rocks instead to weigh it down.

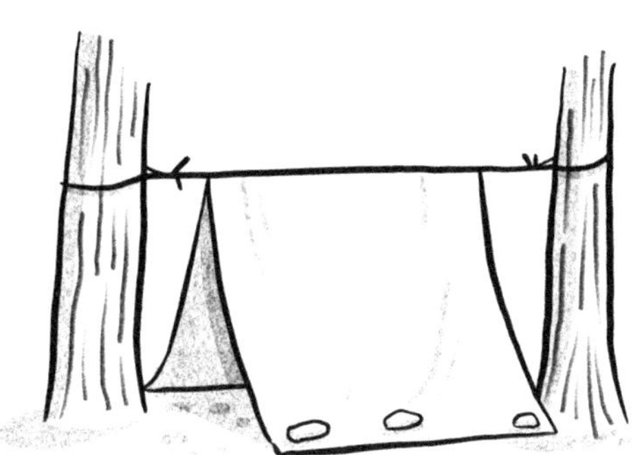

2. ONE-SIDED SHELTER

An alternative is to build a shelter with one side only. The other side will be open, ideally facing your fire to keep you warm. You can build this by securing a long branch between two trees, just below head height, then using sticks and leaves to build the side.

3. BOUGH BED

We lose the majority of our heat through the ground, so being insulated from the ground is even more important than what you place over you. Layering branches from evergreen trees beneath you will insulate you and provide a natural mattress to lie on. Place a log at either end to keep the branches in place. All great Scouts know that when it comes to camping out, one layer underneath is worth two on top.

Rescue

If you're trapped or stranded when out in the wild, it's vital you think about how you'll be rescued. Perhaps you've got an injured member of your party who can't be moved. Or maybe you've climbed to a place where there's no easy way down. In these circumstances, you might just need to wait it out – but there's a lot you can do to help your rescuers.

Rescue is likely to come from the air. But first, you need to attract their attention. The best way to do this is with visual markers, such as a tarpaulin secured on the ground or some skis left in a cross shape outside a snow cave. After all, it's no good being 'safe' in a snow hole if no one can locate you! Make a rescuer's task easier.

Fire is one of the best visual markers, but make sure you're prepared. You might only have seconds or minutes to get a fire going if a plane is flying past – so prepare one, with spare fuel next to it, so you can light it quickly and keep it going.

If you can't light a fire, then remember that any three objects placed neatly together is internationally recognised as a call for help. This can be three fires or three piles of rocks.

Other ways to attract attention include a flare (if you have one), a signalling mirror or a bright flashing light.

If you're lost in a desert or on a tropical island, you can write a giant 'SOS' in the sand (SOS is an internationally recognised symbol of 'requiring rescue'. It stands for Save Our Souls).

In Morse code (which for many years was an international method of communicating using short and long signals, lights or sounds, see page 328), SOS is symbolised with three dots, three dashes and three dots. Like this: **... --- ...** This pattern can be sent as a sound, such as tapping on a water pipe if you're trapped under rubble during an earthquake, or it can be sent visually as above.

To communicate with the pilot of a passing plane, you'll need to learn these signals:

- One arm raised: All is well.
- Both arms raised: Pick us up.
- Arms stretched out at both sides: We need mechanical help.
- Both arms behind your head with your hands on the back of your head: We have a radio.
- Lying down with arms stretched out straight behind you: We need medical help.
- Crouching down with bent knees, holding both arms out straight: Land here.
- Waving a coat from side to side: No.
- Waving a coat up and down: Yes.
- Both arms in the air waving to one side: Do not attempt to land.

If you've sent these signals, how do you know if the pilot has understood?

IN DAYLIGHT:

- Wings waggling from side to side: 'We understand you'.
- Flying in a circular, clockwise motion: 'We don't understand you'.

AT NIGHT:

- Green lights flashing on and off: 'We understand you'.
- Red lights flashing on and off: 'We don't understand you'.

LEAVE MESSAGES

In almost all survival scenarios, you are better off staying put where you are. For example, if your car breaks down in the desert, it is much safer to stay by the car and wait for someone to come along and spot you, than trying to walk to safety.

Stay safe, stay visible, stay hydrated. That's the Scout mantra.

There are only very few occasions when it is better to head off and attempt to self-rescue. One time might be if no one is ever likely to come your way and no one even knows you're missing. (This is why, as a Scout, it is so important that on expeditions, hikes and trips, you always tell someone where you are going and when you are due back. Then, if you are overdue, you know someone will begin a search procedure to try to locate you.)

If you decide to move on instead of waiting for rescue, make sure you leave a message in a safe, visible place. Leave as much detail as possible about who you are, how many are in your party, what condition you're in and where you're heading. Make sure you date your message. Leaving several messages will increase your chances of being found.

Water

Human beings can survive only three days without water (compared with three weeks without food), so finding clean drinking water is a critical-to-life priority. Just a small drop in hydration levels can impact your performance, strength and concentration, so prioritise finding a supply of drinkable fluids.

If water is scarce, doing hard work at night is a smart way to conserve your supply. In a hot desert, you can use urine to make a damp cloth to wrap around your head or neck. This might sound disgusting, but it might help keep you alive for longer. Scouts aren't afraid to do the difficult things in order to save themselves or others.

To find water, first look for a stream. These are easier to spot from a higher position, so climb a tree or hill to give yourself a better view. Follow the angle of the terrain to figure out where water might collect. Animal tracks will often lead you to water, and birds flock towards it at dusk too. Once you find a stream, then you can follow it downhill and it will eventually take you to a larger body of water, such as a river or lake. Civilisation and people tend to congregate around water sources, so rivers and lakes are often your best bet to find help.

Remember, when it comes to staying hydrated, you must boil water before drinking it to kill harmful bacteria. Placing water in direct sunlight for six hours can also kill bacteria, but is less reliable. In an emergency without fire or sunlight, you can strain the water through a homemade filter:

1 Cut a water bottle in half and fill the top section with layers of gravel, sand and charcoal.
2 Pour the water in at the open end and let it filter through and drip out of the mouth of the bottle.
3 Collect the contents and drink.

Boiling water is always the best method though to make it drinkable, but remember, clear water isn't necessarily clean water. Don't take chances with your water. If you get sick, you will get weaker fast. And in survival, you need your strength.

Food

Once you've found water, you can now start thinking about food. Remember, you can survive only three days without water, but you'll live three weeks without food. Plus, the more you eat, the more fluids you need to digest it. So if water is in short supply, limit your food intake.

While there's often plenty of natural plants and animals around, especially in forests and hilly areas, the key is knowing what's safe to eat.

- Acorns. Never eat a raw acorn. Leave that to squirrels.
- Mushrooms and berries. You need to be extremely careful eating both in the wild. If in any doubt, don't. The risk-to-reward ratio isn't worth it. If you get your selection or identification wrong, then you or your Scout troop could find yourselves in serious peril. Many mushrooms and berries can kill you. Locate better, more reliable sources to eat.
- Nettles, clover and dandelions. All make great Scouting tea!
- Grasshoppers. Only eat the body, not the legs, wings and antennae.
- Grubs. Can be eaten raw, and they often taste like peanut butter. Yum!
- Slugs. Might be easy to catch, but they can contain very dangerous parasites.
- Snails. Avoid the ones with brightly coloured shells.
- Worms. Try and boil them first, but they can be eaten raw in an emergency.

How to Survive ...

A Forest Fire

Head to a road or river as quickly as possible. Try to go downhill (fire travels more quickly uphill). If you have a choice, head towards deciduous trees rather than evergreens, as deciduous trees burn more slowly. If you're trapped by fire on all sides, dig a hole and cover yourself in a wet blanket or coat.

Quicksand or Sinking in Mud

Don't make any sudden movements, as you're likely to sink further in. If you're waist deep, lie back and try to float, pulling out your legs slowly, one at a time. Then roll away to the side. Spread your weight as evenly as possible and crawl back the way you came.

A Deep Snowfall

If you're in a wood in deep snow with no shelter, find a large evergreen tree. Dig down at the trunk at least a metre deep. Cover the hole with branches to create your improvised snow hole shelter. Snow is a great insulator as it traps so much air.

An Avalanche

Move out of its way as quickly as you can. The most powerful part is the centre. Stay on your feet as long as possible and grip a strong tree or rock to keep you upright. If you're caught in the moving snow, try and stay on top of it by using a 'swimming' motion – backstroke is best so you can see what's coming. When you start to slow down, make sure you create enough of an air pocket around your head to breathe. When you come to a stop, spit to find which way up you are. Then start digging your way out. The snow will set solid very fast, so speed is essential, as is avoiding avalanche areas and conditions in the first place. Avalanches are incredibly dangerous, hard to escape from, and most can be avoided if you are careful.

Avalanches can be triggered by wind, rain, warming temperatures, snow and earthquakes. They can also be triggered by skiers, snow-mobiles, hikers, and even vibrations from machinery or construction. Avoid avalanche areas once the sun hits the slopes. The most dangerous angle of slopes are steep, convex slopes. Early morning movement is key if you're in steep, snowy terrain.

Deep Water

You should always wear a lifejacket if you're taking part in water activities. However, in an emergency, you can make a flotation device by knotting and blowing up clothing. Pyjama trousers are ideal for this. A carrier bag with handles also makes for a good lightweight emergency float: hold the handles and pull the carrier bag swiftly down into the water, trapping the air inside.

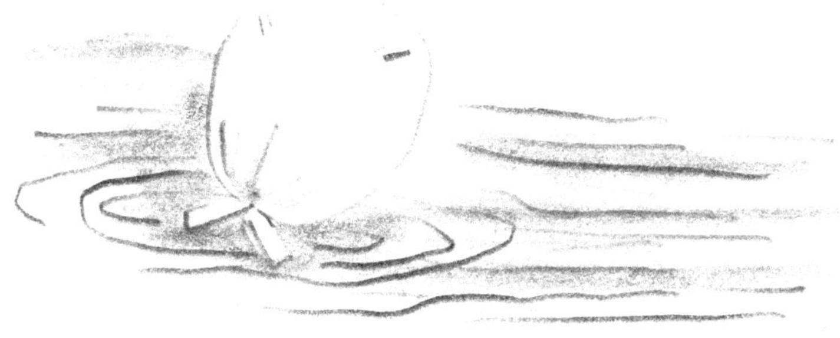

TEN TOP *Survival Tips*

1 Remember to STOP then PRWF (read this chapter again if you can't remember what these mean!).

2 Pack a spare pair of gloves and socks. Losing one can have serious consequences. (If you don't put the socks on your feet, you can always use them as a water filter, food sack or bandage.)

3 Know how to light a fire (without matches). A fire steel and striker is light and small, and easy to include in your gear. This means you'll be able to start a fire even if it's wet (unlike with matches!). Practise using the fire steel with your Scout troop. Practice makes perfect and fire lighting is a key survival skill. So: be prepared!

4 Stay cheerful. If you keep your spirits up you'll live longer. Fact. In a survival situation, a sense of humour is so valuable. (Here's a good Scout joke: What kind of swamp do you cook on a stick? A marsh-mallow!)

5 Keep something that reminds you of home. This could be a photo of your family or best friend. It needs to be something that will give you hope and keep you going.

6 Stash some waterproof bags in your gear. They'll keep your phone and spare clothes dry. You can use them to collect water and store food. And they take up next to no room.

7 Pack a survival kit. A multi-tool is the only cutlery you'll need in the wild, but make sure you know how to use it and carry it responsibly. Make sure you've also got your fire steel and striker and a first aid kit.

8. If it's cold, do all you can to stay dry. You lose heat twenty times faster if you're wet. That's why if you get soaked (whether that's from torrential rain or slipping in a river), you need to get out of wet clothes and next to a fire as quickly as possible.
9. Learn to navigate without your phone. Then, if you lose signal or battery, you won't lose your way. Know how to find north and how to use a map and compass. It could save your life. Remember the sun rises in the east and sets in the west. (See page 150 for more tips on navigating using the stars.)
10. And the most important survival tip of all ... NGU. (You know it by now: never give up!)

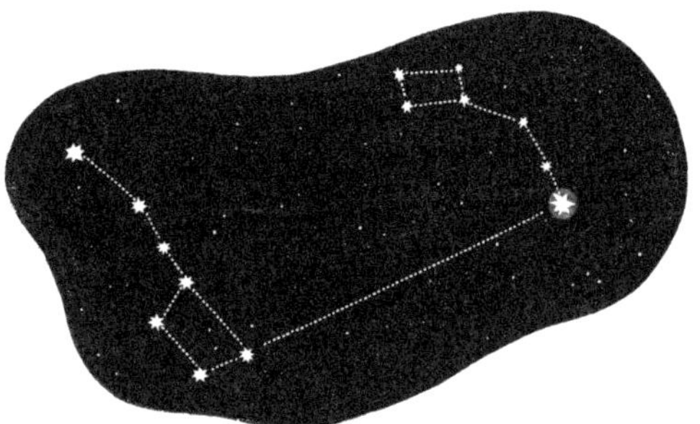

THE POWER OF 'EXTRA'

The difference between ordinary and extraordinary is so often just simply that little word – extra. And for me, I had always grown up with the belief that if someone succeeds it is because they are brilliant or talented or just better than me. And the more of these words I heard, the smaller I always felt! But the truth is often very different. I learnt that ordinary me can achieve something extraordinary by giving that little bit extra, when everyone else was giving up or throwing in the towel. If those things could be a trigger instead, to give more when others give up . . . That simple truth meant the world to me and I really clung to it.

How to give

FIRST AID

EVERY SCOUT SHOULD know what to do when they find someone who's injured or unwell. Acting quickly and decisively can make all the difference in an emergency. You may not always be able to fully treat the injury at the scene, but what you do can keep the person safe and stable until professional help arrives.

The key with any emergency situation is to remain calm. How you act will influence how others behave. It isn't always easy, but your calmness will also reassure the patient that they're in safe hands.

The Primary Survey

The first thing to do is assess the situation. There's a simple process to follow to help you do this, called the primary survey. This can be repeated as many times as needed until help arrives.

1. Check for danger.
2. Check for a response.
3. Open airway.
4. Check breathing.
5. Check circulation.

1 DANGER

Look around you. Are you and the patient safe? Is there traffic coming or any other dangers, such as falling rocks or threatening weather that might risk further injury? Once you're happy that you're safe, move on to the next step.

2 RESPONSE

It's important now to check whether the patient is responsive or unresponsive. Tell the patient who you are and that you're here to help. Get down at their level and ask simple questions like 'Open your eyes' and 'Can you tell me what happened?' If they open their eyes or reply, this means they're responsive.

3 AIRWAY

If they're not responsive, first check whether their airway is clear and open. To open the airway, place the palm of one of your hands on their forehead and use two fingers from your other hand to gently lift their chin. Remove any obstructions you can see from their nose or mouth.

4 BREATHING

Now the airway is open, you need to check for breathing. With your ear over their mouth, listen very carefully for the sound of breathing while looking down the length of their body. Can you hear anything? Is their chest moving? If you can't detect any breathing after ten seconds, you need to act immediately:

- Call an ambulance.
- Start CPR.
- Ask someone to get a defibrillator.

5 CIRCULATION

You now need to check for bleeding. It's vital the patient does not lose too much blood. If they're bleeding severely, apply pressure to the wound and ask someone to call an ambulance.

If they're not bleeding, or if they're breathing but unresponsive, put them in the recovery position and call for an ambulance.

The Recovery Position

Your aim is to put the patient into a safe position until help arrives. If they're sick, for example, being in this position means there's less chance they'll choke. Note: if you think the patient has a head, neck or spinal injury (often caused by a fall or collision) you should not put them in the recovery position, as this could make things worse.

1 Kneel down beside the patient, who should be lying on their back with straight legs.
2 Take the patient's arm that's nearest to you and extend it at a right angle to their body, with their palm upwards. This is to give the patient stability.
3 Now take their other arm and fold it so the back of their hand rests on the cheek closest to you. Hold this in place.

4 Bend the patient's knee that's farthest away to a right angle, with their foot flat on the floor.

5 Now, very carefully, roll the patient onto their side by drawing the bent knee towards you.

6 Their bent arm should now be supporting their head.

7 Make sure their bent leg is at a right angle to their body.

8 It's important now to check their airway again. Gently tilt their head back with your palm and lift their chin. Check for any blockages.

9 Make sure that an ambulance is on the way. Stay with the patient.

10 Keep checking the patient's response and look for any signs of injury, especially bleeding, that you may have missed.

Treating Severe Bleeding

Loss of blood can mean the patient goes into shock (not the same as emotional shock) which can be life threatening. That's why it's so important to stop the bleed.

1 PROTECT YOURSELF
Wear medical gloves if you have them, to minimise the risk of infection to both you and the patient.

2 APPLY PRESSURE
Use a sterile dressing to apply pressure directly to the wound. A clean cloth will do if you don't have a dressing. If there's something in the wound, don't attempt to remove it, as it could lead to more bleeding. Apply pressure to both sides instead.

3 CALL FOR HELP
Without removing pressure on the wound, ask someone to call for emergency help and explain as much as you can about the injury.

4 MAKE A BANDAGE

It's now important to keep the dressing in place with a secure bandage. Don't make it too tight, or else it might cut off the patient's circulation.

5 PUT THEM INTO A SAFE POSITION

Help the patient to lie down. Raise their legs above their heart by resting them on an object such as a chair or ledge. Cover the patient and loosen their clothing.

6 MONITOR THE WOUND

Keep checking the wound until help arrives. If you see blood seeping through, remove the bandage and dressing and repeat the previous steps. You can maintain pressure on the wound by tying the bandage knot directly over it.

Cardiac Arrest

Giving CPR

If the person is not breathing and is unresponsive, call for emergency help immediately. Do not leave the patient as you'll now need to start CPR (cardiopulmonary resuscitation).

1 Kneel down by the patient.
2 Place one hand on top of the other and lock your fingers together.
3 Put the heel of your hand in the centre of their chest, taking care no part of your hand is touching their ribs.
4 Keeping your arms straight, apply downwards pressure to the chest, to a level that's a third as deep as the chest itself.
5 Do this thirty times in succession, to the beat of the Bee Gee's song 'Stayin' Alive'.
6 Now give the patient two rescue breaths: place one hand on their forehead and pinch their nose with the other hand, which should allow their mouth to open. Taking a deep breath, place your lips

over the patient's mouth, making sure there's a seal. Now blow into their mouth until their chest rises.

7 Repeat, alternating thirty compressions with two breaths, until emergency help arrives or the patient starts to breathe normally again.

Using a Defibrillator

Get a helper to switch the defibrillator on and take out the pads. While they're doing this, it's important you carry on giving CPR. Remove the patient's upper clothing to expose the skin of the chest and wipe off any sweat. The defibrillator is programmed to tell you what to do with voice commands.

1 Remove the backing paper from the pads.

2 Apply the first pad to the upper right side of the chest, below the collar bone.

3 Apply the second pad to the patient's left side, below their armpit.

4 Now stop CPR, and very importantly, make sure no one is touching the patient to avoid the risk of electrocution.

5 If the defibrillator says a shock is required, tell everyone to stand well back. It will now instruct you to press the shock button. It will then tell you to carry on CPR for two minutes before it analyses the patient again.

6 If no shock is required, carry on giving CPR for two minutes and wait for further instructions.

7 If the patient becomes responsive (for example, their eyes open, they cough, breathe or start speaking), now's the time to get them into the recovery position. Make sure the defibrillator is still attached. And keep monitoring the patient as you may need to give CPR once again.

Burns and Scalds

A burn is caused by dry heat, while a scald is caused by wet heat.

1. Cool the burnt area immediately by holding the injured part under cold running water for at least ten minutes to reduce the pain and to limit the extent of the burn. If this is not possible, put the injured part in cold water.
2. Cover up the burn with cling film – you can use a clean plastic bag for a hand or foot – or use a sterile dressing.
3. Watch out for shock. If the patient's skin is slightly grey, cold and clammy, they are profusely sweating, experiencing nausea, faintness, increased pulse rate, shallow and rapid breathing, then they could be in shock.

Treating Shock

Remember, this is not the same as emotional shock. It's when the body's organs are deprived of oxygen due to lack of blood circulation.

1. First, treat any obvious injuries using the methods explained in this chapter.
2. Help the patient to lie down on a blanket or similar, reassuring them at all times.
3. Raise their legs above the level of their heart, resting their feet on an object or ledge.
4. Loosen their clothing.
5. Call for emergency help.
6. Do not let the patient eat or drink in case they need an operation and general anaesthetic when they reach a hospital.

If Someone's Choking

1 Deliver five blows to the patient's back, between the shoulder blades, with the heel of your hand.
2 Check the patient's mouth after each blow to see if an object has appeared.
3 If they are still choking, you need to give up to five abdominal thrusts. Stand behind the patient and clench a fist above their navel. Hold the fist in your other hand. Now pull inwards and upwards, sharply. Check the mouth after each pull.
4 Repeat the cycle of five blows and five abdominal thrusts three times. If this does not dislodge the object, call for emergency help, and be prepared to resuscitate the patient.

Broken Bones

These are most commonly caused by a fall or violent collision. There are three common signs to look out for:

1 Pain. Is the person in extreme discomfort?
2 Swelling. Does the area look larger than normal?
3 Deformity. Does it look odd?

Other signs include a snap or grinding noise, and additional pain if you touch, press or move the limb.

The patient may also feel faint, dizzy or sick. Get emergency help as soon as possible, especially if it's a neck or back injury. Do not allow the patient to eat or drink as they may need a general anaesthetic at the hospital.

How to Make a Sling for an Injured Arm

1. Fold a piece of cloth measuring 1 m × 1.5 m to form a triangle.
2. Drape over the injured shoulder with the point facing outwards.
3. Ask the patient to place their hand on their chest over the cloth.
4. Bring the bottom point up so their elbow and forearm are in a cradle.
5. Tie the two ends at the shoulder of the uninjured arm.
6. Use a sock or similar as a shoulder pad below the knot.

Sunburn

Get the patient into the shade, or at least cover their skin with some light clothing. Let them sip cold water. Dab the affected area with cold water. Apply aftersun or calamine lotion.

Heat Exhaustion

This is caused by the loss of water and salt from the body from heavy sweating. The patient is likely to have a headache, cramp, pale skin and a raised temperature.

1. Help them to lie down in the shade.
2. Raise their legs above the level of their heart.
3. Encourage them to drink cold water.
4. Call for emergency help.

Hypothermia

Hypothermia happens when someone's temperature drops below 35°C. Signs of hypothermia include cold, pale skin, shivering, confusion, shallow breathing and a weak pulse.

1. Get the patient out of the wind and rain.
2. Dress the person in warm, dry clothes and make sure they have a warm hat and gloves.
3. Avoid placing the patient in direct contact with the ground, where heat can be quickly lost. Make a base of bracken, blankets or newspapers, for example.

4 Someone should stay with the person at all times and, if possible, also use their body heat to warm them.

5 Give the patient chocolate and hot drinks to increase their body temperature.

6 Monitor their breathing and pulse and begin CPR if necessary.

Insect Stings and Bites

1 Scrape the sting away with your fingernail or plastic bank card. Do not remove with tweezers as this may squeeze more venom from the venom sac.

2 Apply ice to reduce any swelling.

Tick Bites

Ticks are a kind of spider or arachnid (so not strictly an insect). They're parasites that feed on blood. If someone is bitten by one:

1 Remove the tick with tweezers. Get hold of the head as close to the skin as possible and pull firmly, steadily and directly upwards, but don't jolt.

2 Keep the tick in a sealed bag and seek medical help. You may need to show the tick to a medical professional to help them identify any further risks of infection.

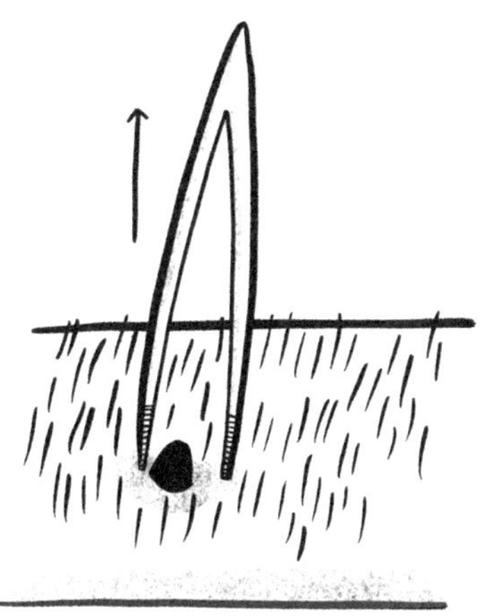

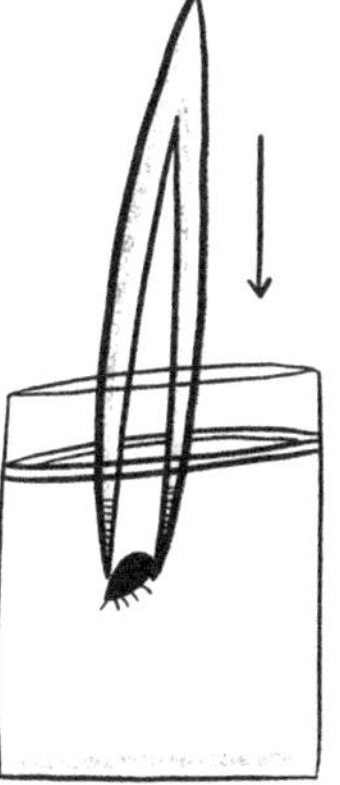

Nose Bleeds

1 Help the patient to sit down.
2 Ask them to tilt their head forward.
3 Get them to pinch the end of their nose (not the hard upper part) and breathe through their mouth.
4 Ask them to stay like this for ten minutes, then release the grip on their nose.
5 Repeat this cycle twice if the bleeding doesn't stop. Tell the patient not to cough, swallow or blow their nose.
6 Once the bleeding has stopped, tell them not to touch their nose, which could start the bleeding again. If you cannot stop the bleeding, call for emergency help.

Your First Aid Kit

On any expedition, make sure you pack a first aid kit. It should contain these items:

- Plasters (different sizes and shapes)
- Sterile gauze dressings (small, medium and large)
- Two sterile eye dressings
- Triangular bandages
- Crepe rolled bandages
- Safety pins for securing bandages
- Sterile gloves
- Tweezers
- A pair of scissors
- Alcohol-free cleansing wipes
- Roll of sticky tape
- Thermometer
- Tube of skin rash cream (hydrocortisone or calendula)
- Cream or spray for stings and insect bites
- Antiseptic cream
- Antihistamine cream or tablets
- Packs of painkillers such as paracetamol, aspirin (not for anyone under sixteen) or ibuprofen
- Distilled water for cleaning wounds
- Eye wash

Make sure all medicines are in date. It's also a good idea to pack a medical handbook (in case you don't have this book with you).

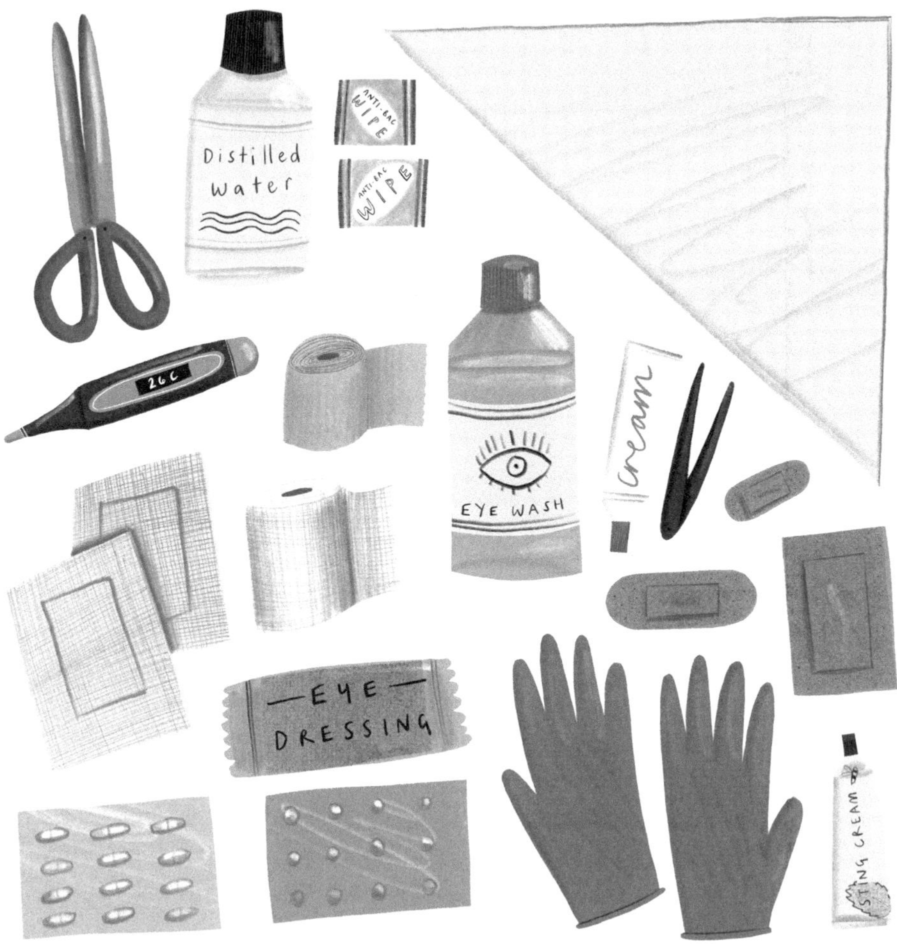

Attend a First Aid Course

You should now be reasonably prepared for a medical emergency. However, none of the advice in this chapter is a substitute for attending a first aid course run by a qualified first aider. The practice and confidence you'll get from this will be indispensable. And keep practising. That's key: staying current and up to date, as techniques and information change.

How to

CAMP

FOR SOME PEOPLE, camping and Scouts are one and the same. I like that. We should be first and foremost an outdoors movement. And camping is a magical part of the outdoors. Long may that continue!

While it is often true that camping and Scouts are one and the same, it's important to remember that we do a whole host of other things just as well! That's one of our superpowers as Scouts: we can do anything and we can turn our hand to anything. We're resourceful.

But why is it that Scouts are so keen on camping? Well, it could be to do with the smell of the woodsmoke, the long nights under the inky skies while gently warming a pot of hot chocolate. But mainly it's because camping out is a lot of fun. Sometimes *rainy* fun, sometimes *cold* fun, but always fun!

The other reason Scouts love camping is because it's where we get to use our outdoor skills. All those Scout evenings spent practising fire lighting, cooking, tent pitching, knotting, chopping and sawing suddenly pay off. Camping is your moment to bring them all together and use them to make yourself warmer, safer and more comfortable.

Suddenly you're not pretending any more. Camping is the real thing.

When we camp, we wake up with the birds. We're up and about in the fresh air as soon as the sun comes up (especially in the summer, when staying in your tent feels like being boiled in a bag). We're outside for fifteen of the twenty-four hours of the day, and even when we're asleep there's only a millimetre of canvas between us and the great outdoors.

We're meant to be outdoors – our bodies are made for movement. To be walking or running, jumping or swimming, playing games or climbing, but not for slumping on the sofa or endlessly scrolling on our phones. When we stop moving, we start decaying – and no one wants that! But running around outdoors, in the fresh air, with sun-light on our face, we come alive.

There's something else too. On camp is where we find out who we truly are. It's only when we face a little bit of hardship and have to rely on ourselves and others, do we discover what we can really do. If you find yourself in a storm and your tent has blown down, then you and your friends have to work together and find or build a shelter fast. That challenge is good. It is when we are challenged that we grow.

Perhaps the other big reason we love camping is because camp is the place where adventures so often begin. Sat round a fire with friends, or lying in your sleeping bag under the stars, it's often in these sorts of places and moments that we have proper time to think, to dream, to imagine. It's here that we have time to chat to friends, to plan, to explore. We can discuss our goals, and share or figure out how to overcome problems. Camp gives us precious time to just be. And it is so often there that we find our heart's true desires.

THE THEORY OF FUN

- **TYPE 1 FUN** is fun at the time, like eating a banana stuffed with melted chocolate or playing a game with your friends. This is the simplest fun of all.
- **TYPE 2 FUN** doesn't feel like fun at the time, but looking back on it, you realise you were actually having fun. Climbing a steep mountain in the rain is a good example of this. You got a blister

on your heel, you fell over twice and your legs ached the whole time. But looking back on it, you realise that the challenge and the achievement was epic.

- **TYPE 3 FUN** isn't fun either at the time or afterwards. A good example of this is sitting an exam. Some people might say this isn't a type of fun at all. And they might well be right!

Where to Camp

If you're at a campsite, you'll be shown roughly where you can pitch your tent. But even in these places, you need to choose your spot carefully.

Do Camp:

✓ On level ground

✓ On dry ground

✓ Where you have permission

✓ In a place you can easily get hold of fresh water and get to the loo

Don't Camp:

✗ At the bottom of a hill (the rain will flow down into your tent)

✗ Under trees (the branches could fall directly on you)

✗ At the bottom of a cliff (where rocks could fall)

✗ Too close to a fire (the embers or a flame could set your tent on fire)

✗ Too near to a river or lake (that could burst its banks in heavy rainfall)

✗ Downwind from a fire (you'll be coughing and spluttering and everything will smell of smoke)

The Anatomy of a Tent

Before you spend a night in one, it's good to know what you're sleeping in.

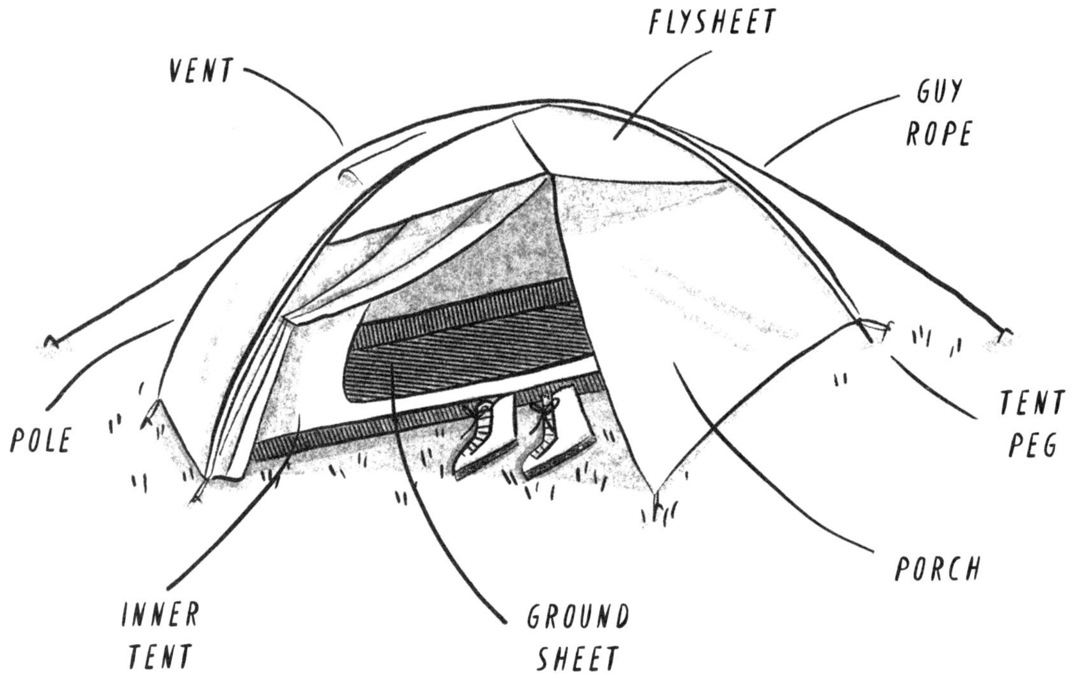

Pitching Your Tent

When it comes to tent pitching, your best friend is the humble tent peg. This is what stops you blowing away in a gale. But as with most things, there's an art to hammering them in. You need to put your peg into the ground at an angle of 90° to your guy lines, then make it extra safe by pegging that down with another peg at the opposite side. In extreme conditions, you could also place large rocks (or piles of smaller rocks) on top of your pegs to make them even more secure.

In Case of Rain

- Dig a trench along the outside of your tent (but only if you have the landowner's permission).
- Inside your tent, hang a 'drip string' from the top of your tent into a bowl or bottle to collect water.
- Duct tape is a good temporary fix for a rip or leak in your canvas.

EXTREME CAMPING

Tommy Caldwell and Kevin Jorgeson successfully scaled El Capitan's infamous 'Dawn Wall' in Yosemite National Park, USA, in 2015. This is a vertical granite rock face considered 'unclimbable' by some – but not by these intrepid mountaineers. Not only did they reach the top, they did so without ropes – an extremely daring (not to say dangerous) form of climbing, called 'free climbing'. During the attempt, they slept on something called a 'portaledge' which dangles at right angles to the sheer rock wall, secured by ropes and pegs. Not for the faint-hearted. I wonder if Tommy and Kevin were Scouts?

Even more extreme is the bivvy bag, which dangles from the cliff face. How soundly would you sleep in one of these? And you'd need to be very careful in the night if you needed the loo!

Fires

After your tent or shelter, your fire is the most important part of your camp. It's your central heating system, your cooker, your front room and possibly also your way of fending off wild animals. That's why knowing how to light one and keep it going is a vital camping skill. Remember that a fire is like being a parent to a child: if we look after the fire when it is small, it will look after us when it is bigger!

How a Fire Works

A fire is just like us – it needs three things: oxygen, heat and fuel. This is called the 'fire triangle'. Take away any one of these things and you don't have a fire. And as a human, we die.

Fire Lighting

The key to fire lighting is being prepared (no surprise there, as a Scout!). So before you even start to light anything, you should make sure you have your fire checklist in order, ready and prepared:

- A fire base (a suitable base to build your fire, away from wet ground or snow if necessary).
- A means to control your fire (such as water or a small portable extinguisher).
- Your tinder (small, dry combustible matter, such as wood shavings, dry grass or the bark of a silver birch tree).
- Your kindling (usually smaller twigs and sticks that will catch easily once your tinder is alight. Use a few pieces at a time, rather than piling it up).
- Your bigger fuel and logs (medium and larger pieces of wood that will keep your fire going. The ideal size is logs the thickness of your arm. You should only collect wood that has already fallen from a tree, and never saw wood from a living tree).

To start a fire, you need to start small – lighting pieces of dry material, which will then help larger logs to catch. You might only have one match, or maybe you only have a small amount of suitable tinder, and if you're not ready with your kindling and everything else, then the tinder will burn out and you will have lost your precious chance to successfully build a life-saving fire.

Types of Fire

There are several different types of fire you can build, all for different spaces and purposes.

STAR FIRE

Ideal for: cooking with a pan

As the name suggests, this fire resembles a star shape. Lay six medium-sized dry pieces of wood in a star shape, all meeting at a central point. Now, using thinner sticks, build a tripod or tepee in the middle, leaving one side open for you to fill with tinder and paper, to help you light it. Then layer on extra sticks to the outside of the tepee, starting with pencil-sized sticks then building to sticks the thickness of your finger. You're now ready to light the fire. Use your match or fire steel and striker to light the tinder and kindling in the open side of the tepee. As your fire burns, you can move larger sticks closer to the centre of the fire to keep it burning.

GROUND FIRE

Ideal for: cooking food in tin foil

Make a raft of stout sticks, each the width of your wrist. This will form the base of your fire. Now start to build a tower on top of this, in the shape of a hashtag, building squares of thinner sticks, roughly the width of your thumb. Build this to a height of 10 cm. Fill the centre with your tinder and kindling, ready to catch light. Carry on building your tower, making it narrower towards the top until the centre is nearly closed. Light the tinder at the base and allow your fire to burn until you have hot embers ready for cooking. Bury your food in tin foil in these.

CRANE FIRE

Ideal for: boiling water

This is a way of suspending a pot or kettle above a fire using a stick as a crane. First, find a long, stout stick. Pin one end into the ground using two sticks, then find a forked stick to act as a rest or support for the stick halfway up. Make a notch towards the end of the stick. You can then hang the pot by its handle from this end and dangle it over your fire.

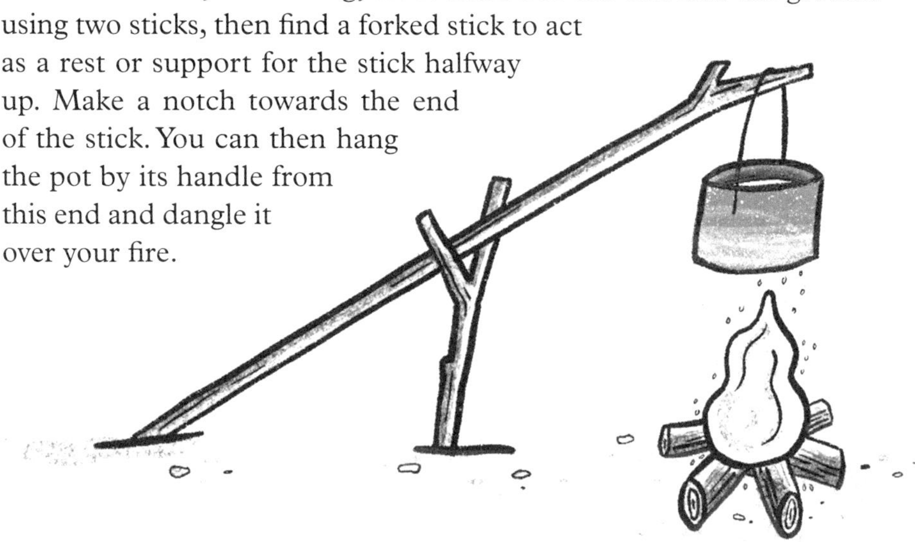

TEN TOP *Fire Safety Tips*

1. Make sure you have the landowner's permission to light a fire. Ideally, use an existing fire pit to avoid scarring more grass.
2. During hot summers, fires are sometimes banned due to the risk of forest fires, so check first.
3. Only build the size of fire you need. A large fire can quickly get out of control.
4. Don't use chemicals or spirits to get your fire going. This can quickly lead to a fire getting out of control, and spillages can lead to burns.
5. Keep a supply of water close by to extinguish your fire in an emergency.
6. Build your fire a safe distance from your tent or shelter.
7. Don't ever leave your fire unattended.

8. Before you go to bed, let the fire burn down as much as possible. Break up large pieces of wood and let these turn to ash.
9. Pour cold water on these ashes, using a stick to make sure the water reaches all parts.
10. Be very careful with any hot ashes left behind. Don't bury these as a passer-by could burn their feet. It can also set fire to tree roots below ground.

Axes and Knives

These are essential items in the wild. It will be much harder to prepare your fire and food without them. But they're only useful if they're sharp and used safely. Always let others know you're about to use an axe or knife so they are aware to be careful around you, and, if ever needed, they can help in an emergency.

How to Chop Wood with a Hand Axe

1. Put the wood you want to chop on a large, stable piece of wood, which will serve as your chopping block.
2. Now grip the wood you want to chop with your non dominant hand, a safe distance from the chopping location.
3. Keeping the lower part of your arm straight, bend your arm at your shoulder and chop the wood.

AXE SAFETY

Make sure you have a clear chopping area, with nothing overhead that your axe could snag on and lots of empty space around you on all sides (equivalent to three times the length of your axe handle). Secure any loose clothing. Wear strong gloves and boots and safety goggles if you have them.

How to Cut Wood with a Knife

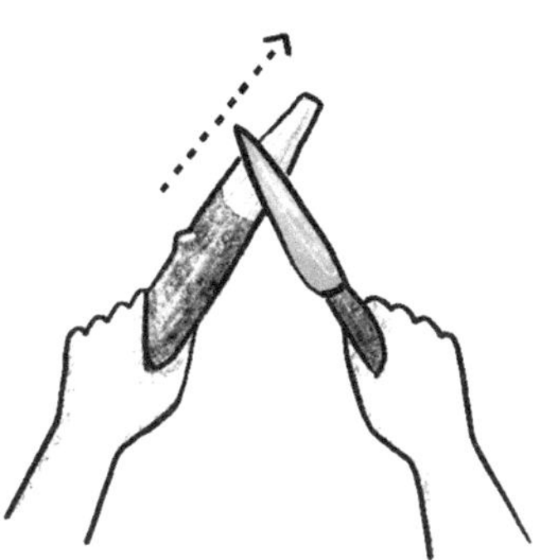

1 To prevent injury, you must always cut away from you.

2 Hold the wood out to one side, around the height of your waist.

3 For efficient cutting, use the power from your shoulder rather than your elbow.

KNIFE SAFETY

Knives should be stored and carried carefully (in the middle of a rucksack) and only taken out when you're ready to use them. If you're sitting, make sure the ground, chair or log you're sitting on is stable and level. Plant your elbows on your knees and cut away from the body.

Be aware of the 'blood circle', which is the danger area of your inner thighs. Never sit with your legs apart, cutting against your inner thigh. Your major artery runs along here and if your hand slips and you cut your inside leg you can find yourself in grave danger. So always kneel down, get stable and cut away from your body.

And remember, a sharp knife is a safe knife. The sharper the blade, the less pressure we have to apply. We can use it in a calm, controlled manner. With a blunt knife, you have to push much harder, and the chances of a blade slipping or 'skipping out' and harming you is much greater.

Different countries have different laws for carrying and storing knives. Legally, you must have a good reason to be in possession of a knife in a public place. In the UK, the legal length for a folding blade that does not lock is 7.62 cm (3 in). Always check first, and remember, ignorance of the law is not an excuse.

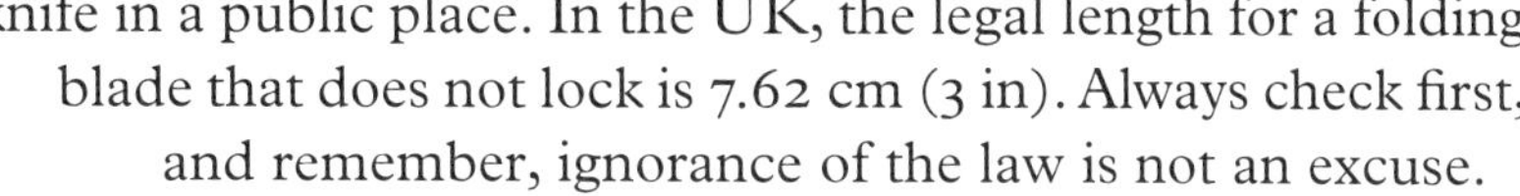

How to Pack Your Rucksack

When you head off to camp, you're likely to have a rucksack on your back. This should contain everything you need for your adventure. But there's a right and a wrong way to pack. Get it right and your trip starts off on the front foot. Get it wrong and you'll end up with an aching back and a sore neck – plus you will need to keep stopping to rummage for the things you need or to rearrange an awkwardly positioned rucksack.

The key thing to think about is weight. No one else will be carrying this but you. That means making some tough decisions. Do you really need that pillow, third pair of trousers or ukulele? Some mountaineers even cut the end off their toothbrushes to save that little bit of extra weight. If in doubt, leave it out.

If you're on an expedition and hiking long distances between campsites, then you'll need to pack light. Remember, as well as your clothes, you'll need to carry your sleeping bag, roll mat, tent, cooking equipment, food and water. Water weighs much more than you think. Here are some of the essentials to take with you.

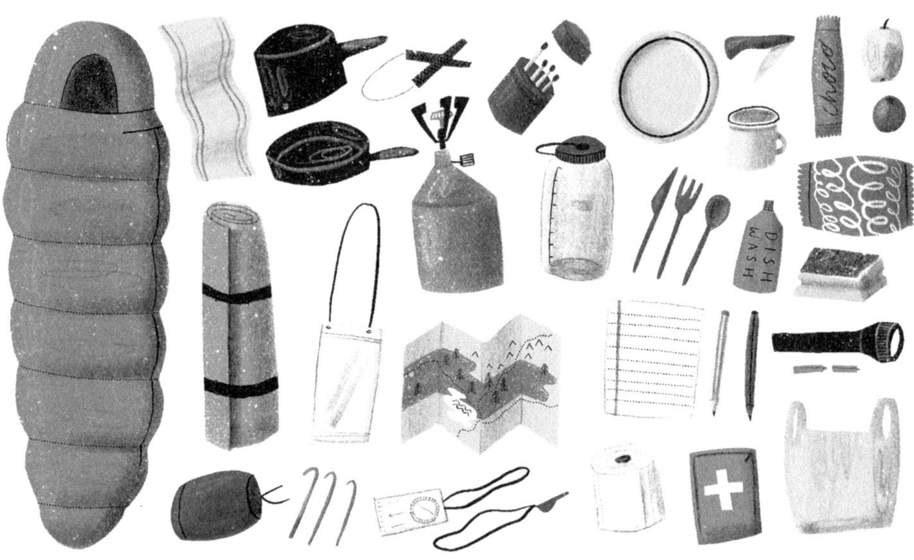

CAMPING AND ADVENTURE KIT

- Tent
- Tent pegs
- Stove
- Fuel
- Pans
- Cutlery set (knife, fork and spoon)
- Plate, bowl and mug/flask
- Washing-up liquid, scourers and cloths
- Tea towels
- Rucksack liners (or plastic bags)
- Sleeping bag and liner
- Roll mat or inflatable mattress
- Bivvy bag
- First aid kit
- Whistle
- Notebook
- Pen
- Suncream
- Torch with spare batteries and bulbs
- Water bottle
- Matches (in waterproof container)
- Fire steel and striker (weatherproof backup for lighting fires)
- Wash kit
- Towel
- Loo roll (mountain money!)
- Hygiene supplies
- Walking poles
- Folding pocketknife
- Map and case
- Compass

CLOTHING

- Underwear
- Walking socks
- T-shirts
- Shirt
- Walking trousers
- Shorts
- Jumper/fleece
- Waterproof overtrousers
- Waterproof jacket
- Warm hat
- Sun hat
- Gloves

FOOTWEAR

- Trainers or flip flops
- Walking boots

FOOD

- Dry food
- Fruit

TEN GOLDEN RULES *for Packing Your Rucksack*

1. Lay out all your kit to check it's in good condition. Now's also the time to decide whether you really need all of it.
2. Put heavy and bulky items, like cooker/stove, pots and pans in first and at the bottom.
3. Any jagged or awkwardly shaped items need to point outwards (so they don't dig into your back).
4. Sleeping bags can either go in the compartment at the bottom of the rucksack or above your stove and other heavy items.
5. Clothing and other kit you won't need while hiking goes in next.
6. Make sure that you pack all clothing, sleeping bags and other items that must be kept dry in rucksack liners or plastic bags.
7. Light items, and things you'll need to get at easily, should go at the top – for example, hat and gloves.
8. Use the side and top pockets for things you'll need really quick access to, like your waterproofs, snacks, water, first aid kit.
9. Keep your rucksack balanced and the weight evenly distributed.
10. Remember, you can attach light and bulky items like roll mats to the back of your rucksack.

WHO INVENTED THE RUCKSACK?

There isn't really any one person who truly invented the rucksack, as the idea of carrying things on our backs has been around for thousands of years. However, Henry Merriam has a reasonable claim. In 1878, he patented a US Army backpack that used sheet metal to distribute the weight of the load. It didn't catch on, mainly because it was so uncomfortable. Four years later, Camille Poirier from Duluth, Minnesota, also in the United States, came up with an improved idea: a square canvas bag that sat halfway down the back and was attached with straps (including a head strap). It looked odd, but was much more comfortable, and therefore quickly became popular.

The word backpack was first used in 1904, and many more versions of the pack appeared over the next century, though none finding quite the right balance between comfort and practicality. The Trapper Nelson Pack (1924) was the first to use an external frame, while the Cunningham Zippered Backpack (1938) was the first – you've guessed it – to have zipped compartments, useful to stop things falling out.

Åke Nordin can be credited with the idea of having a pack that sat higher up and closer to your back with the Fjällräven Wooden Pack (1950), while the Kelty Backpack (1952) was the first to use aluminium frames and have little luxuries we enjoy today, like padded straps.

More recently, Hipbelts transferred some of the weight to the hips, rather than the back and shoulders, while the CamelBak Hydration Pack (1989) was the first that allowed you to drink from your pack (though a tube system) as you hiked along. Ventilated pads, more sustainable and lighter materials, and personalised fitting are all things that have eased the burden over recent years.

Reflection

Your expedition might follow a coastal path, retrace the steps of a great explorer or trek around a great lake. Whatever you choose to do, this is where great memories and friendships are made. They give us a sense of purpose, not to mention some great stories to tell around the campfire.

Plan something local. Maybe it's simply a hike, but do something new that pushes you a little, and do it with those you love. Adventure builds confidence, so just begin. Before you climb any mountain – real or metaphorical – you need to remember that the hard work is done long before you embark on the journey. So get fit, have the right gear and clothing and learn some basic skills.

How to be a

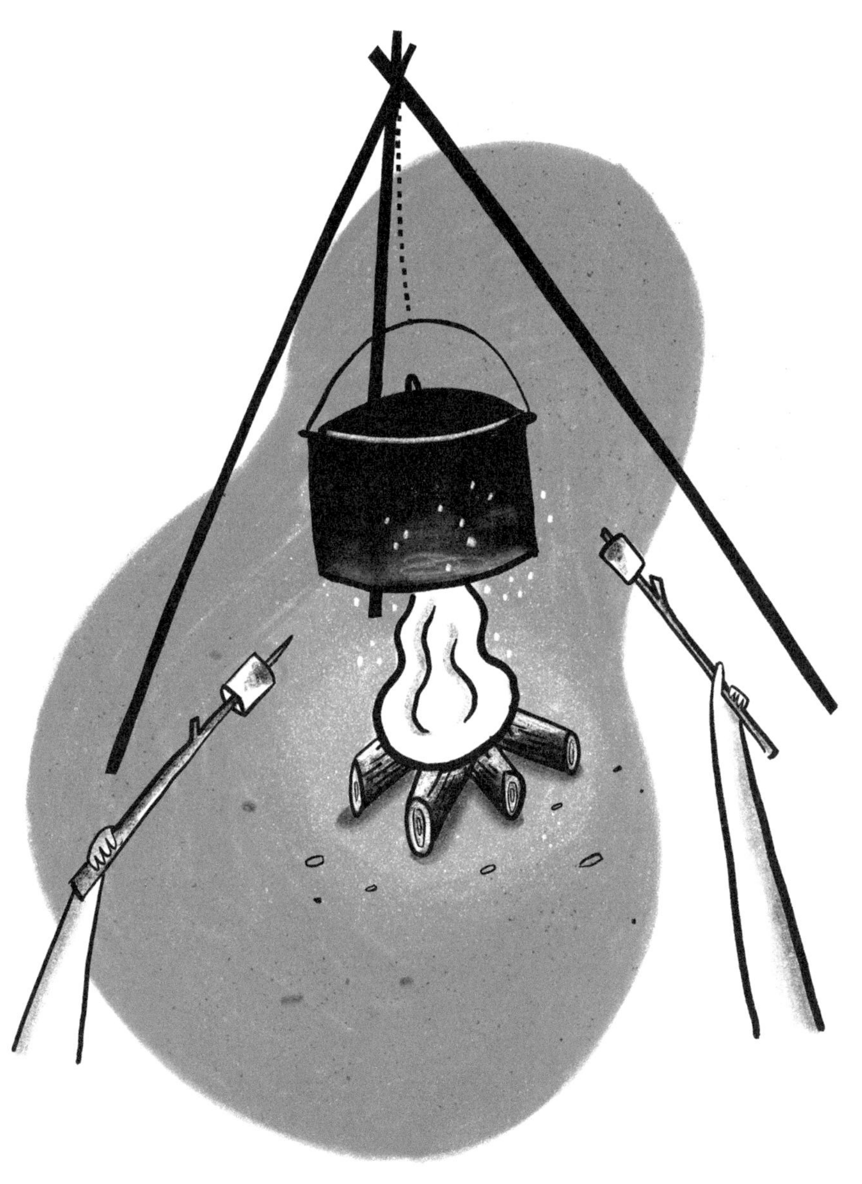

CAMP COOK

IF IT RAINS AT CAMP, we like to call it 'Scouting sunshine'. (You'll have noticed by now that Scouts always look on the bright side, which some people say can be annoying!) But there's one thing that's guaranteed to cheer you up on a cold and rainy camp. And that's great grub. From old-fashioned camping favourites like scrambled eggs to camp treats like s'mores (chocolate, biscuits and marshmallows – need we say s'more?), we've got plenty of tasty things for you to try. And yes, you will end up smelling of woodsmoke!

While on camp, you're outdoors and using more calories than normal. There's always a job to do – from fetching water to tightening ropes, collecting wood or building fires. All of this is hungry work. That's why it's important to take on board the right fuel to keep yourself going. Eat good, simple food that will fill you up and stop you snacking. Remember, food is fuel for life. Better to eat plenty of fruit, some scrambled eggs and a big mug of hot chocolate at the start of the day than to be scoffing crisps halfway up a mountain.

And here's the secret – sitting by your fire and eating something you've just cooked up yourself is better than visiting any five-star restaurant. As Scouts often say: 'What is the world's highest rated restaurant and hotel? The 5 billion-star night sky.'

Did you know? If you put freshly made porridge in a mug, bury it in the ground and cover it with earth, in the morning it will still be hot when you dig it out!

Breakfast

They always say this is the most important meal of the day, and of course, they're right. A good breakfast is the start of a good day.

It's all too easy to pour some milk into a mini packet of sugary cereal then consider breakfast done and dusted. But this will only give you energy for about ten minutes. Instead, take some time over your breakfast and think of it as the way to power yourself through the day. It's also a great time to think through everything you need to achieve.

Scrambled Eggs

One of the great Scouting breakfast traditions is this simple classic. It's quick, easy and most importantly, hot! The perfect remedy for a night in a damp sleeping bag.

YOU'LL NEED:

Lots of eggs!
A splash of milk
Salt and pepper
Butter for frying

HOW TO MAKE IT:

1. In a bowl, beat the eggs, milk and salt and pepper together with a whisk or fork.
2. Heat the butter in a frying pan.
3. Add the eggs and stir.
4. Don't overcook it!

Breakfast Omelette

SERVES 4

YOU'LL NEED:

Butter for frying
4 rashers of bacon, chopped
6 eggs, beaten
Salt and pepper
Cheese, sliced or grated

HOW TO MAKE IT:

1. Heat the butter in a frying pan, making sure it covers the whole base.
2. Cook the bacon until it's crispy.
3. In a separate bowl, beat the eggs then pour into the frying pan.
4. Season with salt and pepper.
5. Sprinkle on the cheese,
6. Fold in half and serve.

Cooking an Egg in an Orange

This is such a fun and easy thing to do, but be warned: your egg will have a slight orange flavour (that's a good thing in our book).

YOU'LL NEED:

1 large orange per person
1 egg per person

HOW TO MAKE IT:

1. Slice the top third off your orange.
2. Scoop out the flesh of the orange (and gobble it down).
3. Gently crack the egg into the orange.
4. Place the orange (still without its lid) into the embers of a fire until the egg is cooked. You should be able to tell by sight when it's cooked, but a few minutes should do the trick.

TOP TIP: if you thread a green stick (without its bark) through your orange (but above the egg) you should be able to get it out of the embers more easily.

Lunch

Pancakes

There are few things more tasty than camp-cooked pancakes. And no limit to the savoury or sweet toppings you can add to them. You just have to use your imagination. I have seen Scouts come up with some truly crazy inventions here – though not all of them have worked! Pancakes topped with liver and honey was a surprising winner, as was chocolate melted with chilli flakes. Whereas pancakes topped with tuna and jelly wasn't one to repeat! (Be aware pancakes should be considered a treat and maybe not for every day. Liver and honey on the other hand . . .)

FOR THE PANCAKES, YOU'LL NEED:

100 g plain flour
A pinch of salt
2 eggs
300 ml milk
Butter for frying

FOR THE TASTY TOPPING(S), YOU'LL NEED:

Ham
Grated cheese
Spring onions
Steak (or liver)
Honey
Sliced banana
Chocolate squares
Anything you can dream up!

HOW TO MAKE IT:

1. Mix together the flour and salt, then set to one side. Now beat the eggs and milk together and pour into the flour mixture. Whisk all of these together into a batter.
2. Heat the butter in a frying pan until it's piping hot, coating the whole base of the pan. Spoon in two tablespoons of batter and tip the pan to get an even amount across the whole base. Cook until crispy, then turn the pancake over (or flip it if you're feeling brave!).
3. As the second side starts to cook, add your toppings – such as ham, cheese and spring onions.
4. Fold in half, remove from the pan and serve.

Dinner

Be a tin foil wizard! When it comes to camp cooking, tin foil is your best friend. Here are three brilliant dinners to cook in foil.

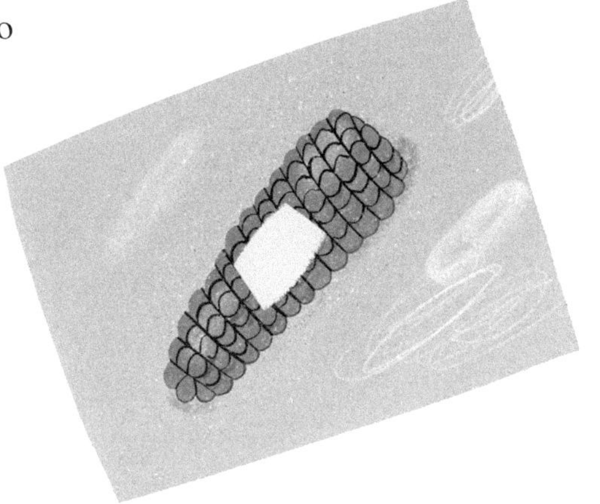

Corn on the Cob

YOU'LL NEED:

Corn on the cob
Butter
Salt and pepper

HOW TO MAKE IT:

1. Tear a piece of foil (approximately 30 cm × 30 cm) and put your corn on the cob in the centre.
2. Place a knob of butter in the centre of the corn on the cob, then season with salt and pepper.
3. Wrap in the foil, then place in the embers of a fire for around thirty minutes, or until golden.
4. Top tip: use sticks to move it in and out of the embers.

Jacket Potato

This is perhaps the simplest (but most delicious) campfire recipe of all.

YOU'LL NEED:

A baking potato
Butter
Salt

HOW TO MAKE IT:

1 Prick the potato with a fork (so it doesn't explode).
2 Place a knob of butter on the potato.
3 Season with salt.
4 Wrap in two layers of tin foil and place in the embers of a fire, piling embers on top.
5 Leave for an hour, turning once after half an hour. The potato should be hot and fluffy on the inside.
6 Add an extra lump of butter and eat straight from the skin (which should also taste delicious).

Tin Foil Stew

Feeling like a tin foil wizard yet? Well, now's the time to try this complete meal – all bundled up in tin foil.

SERVES 2

YOU'LL NEED:

Beef steak or sausages
Small potatoes
An onion and pepper
A few cloves of garlic
A knob of butter
Salt and pepper
Some dried basil

HOW TO MAKE IT:

1 Tear two large sheets of foil (approximately 30 cm × 45 cm) and lay on top of each other.
2 Chop the meat, potatoes, onion and pepper into small chunks, then slice the garlic.
3 Put all the ingredients together in a bowl and add the butter.
4 Season with salt and pepper, then mix in the dried basil.

5 Tip everything onto the centre of the sheets of foil. Make an envelope by bringing together the short sides of the foil, folding over the centre to make a seal, then folding in the long sides of the foil.
6 Cook on a hot grill over a fire for around 25 minutes. The meat should be piping hot and the potatoes and veggies soft and sweet.

Campfire Treats

These are some firm Scout favourites – but be aware, they are not the healthiest. Maybe save them for special occasions!

S'mores

YOU'LL NEED:

2 digestive biscuits
4–6 squares of chocolate
One large marshmallow

HOW TO MAKE IT:

1. Place a digestive biscuit on a plate.
2. Lay the chocolate squares on the biscuit.
3. Toast your marshmallow on the end of a stick, until it's golden brown.
4. Place the hot marshmallow on top of the chocolate squares.
5. Put the other digestive biscuit on top and squish into a sandwich.

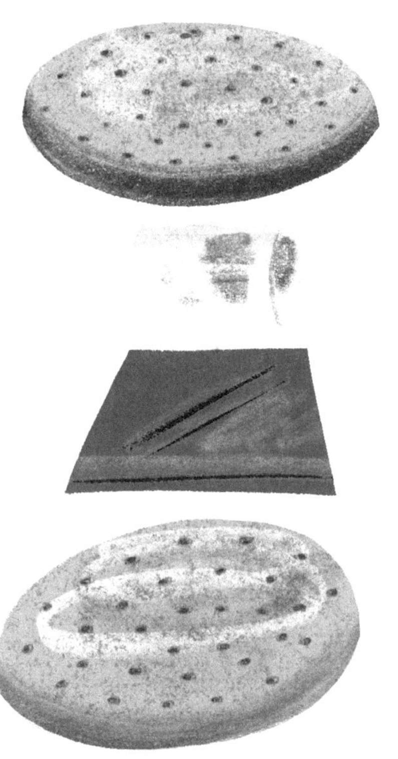

THE MYSTERY OF WHO INVENTED S'MORES

As everyone knows, s'more is short for 'some more' (which is what people generally say as soon as they're finished). In Scouts, you'll hear different stories about the origin of the humble s'more. You might even meet people who claim to have invented it themselves.

One thing we're pretty sure of is that it was invented by Scouts, around a hundred years ago. One of the earliest mentions of 'some mores' is in a book called *Tramping and Trailing with the Girl Scouts* by Loretta Scott Crew, published in 1927. However, it seems the recipe was already popular with Scouts by this time. The shortened version – 's'more' – was first mentioned in a book on summer camps published in 1938. Other names for it were 'Graham cracker sandwich' and even 'marshmallow toast'.

Originally, the American recipe was a toasted marshmallow and half a melted chocolate bar sandwiched between two Graham crackers (President Obama showed me once how to make one of these when we went into the wilderness together. It was a pretty cool moment!)

However, the British version generally uses a marshmallow sandwiched between two digestive biscuits. People have experimented by adding other things (such as peanut butter) over the years, but the 'core s'more' recipe stays the same, and will be enjoyed as long as there are Scouts to eat them.

Welsh Cakes

As the name suggests, these are a traditional sweet Welsh recipe. They work especially well on camp because they can be cooked on a griddle or tray over a fire and don't need an oven. They're sometimes called 'bakestones', which tells you how they were once cooked. Hot and sprinkled with a little fruit sugar, they're a great treat on a chilly evening.

YOU'LL NEED:

125 g butter
225 g self-raising flour
Pinch of nutmeg or cinnamon
75 g fruit sugar
75 g dried fruit, such as raisins or sultanas
1 egg, beaten
Milk
Butter for frying
Raspberries or some jam

HOW TO MAKE THEM:

1. Rub the butter, flour and spices together in a bowl until your mixture resembles breadcrumbs.
2. Stir in the sugar and dried fruit.
3. Create a small hole in the centre of the mixture and pour in the egg. Mix until you've got a good ball of dough, adding a dash of milk if it's too dry.
4. Sprinkle a board and rolling pin with flour, then roll your dough to a thickness of 1 cm. Cut out your cakes with a glass or mug.
5. Heat the butter in a frying pan then fry the cakes, leaving them to cook for about 4 minutes before turning, until they're golden brown on each side.
6. Remove and allow to cool, then add some raspberries or jam as you prefer.

TOP TIP: if you want to make these Welsh cakes 'exceptional', then eat them with some clotted cream! One of the best treats out there.

Chocolate Bananas

YOU'LL NEED:

Bananas
A bar of dark chocolate
Mini marshmallows

HOW TO MAKE THEM:

1 Leaving on the skin, make a slice along the length of the banana.
2 Bury small pieces of chocolate and marshmallow in the slice (you can use honey and berries instead of chocolate and marshmallows if you're looking for a healthier version).
3 Wrap the banana in tin foil and bury in the embers of a fire until the banana is soft and the chocolate and marshmallow is a delicious gooey mess.

TEN TOP TIPS *for Campfire Cooking*

Cooking outdoors isn't quite as easy as working in a fully equipped kitchen. But you have the advantage of fresh air and birdsong. Here are ten top tips to make sure you're prepared.

1 Take some tin foil – you can cook almost anything in a fire by wrapping it in tin foil and placing it (carefully) into hot embers.
2 Keep your food carefully zipped away (and better still, hung up high) so nocturnal visitors like foxes or bears can't pinch it.
3 If your saucepan has a lid, then use it! It'll mean your food will cook much quicker and you'll use less fuel.
4 Coat the underside of pans with washing-up liquid before putting them over an open fire. This will make them much easier to clean afterwards.
5 Keep a bucket of water nearby in case your fire gets out of control or grass catches light, and never leave a fire unattended.
6 Remember, white embers might look cool, but this is actually when they're at their hottest. They can also stay very hot for

several hours. Beware of the wind picking up and spreading hot embers around.

7 Be especially careful when cooking marshmallows on sticks. The gooey marshmallow can be molten hot under the crispy shell. Also beware of pointy sticks near eyes in the dark.

8 Avoid cooking over pine, fir, spruce or cedar wood – the smoke can give your food a very funny taste and can even make you sick. This is because this kind of wood tends to contain a lot of sap.

9 Make sure your food is piping hot all the way through. If in doubt, keep cooking!

10 When it comes to backwoods cooking, make sure you clear up afterwards – take all your rubbish with you or carefully bury any waste food in the ground.

Reflection

After supper and when the fire's burning low, look up and see if you can spot a small cluster of what looks like seven stars. These are called Pleiades, or the Seven Sisters. They glimmer in such a magical way, people once thought they might be heaven itself.

The Ancient Greeks told a story about seven sisters who were in love with the seven judges of Olympus. Artemis, a powerful goddess, found out and transformed them into stars. In fact, there are over 800 stars in the cluster, formed around 100 million years ago, with fourteen bright stars that are visible to the eye.

The cluster is best viewed looking slightly to the left or right, rather than directly at it. It gleams with an ethereal silver-blue glow. As you stare at the Seven Sisters, think of seven good things in your life to be grateful for. These could be people, memories, places, books or films.

How to

FIND YOUR WAY

WE LIVE IN AN AGE of incredible technology. There are apps and gadgets that seem to know every inch of the planet's surface and can track your location with pinpoint accuracy. But what happens when your phone signal disappears, your batteries die and the fog sets in? Your ability to find your way could become a matter of life and death.

No one thanks a Scout who doesn't know how to navigate well and who gets everyone lost! It's a great Scout skill to navigate well and once you master it, it will stay with you a lifetime. It doesn't take long to learn. Start by having a Scout explain how they navigate using a map and compass, then get them to demonstrate it to you, then go and imitate it. That's the Scout way to learn. Explanation. Demonstration. Imitation.

Initially, learning to navigate can feel daunting, but stick with it and practise. It can be so fun to go orienteering with your fellow Scouts and practise all your navigation skills. Start small and keep it simple. Maybe to begin with, set a course of a few hundred metres around your camp. Then when you get good at this, increase the distances and complexity of the checkpoints, and eventually try doing it at night! (But always do this in pairs or more, and always have a solid backup plan if you get lost!)

THE LOST CITY OF 'Z'

Before accurate maps and good navigational equipment, explorers and travellers were forever getting lost. There are legendary tales of intrepid explorers who simply seemed to disappear. Colonel Percy Fawcett, for example, vanished in 1925 while searching for the mythical lost city of 'Z' in the jungles of Brazil. He was attempting to map the area and became convinced that a civilisation unknown to the Western world had created a city with high-rise buildings and a network of roads.

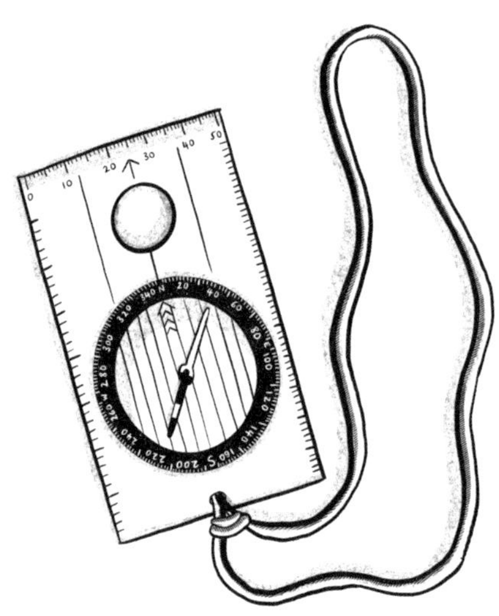

LEGENDS OF THE FROZEN NORTH

Earlier, in 1845, two renowned British sailors, Sir John Franklin and Francis Crozier, set sail on a daring mission to discover the Northwest Passage. Their ships were HMS *Erebus* and HMS *Terror* (named after volcanos in Antarctica). If all went well, it would be a voyage across the top of the American continent on a course that would link the Pacific and Atlantic Oceans. If they could find the fabled Northwest Passage, it would open up a valuable new trade route and make their names.

Things didn't go according to plan. When no word had been heard of the expedition after two years, a rescue mission, at great expense, was sent. And then another. And then many more. Evidence was discovered that suggested the crew had become trapped in the ice over the winter of 1846–47. However, a further disaster had unfolded: the crews had been slowly poisoned by lead from their tinned food. Locals reported sightings of sick men struggling south. Even grislier, when they found the human remains, there were signs of cannibalism. It wasn't until 170 years later that the wrecks of HMS *Erebus* and HMS *Terror* were finally discovered.

These disasters weren't the fault of poor navigation. It was because the maps didn't exist in the first place. It's worth sparing a thought for those brave pioneers who headed into the unknown so we can have accurate maps today.

Using the Stars to Find Your Way

Finding North in the Northern Hemisphere: Locate the North Star

For centuries, the North Star (or Polaris) has helped lost travellers find their way. But first you need to find the star itself. The easiest way to locate it is this:

1. Find the Big Dipper (also known as the Plough), which is saucepan shaped.
2. Draw an imaginary line along the far edge of the saucepan until you see the bright star in the sky.
3. The North Star is at the extreme end of the long handle of the Little Dipper. (It is also about four or five times the distance between the two end stars of the Plough.)

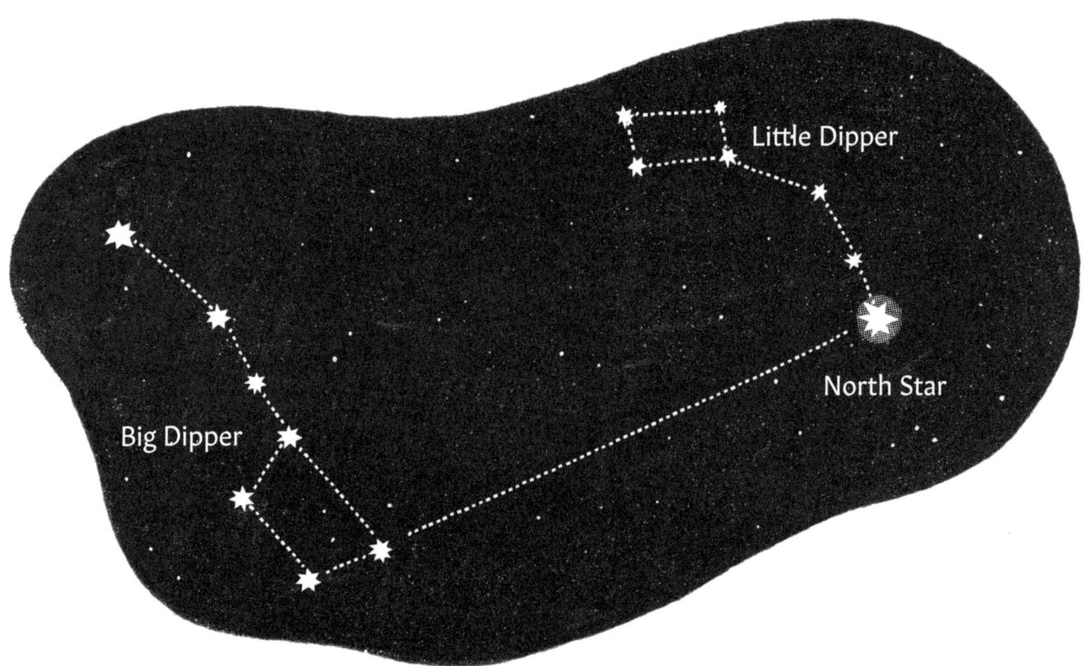

Finding South in the Southern Hemisphere: Use the Southern Cross

The Southern Cross (also known as the constellation Crux) is made up of four bright stars, which form part of the Milky Way. Six thousand years ago, this cross was visible in the northern hemisphere too, but as the axis of the earth has slowly changed, it disappeared from view.

In the southern hemisphere, the Southern Cross is as useful as the North Star for finding your way. To locate south:

1. Draw a long imaginary line from the top point of the cross, extending beyond the bottom point of the cross so the line is four and a half times longer than the cross itself.
2. Go directly down to the ground and you've found due south.
3. Alternatively, draw another imaginary line from the centre of the two Pointers (see picture) to Achernar, a bright lonely star. Draw a line to the ground halfway along the first line to find south.

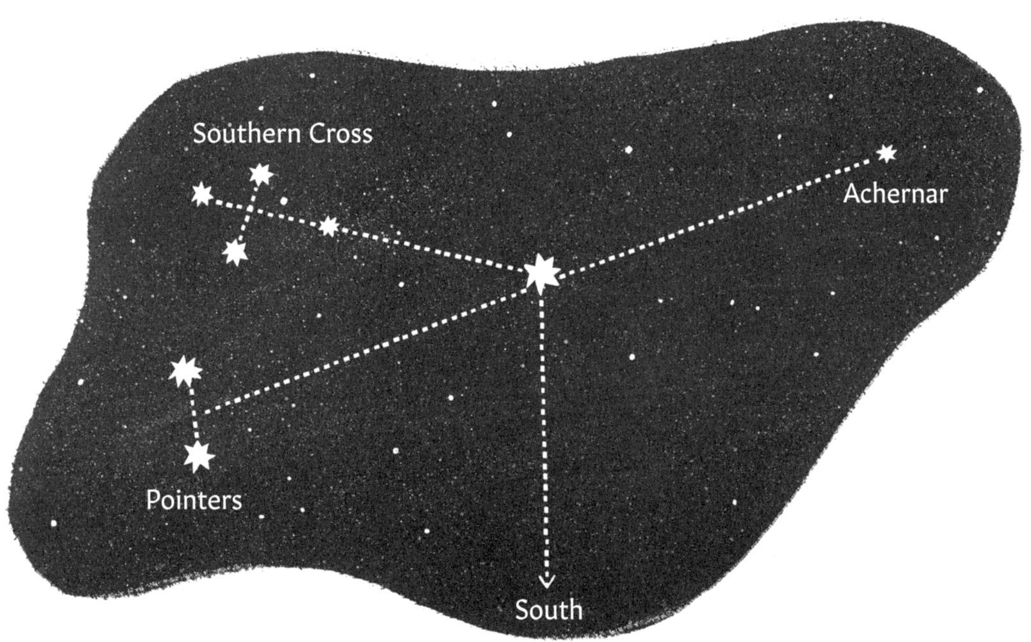

Use the Sun

There's another star that's a little closer to home that can help you find your way too: our very own sun. You probably know it rises in the east and sets in the west, so a glance at its location and your watch will help you find your bearings. If it's midday, you'll need to use another method (but this only works for the northern hemisphere, and north of the Tropic of Cancer):

1. Find some clear ground in full sunlight (away from any shade).
2. Find a stick around a metre tall and push the end into the ground.
3. Look for the shadow it casts on the ground.
4. Place a stone at the very top of the shadow. This point is west.
5. Wait fifteen minutes for the shadow to move.
6. Place another stone at the top of this shadow. This is east.
7. Draw an imaginary line between the two stones.
8. Above the line, and between east and west, place a third stone. This is north.
9. At the bottom of the line (nearest the stick), place a fourth stone. This is south.

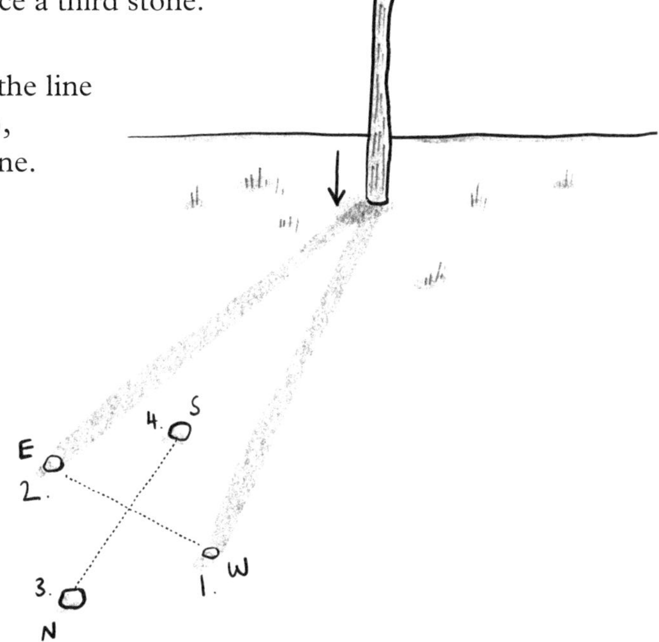

Finding North with Your Wristwatch

If you have an analogue watch (with an hour and minute hand), you can also use this to find north.

In the Northern Hemisphere

1. Hold your watch flat to the ground.
2. Rotate the watch until the hour hand is pointing directly towards the sun.
3. Now find the halfway point between the hour hand and twelve noon and draw an imaginary line. This represents north and south.
4. Now think about where the sun rose that morning. This will be east. Once you know this, you'll know which end of the line points north.

In the Southern Hemisphere

1. Again, lay your watch flat on the ground.
2. Instead of pointing the hour hand to the sun, point the twelve-hour mark towards the sun.
3. Now draw an imaginary line between the twelve-hour mark and the hour hand. This represents north and south.
4. Again, think about where the sun rose that morning. This will be east. Once you know this, you'll know which end of the line points north.

How to Remember NESW

For most kinds of navigation, you'll need to remember the order of the points of the compass (north, east, south and west). A good phrase to remember is 'Never Eat Slimy Worms'.

Parts of a Compass

A compass is one of the world's greatest inventions. First used in China around 200 BC, it uses a magnetised needle that's always drawn to the magnetic North Pole. In a good compass, the needle is sealed inside a liquid-filled container to keep it stable and accurate. It's important to get to know your compass and understand how each of the features can help you find your way.

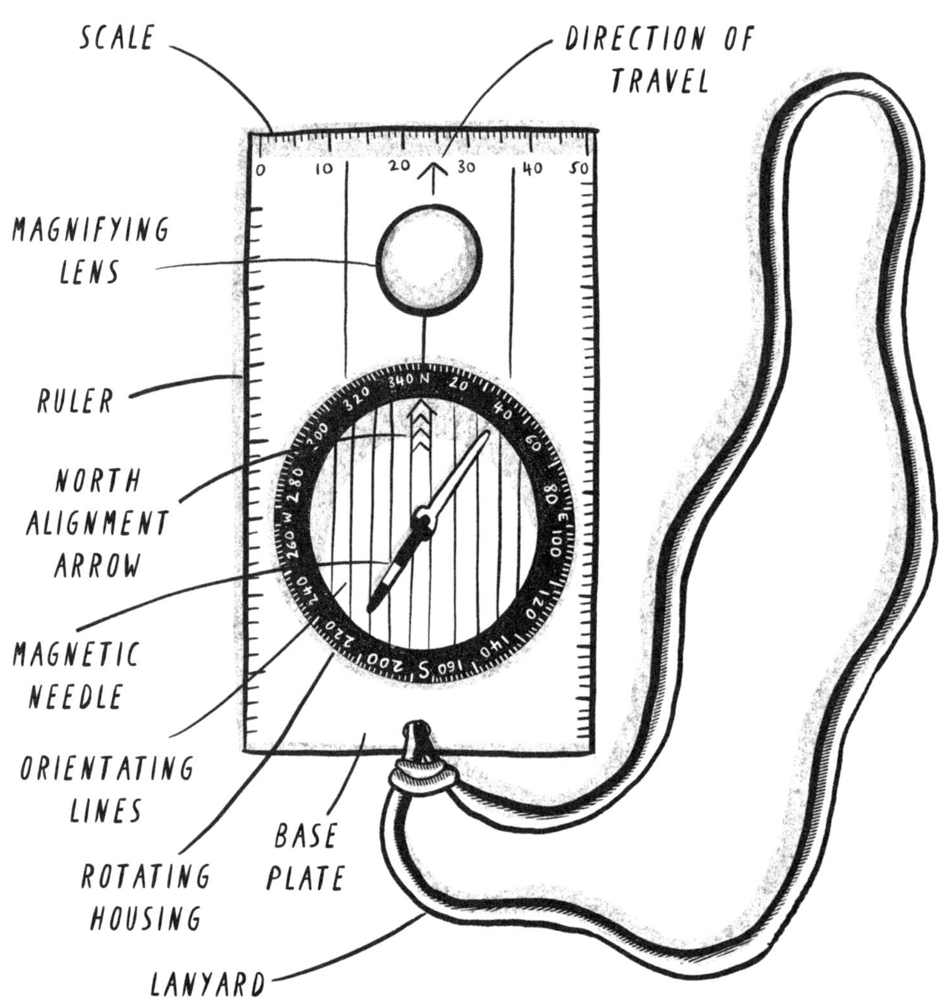

How to Use Your Compass (Taking a Bearing)

This works for any compass with a rotating dial.

1 Hold the compass flat and level in the palm of your non-dominant hand, with the red orienting arrow pointing away from you.
2 Twist the dial until the red orienting arrow and the 'N' line up with the direction of travel arrow.
3 Turn your body until the red compass needle lines up with the two arrows pointing north.
4 You are now facing north.

If you want to travel east, then follow these instructions:

1 Turn your body 90° to the right.
2 Twist the dial until the orienting arrow lines up again with the red needle.
3 You'll see that the letter 'E' at the bottom of the dial now lines up with the direction of travel arrow.
4 You're now facing east.

Walking on a Bearing

You can do this when you can see your destination in front of you. It's especially useful if it's dark or foggy and you're likely to soon lose sight of your destination.

1 Turn the compass housing until your desired bearing is against the index pointer.
2 Turn your compass until the needle is over the orienting arrow.

3 Find a landmark in front of you along the direction of travel line and start heading towards it.
4 Keep checking your bearing and make sure that your destination is still in front of you.

You're now ready to start using your compass with a map.

Using Maps

Maps have been around almost as long as humans. There are cave paintings showing the way back to hunting grounds so that people could find them again. Over time, maps grew more sophisticated and, more importantly, accurate, so that travellers could plan their journeys (and presumably avoid dragons and sea monsters along the way). Maps became extremely valuable to merchants and sailors (especially those treasure hunters where X marks the spot).

Today, digital technology means maps are now found on phones as well as the walls of caves, but there's still no beating an old-fashioned paper map.

Useful maps are drawn to scale, which means all the features, such as hills and fields, are shrunk down to the correct proportions in relation to each other. Most maps are drawn to either:

- 1:25,000 (where 1 cm is the equivalent of 250 m, which gives close-up detail; or
- 1:50,000, where 1 cm is the equivalent of 500 m, which will show more ground, but in less detail.

Always check the scale on the map, and remember that on a 1:50,000 map, the distance will be twice as far as a 1:25,000 map.

Grid References

In the UK, the country is divided into a national grid, with a pair of letters given for each square. Each square covers 100 km². These large squares are then subdivided into smaller squares of 10 km². Blue lines then divide these squares and are numbered 1 to 9. The numbers that go up the map are called 'northings'. Those that go along the map are called 'eastings'.

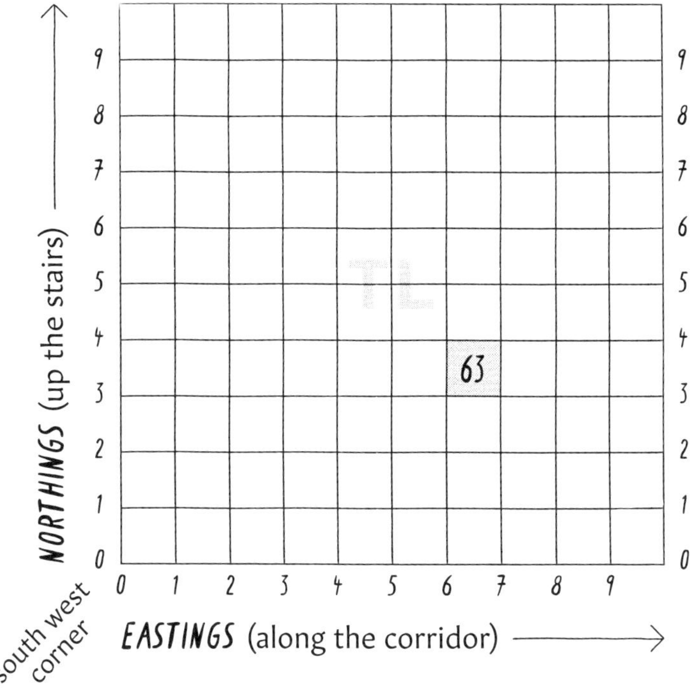

The northings and eastings are used together to give an accurate location for any given spot. The squares are then further divided by ten, but these values aren't shown on the map – you'll need to guesstimate by halving the square, then halving it again. An accurate location within square 63 above may in fact be 625 333.

When giving the values, always cite the eastings first, followed by the northings. You can remember this with the phrase, 'Along the corridor and then up the stairs.'

How to Set a Map with a Compass

1 Line up the direction of travel arrow on your compass with a vertical grid line on your map.
2 Keeping the compass in place, turn the map until the compass needle points north on the compass housing.
3 This will have set your map. Looking ahead, you should be able to start to recognise features from your map.

Remember to Compensate

Because your compass needle points to magnetic north, rather than true north, you'll need to compensate for the difference. This is called the 'magnetic variation', and the difference can be significant. Check the small print at the bottom of your map for the number of degrees you need to adjust your bearing.

If you're working out your bearing from the map to your compass, then you add on the degrees for the magnetic variation. If you are figuring out a back bearing, working from your compass to see where you are on the actual map, then you minus the degrees. Remember this phrase to help you with your magnetic variation calculations: 'Grid to mag, add. Mag to grid, get rid.'

How to Set a Map Without a Compass

1 Find a recognisable feature in the landscape and stand beside it.
2 Find the same spot on your map and mark this with your fingertip.
3 Now rotate the map, keeping it parallel to the ground, until the other features in the landscape correspond with their location on the map.
4 Your map is now set to the landscape.

Navigation Markers

The way I navigate, and I have used this on expeditions all over the world, is to use something I was taught when I was on Selection for 21 SAS (the British Special Forces). I simply use five navigation markers that I remember with this phrase: Bear Drinks Tea For Breakfast. This stands for: Bearing, Distance, Time, Features, Backdrop. Using these five elements, you can break down each leg that you have to navigate into simple markers:

1. BEARING. What is the compass bearing that you are following? For example, I am following a compass bearing of 80°.
2. DISTANCE. How far am I going to be travelling in order to reach the next checkpoint or destination? For example, 6 km.
3. TIME. How long should it take to travel the 6 km? In the mountains, moving fast and efficiently, we would cover 4 km in one hour, so it would take ninety minutes to go 6 km.
4. FEATURES. What features should I be noticing along my route? Maybe it is a river that should always be on my left, or a high peak should be just off to my right in the far distance.
5. BACKDROP. What will I see if I have gone too far? Maybe if I start going downhill, or if I reach the shore of a lake? Those things can let you know you've passed your destination.

All these elements are simple key markers to take note of as you travel. Just a compass bearing and a final destination aren't enough to guarantee you will reach your mark without getting lost. You want to be continually using pointers and indicators that keep you on track. And the simple phrase 'Bear Drinks Tea For Breakfast' – Bearing, Distance, Time, Features, Backdrop – has saved me so many times.

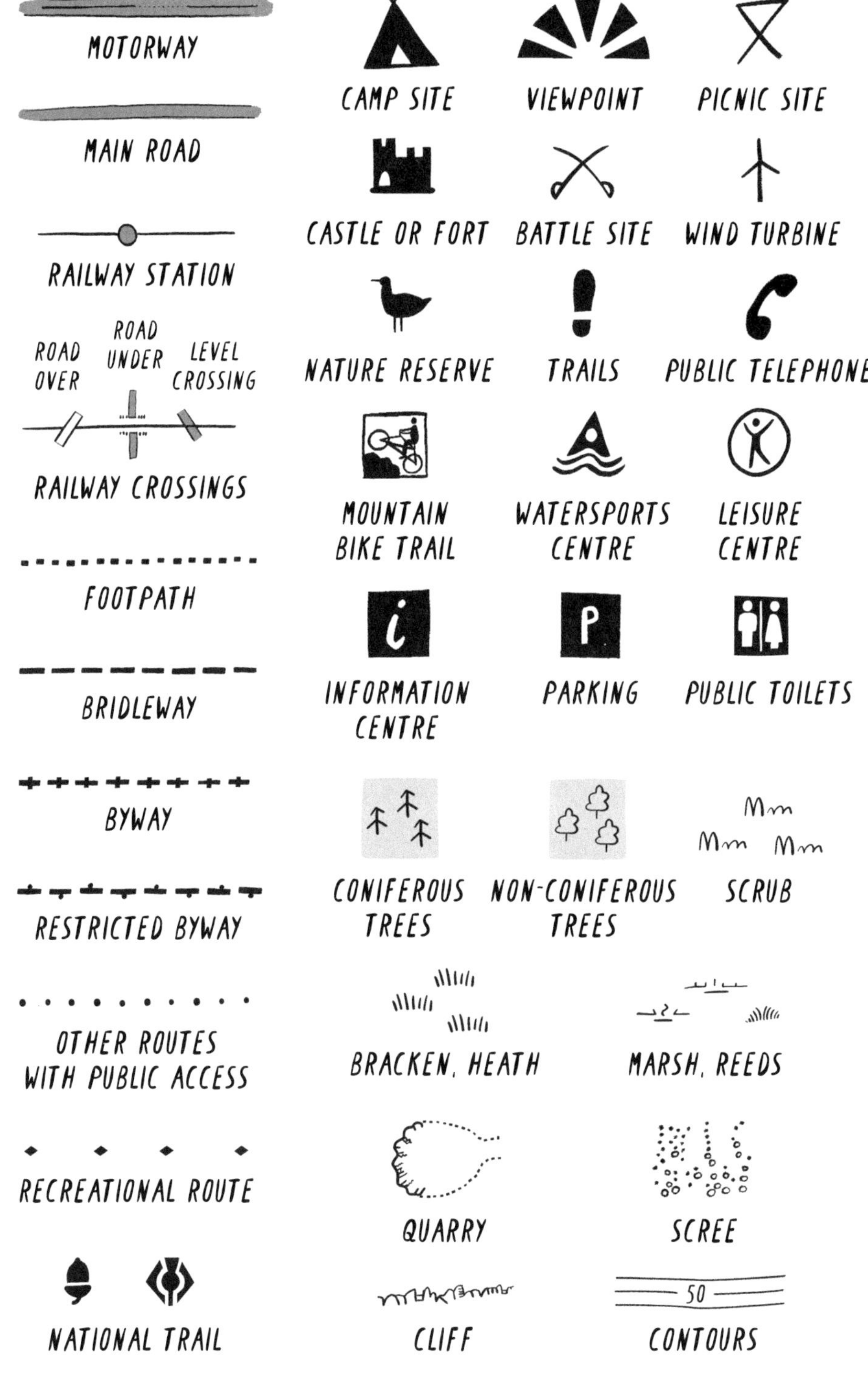
MOTORWAY
MAIN ROAD
RAILWAY STATION
ROAD OVER
ROAD UNDER
LEVEL CROSSING
RAILWAY CROSSINGS
FOOTPATH
BRIDLEWAY
BYWAY
RESTRICTED BYWAY
OTHER ROUTES WITH PUBLIC ACCESS
RECREATIONAL ROUTE
NATIONAL TRAIL
CAMP SITE
VIEWPOINT
PICNIC SITE
CASTLE OR FORT
BATTLE SITE
WIND TURBINE
NATURE RESERVE
TRAILS
PUBLIC TELEPHONE
MOUNTAIN BIKE TRAIL
WATERSPORTS CENTRE
LEISURE CENTRE
i
INFORMATION CENTRE
P
PARKING
PUBLIC TOILETS
CONIFEROUS TREES
NON-CONIFEROUS TREES
SCRUB
BRACKEN, HEATH
MARSH, REEDS
QUARRY
SCREE
CLIFF
50
CONTOURS

Understanding Map Symbols

Features such as roads, churches, train lines and footpaths will be marked on your map. Mapmakers use symbols to represent these, and they vary from country to country. Before you set off, it's important to know what each of the symbols mean. Opposite are some examples from a UK Ordnance Survey map.

Latitude and Longitude

If you look at a globe, you'll see that it's criss-crossed with vertical and horizontal lines. These are a system of lines that are used to find any location on earth.

Lines of latitude run east to west, and circle the earth. The equator, which is an imaginary line that circles the centre of the earth like a belt, is 0°. The lines above the equator are measured 1° to 89° N and those south are measured – you've guessed it – 1° to 89° S.

Lines of longitude run north to south (from the North Pole to the South Pole). The line that marks 0° runs through Greenwich, in South London.

Put these lines together and you can pinpoint anywhere on earth.

TEN TOP TIPS *for Finding Your Way*

1 WATCH THE LANDSCAPE AS WELL AS THE MAP

Get into the habit of regularly matching physical features to what's on your map. This will help you stay on course. It's amazing how far people will walk in the wrong direction because they don't do this.

2 HAVE A BACKUP FOR YOUR BACKUP

Take your phone or GPS with you, but make sure you pack your map and compass too. And a spare. Remember, technology often fails at the worst of times! Be prepared.

3 LOOK FOR CONTOURS

Remember that the contour lines on your map will show you how steep the route ahead will be. The closer together the contours are, the steeper the climb (or descent). What looks like a short distance to travel could mean hours of struggling over steep, dangerous terrain. Naismith's rule says that for every extra 10 m you climb in height, add an extra minute walking time to your journey.

4 TELL SOMEONE WHERE YOU'RE HEADING

Leave details of your route and departure time with someone you can trust. That way, if you run into trouble, they'll know when and where to raise the alarm. Don't forget to let them know you've arrived too. This is one of the most important tips to navigating and hiking in back country. The worst feeling is being lost and no one being aware that you're in trouble.

5 WALK THE ROUTE ON YOUR MAP FIRST

This way you'll be familiar with the main features you'll see on your journey, and hopefully won't run into any nasty surprises along the way. Check that the bridge across the river isn't just a smudge on the map.

6 CHECK THE WEATHER

Checking the weather is vital to every outdoor endeavour. A dense fog or storm could make your route impassable.

Get the most up-to-date local weather forecast before you set off. Get used to doing this before all trips. Don't be the numpty who gets caught out and didn't know there was a storm coming!

7 LOOK FOR 'HANDRAILS'

These are linear features like rivers and roads that you know you'll see along the route. Once you catch sight of these, you can relax a little, knowing they'll always be on your left or right. But keep checking your map and compass to make sure you're following the right handrail. Or left.

8 BE ABLE TO START AGAIN

If you become hopelessly lost, don't panic. Take a deep breath and start again. This process is called 'relocating'. It's better to admit a mistake and rectify it early than to plough on in denial and then find yourself truly lost and exhausted further down the line! If in doubt, stop, check, confirm with others and then continue. People will respect that. If still nothing looks familiar, find a handrail, such as a road or river, and follow that until it takes you to civilisation.

9 PROTECT YOUR MAP

Out in the wild, your map is more precious than chocolate. Hard to believe, I know! Make sure you carry it in a waterproof map case that allows you to read it on the move without it turning to soggy mush.

10 ASK THE WAY

Finally, don't forget you can always stop and ask someone local for the way. They might know the area well and be able to point you in the right direction. Just make sure that they're not lost too! Don't be too proud to ask for help.

How to

TRACK

THE ORIGINAL SCOUTS were those who headed out alone or in small groups to find out what lay ahead. They would move quietly through the woods and fields, carefully surveying the terrain and reading signs in nature. To help others who followed them, they left tracking symbols, not only to give directions but to warn them of dangers they might encounter.

Today, Scouts still learn this skill, which becomes essential in a survival situation. Imagine your party has run out of food and water and you have an injured person with you. One of you may have to go on ahead to look for food and shelter or seek help. The others may then follow at a slower pace, using the symbols you leave behind to get to safety. If you plan to return to the party, you may also want to leave a trail of symbols for yourself so you can more easily find your way back.

Scouts are quick thinking and resourceful, so they make tracking symbols out of whatever natural materials they find, from sticks and stones to long grass, and even scratching messages into soil. However, when leaving your symbols, think carefully about how long they'll last. Will rain wash away messages left in the dirt, or will wind blow away your sticks? You'll need to adapt your materials to suit the conditions – for example, using larger sticks if there's a strong wind blowing, or even leaving symbols in the branches of trees so they can still be read after a snowfall.

If you need to leave an important message, it's a good idea to leave it on top of a cairn – a tall pyramid of stones that you can make and which will attract attention as it's obviously made by a person.

WHY TRACKING IS IN OUR DNA

Tracking's not just a skill passed down through countless generations, it's in our DNA. As hunter-gatherers, our ancestors relied on their tracking skills to hunt for food. Even if our parents or grandparents didn't pass this knowledge onto us directly, it's something hard-wired into our brains through evolution. Instinctively, we'll look for tracks to see where others have gone before us. It's the reason we have good eyesight, a keen sense of smell and the ability to deduce information from what we've observed.

The great fictional detective, Sherlock Holmes, created by Sir Arthur Conan Doyle, was a master of observation and deduction. He said, 'People see everything but do not observe it. And this is the difference between people and me. The world is filled with such obvious things that no person can ever see.'

In the course of his adventures, Holmes deduces the type of dog a man owns by the teeth marks it leaves in a walking cane; where a man has walked by looking at the brand of cigarette stub left on the ground; and whether someone has been walking in the rain by how recently and well his boots have been cleaned.

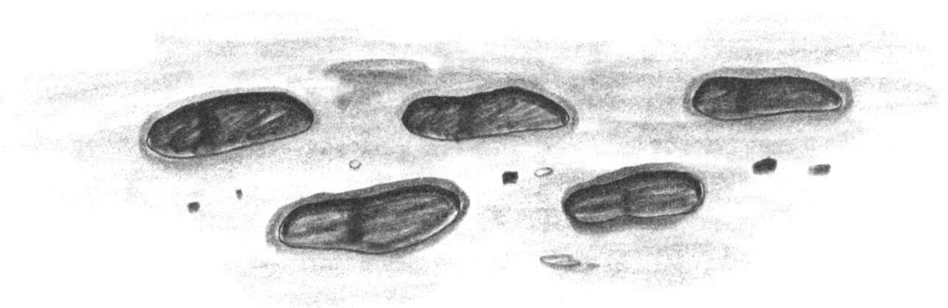

Tracking Symbols

These are some of the most common tracking symbols, which you should memorise and practise laying. When you're ready, why not try your skills with a friend or two, with one person laying the track and the others following?

	STICKS	STONES	GRASS	MARKS
THIS WAY				
TURN LEFT				
TURN RIGHT				
PACES TO A NOTE				3
DANGER HELP				HELP
NOT THIS WAY				
I HAVE GONE HOME				

BADEN-POWELL: THE ORIGINAL SCOUT

Robert Baden-Powell, the founder of Scouting, was a highly skilled tracker and passed his knowledge on to the men he trained in the army.

He led many tracking parties himself while he was a soldier in Africa. He was so skilled, he once found his way back to his base in the dark simply by feeling for, and then following, his own footprints.

In his book, *Scouting for Boys*, he gave this advice: 'Let nothing be too small for your notice; a button, a match, a cigar ash, a feather, or a leaf might be of great importance. A Scout must not only look to his front but also to either side and behind him.'

Baden-Powell claimed, 'From a man's track, that is, from the size of his foot and the length of his stride, you can tell, to a certain extent, his height.' He could also tell the speed of a horse by the distance between the hoof marks. However, he also warned his men to beware of false tracks. For example, highwaymen used to put their horses' shoes on the wrong way round to make it appear they were travelling in the opposite direction.

Speculative and Systematic Tracking

There are two different types of tracking, but they both have the same goal: to follow signs and find what you're looking for. Speculative tracking is about thinking like the person or animal you're following. Where might they go at this junction? Are they looking for water? Are they heading downhill? Are they injured? Would they be taking the easiest path? (Maybe not if they are trying to stay hidden, for example.) Thinking like your prey is speculative tracking.

Systematic tracking is looking and searching to pick up physical clues that indicate a direction of travel and how long ago they were at a place. It's the technical side of recognising signs. Great trackers perfectly blend both techniques of tracking to bring successful results.

Tracking by Observation

Of course, it's possible to track people even if they haven't left deliberate symbols. Often, police will bring in tracking experts if they're on the trail of a criminal or escaped prisoner. This is also a vital skill if you need to search for someone who has become separated from the main party. Mountain rescuers use tracking techniques to look for lost climbers or to find people who may be injured or exposed as night falls.

Footprints

The first thing to look for is footprints, or more likely, boot or shoe prints. Think carefully about the person you are tracking, their size and likely shoe size. Can you remember an exact style of shoe or boot? Could they be barefoot?

When you find some footprints, check first that they're not your own, or haven't been made by a member of your own party. See if the print looks wet or dry. If it's still wet, then you know it hasn't been there long and the person may still be near. If it's dry, they could now be a long way ahead.

Even if there's no soil, mud, sand or snow, you might still be able to see where someone has walked. Look for long grass that's been trodden down, or sticks that have snapped in two where they've been trodden on.

Resting Places

Ask yourself where you would stop to rest if you were the person you're tracking (speculative tracking). Then look for signs to back up your theory (systematic tracking). For example, a pair of boot prints close together, or side by side, might show they've been sitting down. Can you see any food wrappers, dropped berries, nutshells or similar where they might have stopped for a snack?

Clothing or Personal Items

Is there a piece of torn clothing on brambles, branches or barbed wire? Think back to what they were wearing to see if any torn clothing you find could be theirs. Have they dropped any items, like money or a phone? Do they chew gum or like a particular kind of sweet or chocolate? Can you see any evidence of these? If the person is injured, they may also have left traces of blood.

Think Yourself Into Their Shoes

What would you do if you were them? Would you attempt to wade across a river or follow a riverbank until you found a bridge? Often, this is the most effective way to track someone, but you should look for evidence to support your hunch. And remember, it's important that you don't find yourself stuck or lost. It's not good if the rescuer has to be rescued!

Ask People You Meet

Be prepared to give an accurate description of the person you're tracking. Someone may have seen them, or even spoken to them to give directions.

Tracking Animals

Our fields and forests are full of tracks revealing who's been there before us. Because of their acute sense of smell and hearing, most woodland animals will make themselves scarce before we can catch a glimpse of them. But there are still plenty of telltale clues they leave behind.

Droppings are a very good clue to which animals have passed by:

- Badger: long, dark, wet tubes
- Deer: clumps or scatterings of gleaming balls
- Fox: dark with fur and seeds

- Hedgehog: dark brown or black, slightly pointed and sparkly from beetle skeletons
- Rabbits: small, brown-green balls

How to Conceal Yourself

If you're tracking an animal and don't wish to scare it away, you'll need to try and hide and conceal yourself. That means from sight and from smell.

- Stand downwind of the animal so it can't smell you.
- Stand very still. This is one of the best ways to disguise yourself, even if you're caught in the open and have nowhere to hide. (Try it when you next play hide and seek.)
- Walk lightly. Baden-Powell recommended walking on the balls of your feet rather than on your heels.
- Keep low. Don't let your silhouette appear on the horizon line. Lie close to the ground or in a ditch, raising your chin only very slightly to look ahead.

Remember: Shape, Shine, Shadow, Sound and Silhouette – the five Ss of great camouflage.

1. SHAPE. The human figure is very distinct. Especially our head and shoulders. Try and blend these together to break up that human pattern. Maybe drape a coat over the back of your head and shoulders.
2. SHINE. Think about anything that glistens. Watch faces, jewellery, rings or earrings. Cover them.
3. SHADOW. As you move by day or night, the sun or moon can cast a huge shadow from your actual figure. This will make you much more visible. Stay in the shade to avoid this.
4. SOUND. Move stealthily and softly. No metal mugs jiggling off your backpack making a noise!
5. SILHOUETTE. Don't get 'skylined' on a ridge where your human profile is so visible against the sky behind you. Drop

down a few metres off a ridge, so your backdrop is the hill itself and not the sky.

Identifying Animal Tracks

Get to know the subtle differences between different kinds of paw and hoof prints. You'll notice the fore (front) and hind (back) prints are often quite different. For example, the hind feet of a rabbit or hare are much larger, due to their powerful hindquarters for running and leaping as they escape predators.

Look for Their Homes

Another way to discover which animals are in the area is to look for their homes. Become an animal estate agent and get to know the different kinds of dwelling.

For example, a badger sett has large, mouth-shaped entrance holes around 30 cm wide. You'll find these sloping downwards, often at the foot of a tree. They lead into a network of underground tunnels and hollows. You might notice signs of animal activity nearby, such as piles of loose soil from recent digging, or badger latrines – a hole filled with slimy poo (especially slimy if they've been feasting on earthworms). Watch your step!

Each animal home has its own special name. Here are just a few of them:

- Badger – sett
- Bat – roost
- Bear – den
- Beaver – lodge
- Bee – hive
- Bird – nest
- Eagle – eyrie
- Fox – earth
- Hare – form
- Otter – holt
- Rabbit – warren
- Squirrel – drey
- Wasp – nest
- Wolf – lair

BADGER
OTTER
FOX
WEASEL
WOODMOUSE
BEAVER
HEDGEHOG
MINK
RABBIT
GREY SQUIRREL
HARE
RED SQUIRREL
DOMESTIC DOG
DOMESTIC CAT
ROE DEER
RED DEER
FALLOW DEER

How to

LOOK AT THE NIGHT SKY

THE STARS, MOONS and planets have filled us with wonder since we first walked the earth. For Scouts, one of the greatest things about camping is sleeping beneath a sky filled with stars which scatter the heavens like the embers of your campfire.

It's perhaps no coincidence that Scout camps have inspired generations of astronauts. As we've learned, an incredible eleven of the twelve people to walk on the moon were Scouts, while others became Space Shuttle pilots and crew aboard the International Space Station. The astronaut, Tim Peake, said that 'becoming a Cub Scout was the first step on the path that took him into space'.

Recognising the celestial bodies and the different star constellations isn't just useful for navigation (see page 150). It's an important part of being a citizen of the solar system. We can only really find our place on earth when we understand our place in the universe.

The tricky thing about stargazing is that the stars and constellations appear to move around at different times of the year, making them hard to identify. But, of course, they aren't moving so much as we are.

The earth is a giant blue and green spaceship orbiting the sun at 67,000 mph (so fasten your seatbelt). The earth takes a year to complete this cyclical journey. This is why the night sky looks different in different seasons.

Constellations

The constellations are families, or patterns, of stars that have been given names by our ancestors. They've joined the stars like dot-to-dot puzzles to create animals and figures to help us recognise them. In reality, many of these stars are not close to each other at all; they're millions of light years apart. However, to our eyes, they can look like they're neighbours.

Northern and Southern Hemispheres

The night sky looks different depending where you are on earth. You'll see different constellations in the northern hemisphere to the southern hemisphere.

NORTHERN HEMISPHERE
Andromeda
Cassiopeia
Perseus
Cygnus
Cepheus
Lyra
Draco
Ursa Minor
Auriga
Hercules
Ursa Major
Gemini
Bootes
Piscis Austrinus
Phoenix
Capricornus
Eridanus
Pavo
Hydrus
Sagittarius
Columba
Triangulum
Australe
Carina
Puppis
Scorpio
Vela
Centaurus
SOUTHERN HEMISPHERE

The Moon

The moon is a natural satellite of the earth, orbiting our planet just like the earth orbits the sun. It's made of similar stuff to the earth – rock and metal – but is only a quarter of its size.

Our moon is around 4.53 billion years old (compared with the earth, which is 4.54 billion years old). There are different theories about how it was formed, all of which are fascinating. The first idea is that the moon was once what's called a 'wandering body': a giant rock that was passing through our neighbourhood and was captured by the earth's gravity. Another theory is that a piece of the earth broke off as it spun, and has remained orbiting the earth ever since.

However, the most popular theory is also the most dramatic. Most scientists now believe that the earth once had a smaller sister planet called Theia, located close to us in the solar system, and roughly the size of Mars. At some point in our very early history, Theia smashed into the earth. From the chaos, a new planet formed, combining elements of both earth and Theia. It's believed that a piece of this new combined planet spun away to form the moon. The moon, therefore, is almost like a child of earth and Theia. Pretty amazing!

The moon is roughly 240,000 miles away, and so far is the only other non-earth body where humans have ever set foot. NASA and SpaceX's plans to land on Mars in the next few years may change that.

Unlike the earth (and like a boring party!), the moon has no atmosphere. This means there's no breathable air, and it can have extremes of heat and cold. The moon takes a month to orbit the earth, and twenty-seven days to spin on its axis. The moon's gravitational pull governs the earth's ocean tides.

Phases of the Moon

The moon doesn't have any light of its own. All the light you see is a reflection of the sun. During each month, it also appears to change shape. Of course, the moon doesn't change shape at all – all that changes is what we see of it. As it orbits the earth, we see more or less of it depending on its position in relation to the earth and how much of the sun's reflected light is visible. A 'waxing' moon means it appears to get bigger, while a 'waning' moon means it seems to get smaller.

These are the phases of the moon:

- NEW MOON. The side of the moon facing the sun is in full sunlight, but the other is in complete darkness, so we cannot see the moon at all.
- WAXING CRESCENT MOON. You'll see this moon rising during the day and it will be invisible by midnight.
- FIRST QUARTER HALF MOON. Half of the moon is now visible.
- WAXING GIBBOUS MOON. This is now almost full and is mostly visible. Gibbous means 'bulging' or 'rounded'.
- FULL MOON. This is the moon in all its glory and it will light up the woods and the fields in its silvery-blue glare. The sun, earth and moon are fully aligned.

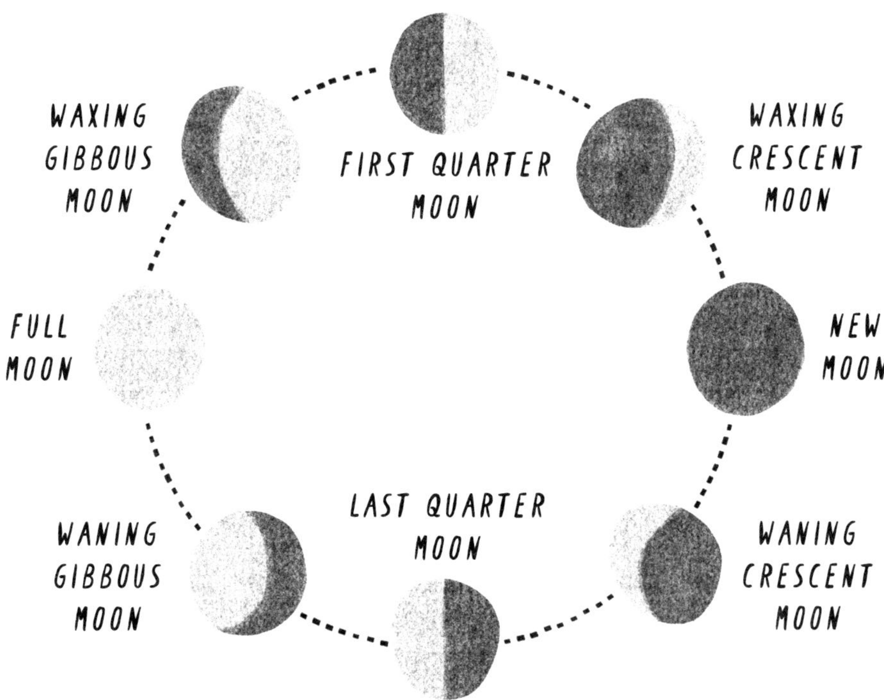

- **WANING GIBBOUS MOON.** Now the moon starts to look smaller. You'll notice it has a reddish colour when it's near the horizon.
- **LAST QUARTER HALF MOON.** The light is now disappearing and only half the moon is visible.
- **WANING CRESCENT MOON.** It's almost time to say goodbye, before the next (invisible) new moon.

The Seas of the Moon

People once believed there was liquid water on the surface of the moon, and therefore thought that the dark patches were seas. We now know that these are basaltic plains created by volcanic activity triggered by asteroid collisions on the opposite side of the moon.

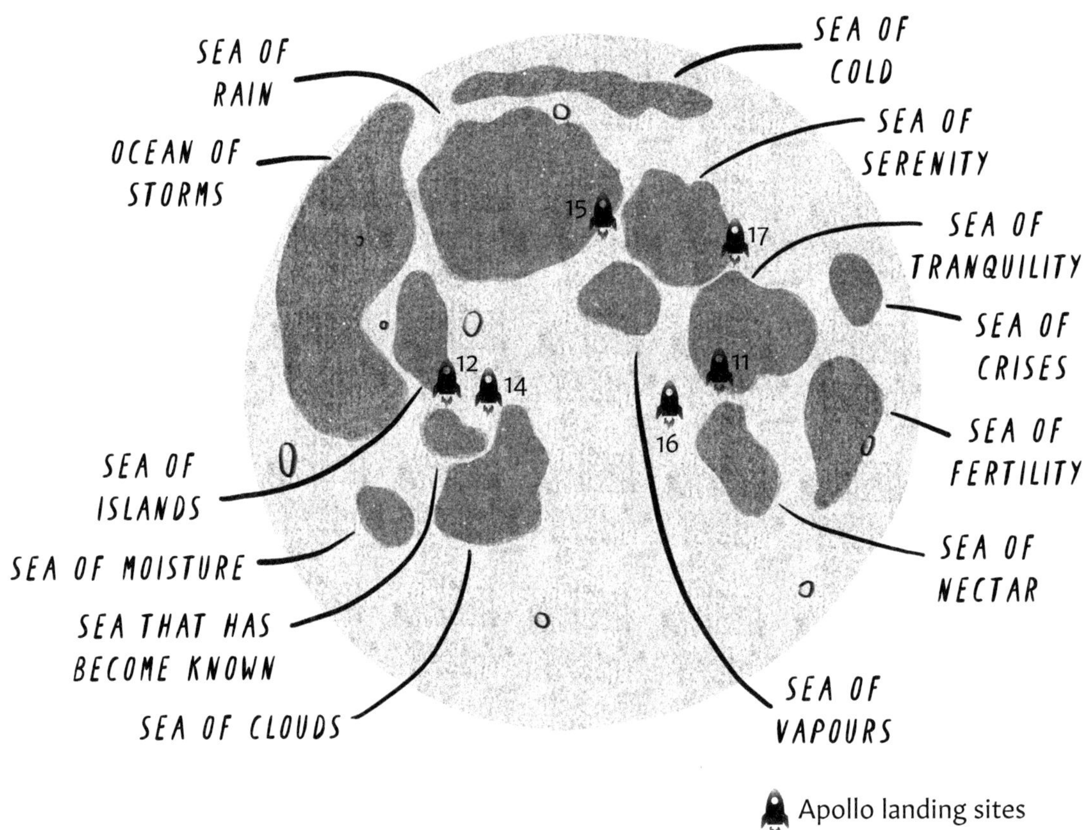

The 'seas' are less reflective (and therefore darker) than other parts of the moon because they're rich in iron. However, the idea of calling them seas has stuck. You'll probably know that it was on the Sea of Tranquillity where Neil Armstrong and Buzz Aldrin took their first steps on the moon.

The map on the previous page shows the seas of the moon and the landing sites of all the Apollo missions. See if you can spot these seas on the moon when you next see it in the night sky.

The Moons of the Solar System

Would you be surprised to know the moon isn't the only natural satellite in our solar system? In fact, there are 214 moons (or provisional moons – the ones waiting for the boffins to confirm they're actually there). But our moon is the only one just called 'the moon'. What would you call it instead?

Our nearest planetary neighbour, Mars, has two moons. Both are slightly lumpy and misshapen, and not nearly as lovely as ours, but we shouldn't have favourites, should we?

Here's a rhyme to help you remember the names of the moons of Mars, and also to remind you which one is bigger:

The moons of Mars aren't famous.
But that doesn't mean that they're not there.
There's Phobos and there's Deimos,
Which is smaller in compare.

Superstar Moons

Some moons in our solar system are so large or strange they're almost like small planets. Here are some of the most spectacular:

- GANYMEDE is Jupiter's largest moon and is also the biggest in the solar system. It's thought to have a saltwater ocean beneath a shell of ice. Some even believe this might be home to primitive life forms.
- EUROPA, another of Jupiter's Galilean moons, has probably created the most excitement among scientists, explorers and sci-fi fans. This is because it's the moon that seems most likely to be able to sustain some sort of extraterrestrial life. Not only does it have oxygen in its atmosphere, it has a liquid ocean of water beneath its icy surface. A plume of water 120 miles high has been spotted shooting out of the ice near the south pole of Europa. Now that's what you call a water feature!
- TRITON behaves very strangely indeed. It spins in the opposite direction to its parent planet, Neptune, a phenomenon known as a retrograde orbit. This has led astronomers to believe it was once a dwarf planet. Like Neptune itself, Triton is named after a sea god. It has oceans of frozen nitrogen above a crust of water ice.
- TITAN, as the name suggests, is the biggest of the moons of Saturn. It was probably formed by other moons smashing together to create a super moon. Beneath its thick, brown, hazy atmosphere is a solid surface, and there are mountains and deserts, rivers and lakes of liquid methane. It also rains liquid methane, and there are even seasons. With a surface temperature of -180°C, however, it's still not an obvious holiday destination.
- MIRANDA is one of the moons of Uranus, which are all named after characters from works by William Shakespeare or Alexander Pope (Miranda is Prospero's daughter in one of Shakespeare's last plays, *The Tempest*). Miranda is beautifully imperfect. The surface, mostly made up of water ice, is gloriously uneven and it looks like several lumps of clay have been smashed together. Some believe that the planet may have been obliterated by a cosmic collision, then slammed back together in a random fashion (rather like

earth and Theia). Miranda is also home to the tallest cliff in the solar system, Verona Rupes, which is an astonishing twelve miles high!

The Planets No One Ever Talks About

You'll be familiar with the map of the solar system, showing the planets from Mercury, nearest the sun, to Neptune, furthest away. Older maps will also show Pluto at the edge, before it was reclassified as a dwarf planet in 2006.

Mercury | Venus | Earth | Mars | Jupiter | Saturn | Uranus | Neptune

In fact, the real order (including dwarf planets) looks like this:

Mercury | Venus | Earth | Mars | Ceres | Jupiter | Saturn | Uranus | Neptune | Pluto | Haumea | Makemake | Eris

- CERES, named after the Roman god of agriculture, can be found in a place called the asteroid belt, between Mars and Jupiter. Ceres was discovered in 1801 by the Italian astronomer Giuseppe Piazzi. In March 2015, 214 years after it was first spotted, the NASA spacecraft, *Dawn*, made a flying visit to Ceres.
- HAUMEA is a strange, egg-shaped moon, discovered in 2004 and named after the Hawaiian goddess of childbirth.
- MAKEMAKE, discovered in 2005, is another dwarf planet found, like Haumea, in the Kuiper belt on the edge of our solar system.
- ERIS was discovered around the same time as Haumea and Makemake and is named after the goddess of strife and discord. White in colour, it has a moon called Dysnomia, the goddess of lawlessness, daughter of Eris.

THE GIRL WHO NAMED A PLANET

Did you know that the dwarf planet Pluto was named by an eleven-year-old girl? Venetia Burney (born in 1918, later Venetia Phair) was living in Oxford with her family when inspiration struck. Her grandfather, Falconer Madan, was the librarian of the Bodleian Library in Oxford, and well connected at the famous university. (Remarkably, his brother Henry was the person who came up with the names Phobos and Deimos for the moons of Mars.)

When Madan mentioned the discovery of the planet to Venetia, after reading about it in his copy of *The Times* on 14 March 1930, she proposed the name Pluto, the god of the underworld who could make himself invisible – just like the planet had been all those years. Madan liked the idea and mentioned it to his colleague, the astronomer Herbert Hall Turner, who in turn mentioned it to his counterparts at the Lowell Observatory in Arizona, USA, where it was discovered by Clyde Tombaugh. They all agreed it was the perfect name, and Pluto became the official name. Venetia lived to the grand old age of ninety and died in 2009. Six years later, the *New Horizons* spacecraft visited Pluto and on board was a scientific instrument named in her honour.

How to Use a Telescope

Many stars and planets can be seen with the naked eye. However, you'll need some equipment if you want to get a really good look at the night sky. A good pair of binoculars will improve your view of the moon – for example, revealing much more detail.

If you're serious about your stargazing, you'll want to think about investing in, or borrowing, a telescope. These vary wildly in price and sophistication, from an inexpensive model available from your local supermarket, to the $9.7 billion NASA spent on the James Webb telescope, which orbits the sun and uses infrared to observe the formation of stars and galaxies.

Other Things to Look Out for in the Night Sky

- COMETS are icy objects that streak across the sky, leaving a trail of gas behind them. They're typically made up of ice, rock and dust and can vary in size from tiny fragments to huge formations the size of a town. The tail can be millions of miles long.

  There are 3,743 known comets, and some, like Halley's Comet, which is visible from earth every seventy-five years or so, have become famous. This is the comet that features on the Bayeux Tapestry, recording the Norman invasion of Britain in 1066. As it also appeared in 12 BC, close to the historical birth of Christ, some have also speculated this was the star of Bethlehem, followed by the Magi in the Christian faith's nativity story. The comet last appeared in 1986 and will next be seen in 2061. Make a note in your diary!

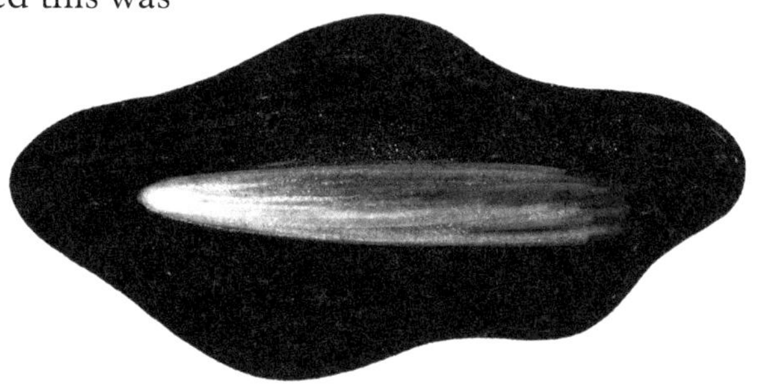

- METEOROIDS are space rocks of varying size that travel through space.
- METEORS are meteoroids that burn up as they enter our atmosphere.
- METEORITES are the rocks that survive the trip through our atmosphere and land on earth. In July 2010, a meteorite hit the ground during a county cricket match between Middlesex and Sussex in Uxbridge, near London. It split in two, with one fragment hitting a spectator, luckily not injuring him. It was also lucky a fielder didn't mistake it for the cricket ball and try to catch it!

How to

PREDICT THE WEATHER

ONE OF THE best things about the outdoors is that it keeps changing. The changing seasons put on a different show for us every time. The same patch of woodland or field can look like the surface of the moon in winter and a magical green kingdom in the summer. The same goes for the weather: wind and rain can transform a landscape in minutes and bring with it plenty of dangers. Learning how to predict the weather (and knowing how to stay dry) is a skill every Scout needs to know.

People have been predicting the weather for as long as they've looked up at the skies. Folklore passed down through generations has helped us get a better idea of what to expect, long before weather forecasts or weather apps were a thing. This ability to predict the weather was especially important to farmers, sailors and others who lived and worked in the wild.

Today, for those of us planning expeditions and adventures, knowing how to predict the weather will help us know what gear to pack and what clothing to wear. No one likes getting wet and cold, and developing a good sense of the weather by observing nature will keep you both drier and happier. A good sense of humour helps too. (And by the way, what does a cloud wear under his raincoat? Thunderwear.)

'There's no such thing as good weather or bad weather,' said the author Louise Hay. 'There's just weather and your attitude towards it.' I'd also add: there's just weather and your equipment within it! Because the right gear, such as waterproofs, or even just an umbrella, can transform bad weather into a great, fun adventure.

Weather Wisdom

These are just some of the many phrases people have used for centuries to predict the weather by observing nature.

'Red sky at night, shepherds' delight. Red sky in the morning, shepherds' warning.'

This rhyme is at least as old as the Bible, where it first appeared in the book of Matthew. When we see a red sky, we're actually seeing dust and other tiny particles locked into the atmosphere by high pressure. A red sky at night means that high pressure is coming in from the west, bringing us good weather. However, if we see it in the morning, heading east, this means the best of the dry weather has already gone, to be replaced by wind and rain.

'Cold is the night when the stars shine bright.'

Have you noticed that the nights seem much colder when there are no clouds, and you can see more bright stars than usual? This is because there's less water vapour in the atmosphere, causing temperatures to drop.

'Mackerel sky and mares' tails make tall ships carry low sails.'

Sailors are experts at predicting the weather as they see so much of it. A mackerel sky means that it's full of altocumulus clouds, which look like the scales of a mackerel – a kind of fish – while mares' tails are wispy cirrus clouds, like a horse's tail. These clouds normally mean that the weather is changing and that rain and storms could be on the way. Sailors lower their sails in these conditions.

'Dew on the grass, rain won't come to pass.'

Dew is the water droplets you see clinging to the grass. If you see this in the morning, it usually means the sky is clear of clouds, promising a day of good weather ahead.

'Rain before seven, fine after eleven.'

This means that if it rains early in the morning, it should be dry again by late morning. This is based on the wisdom that most rain fronts will pass in three to four hours.

'If there's a halo round the sun or moon, then we can all expect rain quite soon.'

A halo appears to form around the sun and moon because of light refracting through ice crystals of cirrostratus clouds, which are an indicator of changing weather.

The Pine Cone Predictor

Pick up a pine cone from the ground and take a look at the scales. If it's open, and the scales are dried up and fanned out, this means good weather is on the way. If they're closed, it means there's water in the atmosphere and rain is coming.

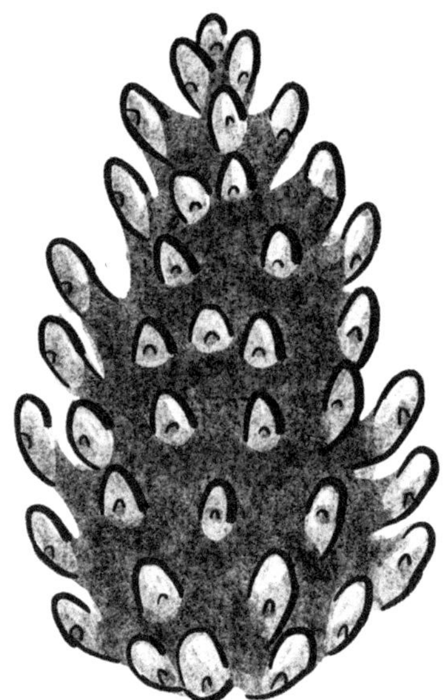

Watch the Cows

Cows will often lie down before rain. They instinctively seem to know when rain is coming, detecting moisture in the air. It's thought perhaps they lie down to make sure they get a dry patch of grass before another cow gets there first.

How to Read the Clouds

Most of us know that dark clouds are usually full of rain and that when you see them it's time to look for cover. But getting to know the different kinds of clouds will help you get even better at predicting the weather.

Low Cloud

CUMULUS

These puffy clouds, like sheep floating in the sky, are low-lying. Very simply, if they're white, that spells good weather. If they're darker, rain is coming.

STRATUS

These are those long clouds that can completely obscure the sky. When they're very low-lying, and come down to ground level, we call it fog. However, while it can feel damp, these clouds don't produce a great deal of rain.

NIMBOSTRATUS

These dark grey sheets mean some heavy rain is on the way.

STRATOCUMULUS

These clouds can look a little like lumpy porridge, and often bring light rain.

CUMULONIMBUS

These are giant stacks of cloud that look like mountains or castles looming over us. They rise as high as 12,000 m and bring rain, hail and storms.

CIRROCUMULUS
CIRRUS
CIRROSTRATUS
ALTOCUMULUS
ALTOSTRATUS
NIMBOSTRATUS
CUMULONIMBUS
CUMULUS
STRATUS
STRATOCUMULUS

Mid-Range Cloud

ALTOCUMULUS

These patchy clouds rarely mean rain and are usually nothing to worry about.

ALTOSTRATUS

These elongated clouds can screen out the sunlight and mean the weather is probably changing for the worse.

High Cloud

CIRROCUMULUS

These high clouds are the famous mackerel skies, which you'll often see in winter. They're an indicator that the weather is changing.

CIRRUS

These are the wispy clouds that can look like horse's tails or angels. They also mean the weather is changing, but don't contain much rain in themselves.

CIRROSTRATUS

These are the clouds that can create the halo around the sun or moon. They contain ice particles which can fall as light rain.

How to Cope in Wet Weather

Learn the Wet-Dry Routine

A good tip in an environment where you're going to get wet is to learn the wet-dry routine. Make sure you've got a dry set of clothes in your waterproof bag. If you get wet, don't be tempted to change immediately. If you're on the move, your body temperature will start to dry the clothing. Keep going. But in the evening, change into the dry kit and get a fire started. If you can, try to dry your wet gear over the fire during the evening. In the morning, take your dry clothes off and put on your others – even if they are still wet or damp.

It might feel horrible putting on wet clothes, but it doesn't stay horrible for long. Five minutes later, when you're moving, it's all fine. Anyway, you'll no doubt be getting wet again imminently – especially if you're in the jungle – but this way, at least your dry set is always dry for the night time. The worst thing is ending up with two sets of wet kit! Protect one set – and keep it dry at all costs.

That's the wet-dry routine, and every Scout should master it and not be afraid of it. After all, Scouts are tough and they are able to do the difficult things, especially if they are the right things. (Still, putting on cold, damp clothes in the morning is never fun!)

Beware Flash Floods

Just because there are blue skies doesn't mean you can't be quickly hit by a flash flood. This might be a sudden downpour of rain up to thirty miles away, and it can be clear where you are, but that rain has to go somewhere, and it follows the path of least resistance. That often means a 'wall' of water can charge down a ravine, and this has caught many a rookie camper out in the past. Clear skies don't mean you're safe from flash floods.

The first sign of a flash flood will be a strong wind and deep rumbling in the distance. This is the water moving and pushing the wind ahead of it. Seek high ground at once.

If you're on a big expedition, especially in unfamiliar country, don't just rely on nature observation. Get a proper weather forecast of the wider area before you set off.

Avoid Cotton Clothing in the Rain

When it's pouring with rain, don't go out in cotton clothing. There's a saying: 'In the hills, cotton kills.' The reason is that cotton absorbs water so quickly that with the wind factor, it can lower your body temperature mega fast.

TEN TOP TIPS *for Camping in the Rain*

Let's face it, camping is a lot less fun when it starts to rain. But there are all sorts of things you can do to stay warm, dry and happy.

1. Water travels downwards. In the same way, cold air sinks at night. So never pitch your tent at the bottom of a big valley or in the bottom of a ravine or dry river bed.
2. If you have one, rig up a tarpaulin between some trees to keep you dry while you set up your tent.
3. Make sure your kit and groundsheet stay dry while you pitch your tent.
4. Once inside your tent, keep all your gear, and especially your sleeping bag, away from the sides of the tent. As soon as something touches them, water will start to come in.
5. We should all cut down on our plastic use, but plastic bags are vital when camping in the rain to keep clothing and other essentials dry. If you're expecting rain (and even if you're not – it has a nasty habit of surprising us), pack things into ziplock plastic bags before putting them in your rucksack.
6. Remember the wet-dry routine, and always have a dry set of clothes to change into.
7. Even if everything gets wet, make sure you have a spare pair of dry socks, at least. I also always take a small down jacket, compressed down and kept dry inside a ziplock plastic bag. Both these items can transform a survival situation for the better. And you can use the plastic bags to collect water.

8 Make sure you're zipped up. A lot of rain can get through a very small gap.

9 A long day or evening stuck in your tent because of the rain can get a little boring. Pack a book, or pack of cards if you're with a friend.

10 Stay cheerful. That counts for a lot when it's raining. In fact, it counts for everything! As the Scout saying goes: 'Good morale is a state of mind – with it all things are possible!'

When Lightning Strikes

Thunder and lightning feel much more frightening when you're in the outdoors. You feel the full force of nature's power all around you. Worldwide, a quarter of a million people are injured by lightning strikes each year, and around 6,000 die. It's a good enough reason to know how to look after yourself in these conditions.

Thunderstorms are caused by electric charges that build up inside clouds. These cause water droplets and ice particles to rub together. The upper part of the cloud becomes positively charged, and the lower part negatively charged. Below the cloud, the ground also becomes positively charged. Together, this becomes an explosive combination. When the charge is strong enough, a bolt of lightning will be produced, travelling either through the cloud, from cloud to cloud or – most dangerously for us – down to the ground.

What to do in a lightning or thunderstorm:

Do:

✓ Get to shelter immediately, ideally in a solid structure with walls. Inside a car will do if there isn't a building nearby, but don't touch any metal.

✓ If there isn't good shelter, find low ground or a ditch and get yourself into the 'crash position' with your head between your legs, balancing on your heels, and cover your ears. Never lie down in the open ground during lightning.

✓ If you're in, or on, water, get to land as quickly as possible, as water is a strong conductor of electricity.

✓ Wait in your shelter or safe space for as long as possible. Thunderstorms still pose a risk up to half an hour after the storm has appeared to have passed.

Don't:

✗ Shelter beneath a tall tree.

✗ Hold an umbrella, phone, walking pole, golf club or any other metallic object.

NOTE: large caves and valleys are relatively safe places to be during a storm. Small caves, overhangs and wet stream beds are more dangerous though, because water conducts electricity and electricity can jump gaps between rocks.

How to Judge Your Distance to a Thunderstorm

You can do this by first counting the number of seconds between the moment you see the flash of lightning and when you hear the rumble of thunder. Divide this by three to get the distance in kilometres. Six seconds between the lightning and thunder, for example, means the storm is 2 km away. If the lightning and thunder happen at the same time, it's happening right overhead, and you're in maximum danger.

Protecting Yourself from the Sun

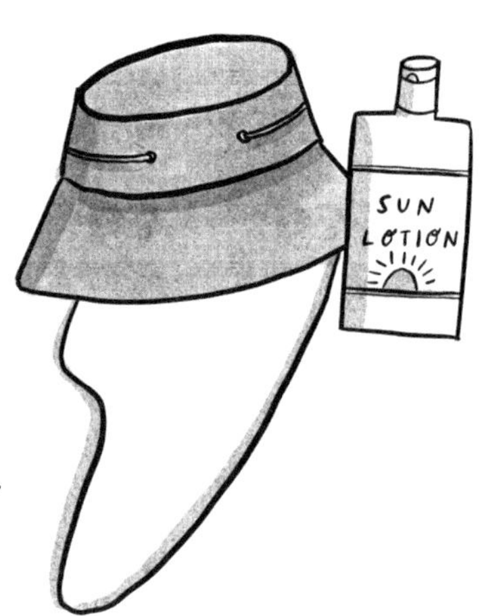

Getting some sunshine on your body every day is important for good physical and mental health, but like so much in life, too much of a good thing can be dangerous. Overexposure to the hot sun, especially in the middle of the day, can be dangerous if you're not used to it or if you are especially fair-skinned.

To protect yourself:

- Be especially mindful of what time of day you're getting your sun exposure. It is better to spend time in the sun during the morning or late afternoon, and to avoid too long in the midday heat.
- Cover up well with long sleeves and trousers to avoid sunburn.
- Always wear a hat.
- Drink plenty of water.
- If you feel yourself becoming unwell, seek shade, remove layers and cool yourself down by drinking water and applying wet cloths or sponges on your body. If you can find a shallow, safe and shaded stream to cool off in, then all the better. The key is to lower your temperature.

Note: it's important we aren't scared of the sun. It is a life-giving force and as humans we need it. The vast majority of people in the northern hemisphere are vitamin D deficient from not enough time in sunlight, and this can have a really detrimental effect on our health. So make sure you get sufficient time in the morning or late afternoon sun if you can. Look at how cats and dogs seek out the sunshine and soak it up. But remember, they have more fur than you as added protection!

Wind Watching

Wind is produced when hot and cold air interacts in our atmosphere. Warm air rises, and cool air takes its place. If you're in the outdoors, wind can pose several threats:

- If you're poorly dressed, the wind can make you feel very cold, very quickly. A strong wind will make the actual temperature feel much lower. Wrap up well.
- If you're high up and exposed, the wind is likely to be stronger. If you're climbing or walking in the hills, take special care as it can blow you off balance. (Wind accelerates as it passes over the top of a hill. Essentially, it gets 'squeezed' over the summit and picks up velocity. This is called the Venturi effect – where wind accelerates as it is compressed.)
- If the wind is really wild, then seek shelter, but beware of overhead branches or damaged walls which could collapse on you.

Choose the Right Clothing

Whatever the weather, the one thing you must do is choose the right clothing.

- Winter: wear a thermal under-layer with a waterproof garment over the top. Choose strong boots with good grips, and a warm hat, scarf and gloves.
- Summer: wear a long-sleeved shirt and trousers to reduce the amount of skin exposed to the sun. A broad-brimmed hat will give more protection than a peaked cap.
- In all seasons: never forget your extra set of dry clothes. Remember, rain loves every season.

How to

GET TO KNOW THE TREES

TREES ARE SOME of the most awesome living beings on planet earth. In fact, it's hard to imagine our world without them. They're symbols of strength and stability, continuity and growth. They outlive us, outnumber us and outgrow us.

There are an astonishing 3.04 trillion trees in the world. If we were to divide them up between everyone who lived on earth, we would have 422 each. That's a small wood for every one of us.

But if that sounds a lot, it really isn't. Before humans came along, the planet belonged to the trees; there were more like 7 trillion. Humans cleared the land of many trees to grow crops, and build villages, towns and cities. They felled the forests to make ships and houses.

Trees mark the changing seasons with their colours and annual cycle. They represent hope and renewal and remind us of our own lives: just as trees shed their leaves in the autumn and winter, we go through tough patches before finding our purpose again, blossoming and growing.

They're much-loved landmarks, and when an old tree dies, a community will remember it like a much-loved person. When there are great storms and whole woods are devastated, we feel a collective sense of loss. Trees are connected to us on an emotional level.

The Gift of Trees

With their welcoming branches, majestic canopies and green-fingered leaves, trees seem to look after us, giving us shelter from the wind and rain, and shade in the summer.

When travellers are lost in the woods, they rest at the feet of trees. With their outstretched limbs, it's as if the trees are extending the hand of welcome and friendship.

They give us gifts of fruit like peaches and pears, spices like cinnamon and cloves, and nuts like almonds and cashews. Most importantly, they give us our life-giving oxygen.

Trees are also home to birds and animals: vertical cities full of thousands of living things.

How Trees Talk to Each Other

Trees are living things and we can sense their energy. While trees are not conscious and cannot think in the same way we do, they respond to their environments in highly sophisticated ways. Each tree has its own complex ecosystem, but they do not live alone – they're part of a wider, connected system. As odd as it sounds, they actually communicate messages to each other. Speaking a language we can neither hear nor yet fully understand, trees warn other trees of danger or disease, by sending chemical, electrical and even sound signals, while passing nutrients and water through underground systems of fungi called mycorrhizal networks. Trees can 'sense' through these fungal connections when other trees are dying or in distress, and will transfer what resources they can spare to help. Pretty amazing!

Older, established trees look after the saplings (baby trees) in a way that feels almost kind, or human, helping the younger trees to flourish and grow. Perhaps most extraordinarily of all, trees seem to be able to smell and taste. They can tell when they're threatened by disease and can communicate this to other trees nearby by releasing hormones through the air or pulses through their underground systems.

One of the most inspiring things about trees (which Scouts and trees have in common) is that they don't just look after their own kind. Oaks don't just talk with other oaks. Trees look after each other, no matter what they look like. Deciduous trees (the ones that lose their leaves in winter) will help evergreens (the ones that don't) just the same. It's this interconnectedness that makes a forest buzz with an energy all of its own. It's as if the forest itself is a single organism and fully alive. You'll never think of trees the same way again.

Forest Bathing

Spending time among trees has huge benefits to our mental well-being. In green spaces, away from the stresses of urban environments and technology, we're able to connect with nature and our true selves. The forests and woods were our first homes, and there's something deep within us that seems to remember that.

Forest bathing is becoming popular across the world. I now realise I have been doing this 'forest bathing' for years, but without realising it was a real thing! In Japan, they call this *shinrin-yoku* (or 'forest bath'). It's about opening yourself completely to the forest and experiencing the trees around you with all your senses. Be still and you'll hear the sounds of the birds twitching in the branches, see the sun glinting through the leaves, smell the earth after rain, taste the loamy air, and feel the spongy bark against your fingertips. You can walk slowly between the trees or sit quietly with them. But if you allow your mind to take all this in, you'll feel an extraordinary sense of calm and connectedness. And when your mind feels calm, it reduces the release of stress hormones in the body, which means a stronger immune system and better sleep too.

A tree is a bit like a Scout: if it has its roots in good soil, it can reach to the sky; in order to breathe, it must be grounded; and no matter how high it reaches, it's from its roots that it draws its strength.

Identifying Trees

A great Scouting skill is to be able to recognise different kinds of trees. And the best and easiest way to do this is by looking at their leaves. Each has its own shape. Some are confusingly similar, but after a little practice you'll get to know these by sight.

Learn the simple ones first, like the horse chestnut (which produces those shiny brown conkers that gleam like a horse's eye). Its leaf looks like a hand of fat fingers. Then there's the oak leaf, which looks a little like a squirrel's paw print.

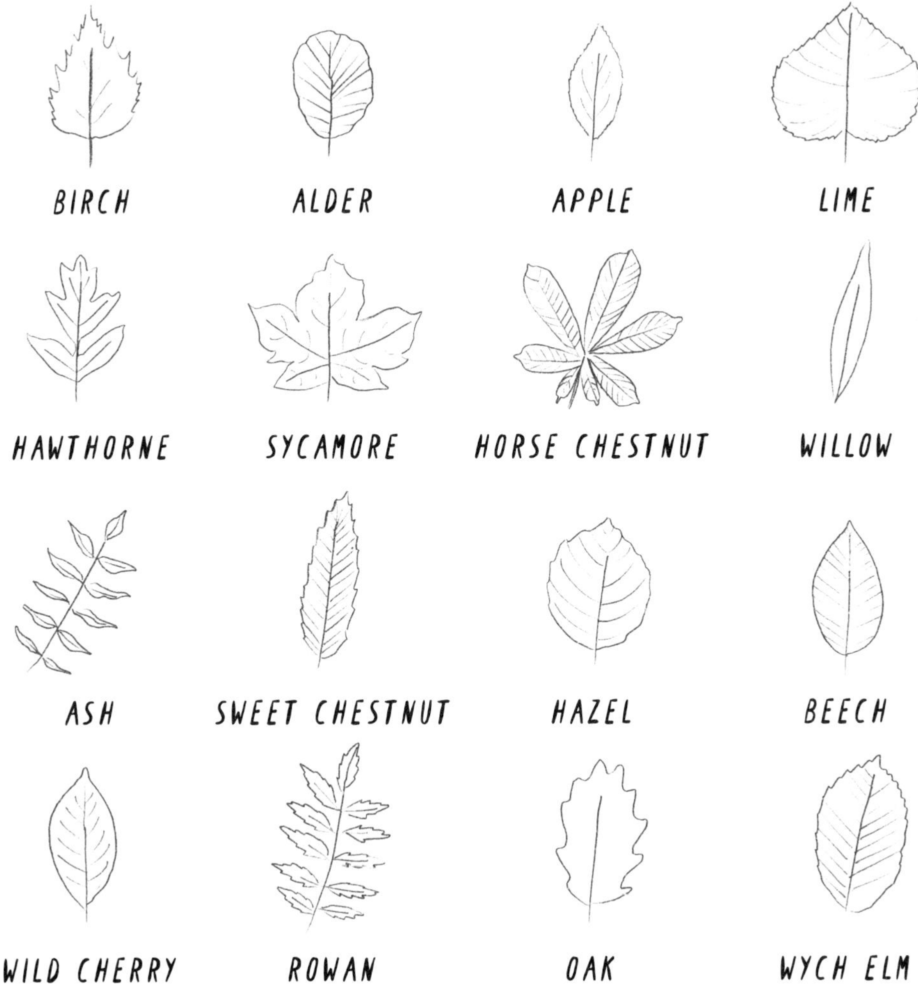

You can also tell trees apart by looking at their shape. The trunks, branches and tree canopies, colours, fruit and nuts will all help reveal their identity.

How to Use Trees to Find Your Way

Young trees will be lighter on the south side and darker on the north. Branches grow out sideways to the south but upwards to the north. A tree on its own will have more moss on the north side. Trees growing on a slope that faces south will be taller and thicker. This will be the opposite in the southern hemisphere.

How to Age a Tree

The oldest tree in the world is believed to be a Great Basin bristlecone pine, still growing in California, USA. Incredibly, it's now 5,000 years old, which means it started its life at the same time Stonehenge was built on Salisbury Plain, in the south of England, or some 3,000 years before Jesus walked on the earth.

While sweet chestnuts and oaks can live up to 1,000 years, the yew tree is the oldest living tree in the UK. The Fortingall Yew in Perthshire could be 3,000 years. To trees like these, a human life – even one lasting a hundred years or more – is little more than the blink of an eye (or the twitch of a leaf).

Count the Rings

You can tell the age of a felled tree by counting the rings in a cross section of its trunk. Look carefully and you'll see lots of concentric circles, starting small in the centre and becoming wider as they grow outwards. These are called growth rings and each one represents a year in the tree's life.

You can learn even more from these rings. The thick rings will tell you conditions were good for growing that year, probably with lots of rain. Dark rings will tell you it was a dull summer without much sunshine. You might even be able to see damage from insect attacks or dark scars from forest fires that the tree endured throughout its long life.

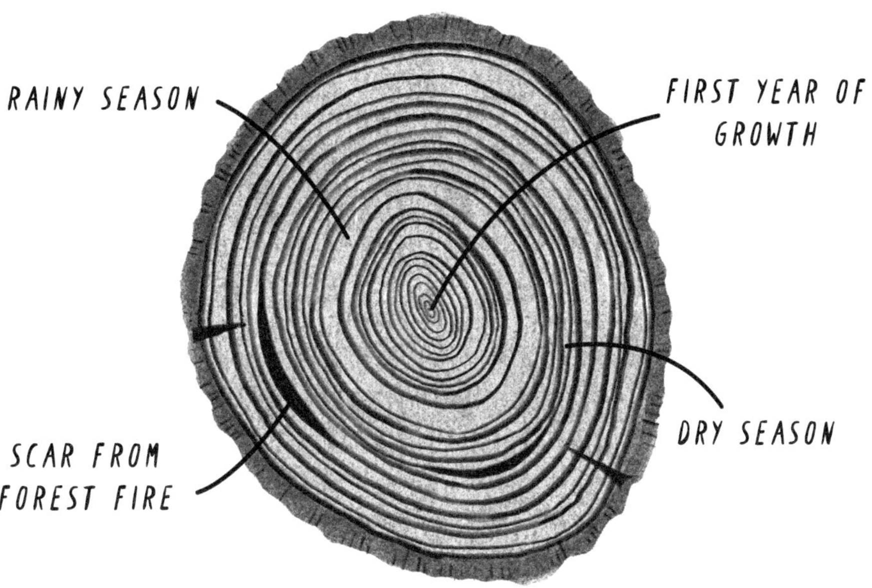

Use Some Fancy Maths

For pine trees, there's a mathematical way to age the tree. (Pay attention, this is worth knowing.)

1. Measure the tree's circumference at chest height (around 1.4 m above the ground).
2. Calculate the diameter. This is the circumference divided by pi (3.142).
3. You can now find out the age of the tree by using this formula:

   Age = Diameter × Growth factor

   You can see a table of growth factors on page 331.

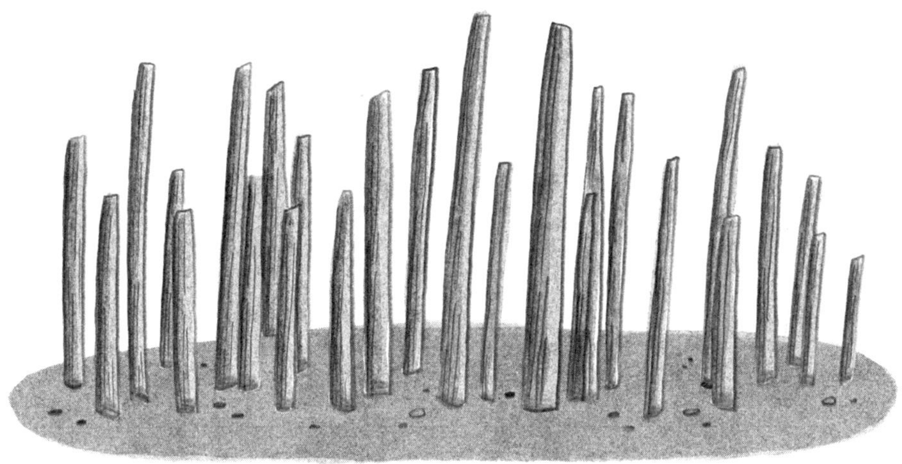

WOODHENGE: THE FOREST CLOCK

Did you know that close to Stonehenge, the prehistoric monument, there's another famous circle? This one is called Woodhenge, and, you've guessed it, it was made out of wood. Made up of six concentric rings of tall, vertical, wooden posts, standing inside it would have felt like being in a strange forest.

Built around 2500 BC, it's only half the age of Stonehenge, but equally mysterious. It was only discovered in 1925, when a photograph taken from the air revealed dark spots and rings: the sockets for the wooden postholes and outline of the earth banks.

Just as Stonehenge is associated with the summer solstice, Woodhenge lines up with the midwinter sun, and it seems that its creators were equally aware of the changing seasons. It's possible they thought of it as a giant calendar or cosmic clock.

There's evidence of feasting and animal bones at Woodhenge, none of which are found at Stonehenge. An intriguing theory is that Stonehenge was for the dead – the ancestral ghosts – and Woodhenge was for the living. Ancient people may have travelled between the two sacred places to show the journey from life to death.

How to Measure the Height of a Tree

For this, you'll need to work out a 45° angle. You can either estimate this or use a phone to help. After that, it's just a question of simple maths. Have a go yourself.

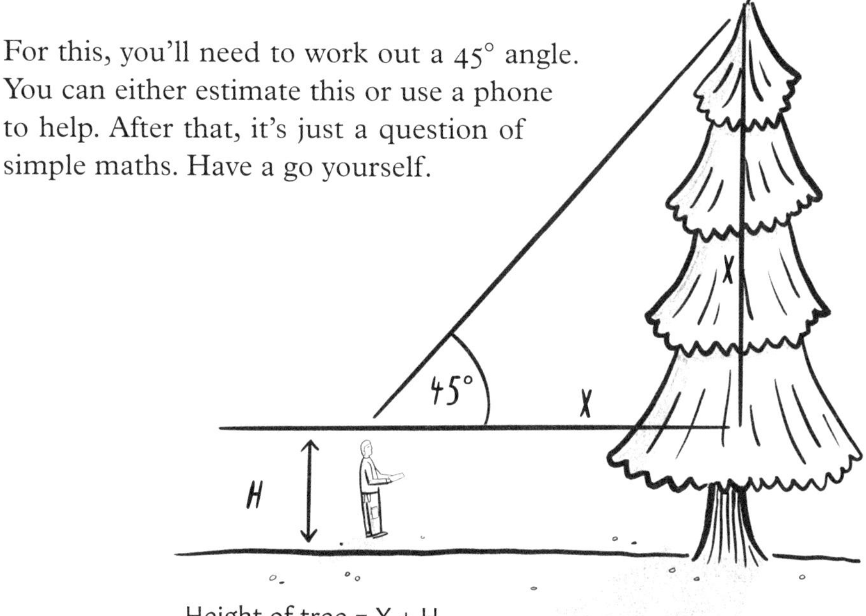

Height of tree = X + H

TEN THINGS to Know About the Amazon Rainforest

The Amazon rainforest, in South America, is the largest forest in the world. Here are ten tree-mendous things to know about it.

1 The Amazon rainforest covers a whopping 2.3 million square miles.
2 It's home to around 400 billion trees.
3 The rainforest is so big it spans nine different nations.
4 The largest part is in Brazil, accounting for roughly 60 per cent of the overall forest.

5 It's 55 million years old, and has been home to countless generations of trees.
6 What helps the trees grow isn't just the soil of South America but also dust rich in phosphorus that blows in from the African Sahara.
7 Roughly 2.5 million species of insects live there.
8 The deadliest creatures in the forest include piranhas, electric eels, cougars, anacondas and jaguars.
9 A million indigenous people live in the rainforest.
10 The most common type of tree species in the forest is a kind of palm, the Euterpe precatoria.

Threats to the Rainforest

The Amazon rainforest produces an astonishing 20 per cent of the world's oxygen. It also acts as a 'sink' for the carbon dioxide we produce, which its leaves turn back into oxygen. You would have thought this would be a pretty good reason to leave it well alone. And until the 1960s, we very sensibly did. There were special protections for the wildlife, trees, people and plants.

However, over the last sixty years, there has been rapid deforestation. Forests have been cleared to build roads and homes, and for commercial use. Nearly 20 per cent of the forest has been destroyed in this way. Without proper protection and regulation, and with money and greed driving negative change, this looks set to continue.

Another key threat is forest fires. These have always been a feature of forests, but they appear to have become more widespread over recent years, with tens of thousands of fires in the rainforest every year – again caused by poor regulation.

Finally, and perhaps most serious of all, is the impact of climate change. If global temperatures rise by 2–3°C, up to 30–60 per cent of the rainforest could become a dry savannah, which cannot sustain the incredible biodiversity of the rainforest today.

THE BIGGEST TREEHOUSE IN THE WORLD

Have you ever slept in a treehouse? It's a magical feeling being cradled in the branches of a tree. It's the perfect place for bird watching, cloud spotting or simply dreaming.

Most treehouses are thrown together from just a few planks of wood. But some are planned on an altogether larger scale.

The biggest treehouse in the world was created in Tennessee, USA. It was ten storeys high and propped up by six mighty oak trees. It took fourteen years to complete and used a quarter of a million nails. The treehouse was so big it had its own basketball court in the middle, a church bell and a cabin at the top to look out over the forest. Sadly, it was burnt to the ground in October 2019.

Reflection

Take a walk through a wood or forest. Choose a tree and peer up into its branches. How long do you think it's stood there? Place both your hands on its bark. Think about all the years it's grown and all that it's seen. Think about how it changes in the different seasons, and the roots beneath your feet. Feel it, close your eyes and see what it makes you feel.

What's the view like a little higher up? See if you can climb a short distance, making sure you have three points of contact at all times – either two hands and one foot, or two feet and one hand. Don't climb too high (unless you have the safety equipment and training to do so, in which case, go for it!). Climb high enough to get a different view of the world. Take a moment to be thankful for all living things, and to appreciate the miracle of being alive in such a beautiful world.

How to

GET TO KNOW THE BIRDS

BIRDS ARE OUR constant companion in the outdoors, rowing through the heavens, swooping and diving as we get on with our day. They lift our spirits with their graceful flight, varied colours, curious habits and bewitching songs. It's a great gift to be able to identify birds by their songs, shape and plumage.

Did you know that birds and crocodiles are related? It seems unlikely, but in fact they're both surviving members of a family of reptiles called archosaurs. Birds first lifted off around 150 million years ago, having gradually evolved (and shrunk in size) from their origins as the great dinosaurs.

Feathers and wings that may once have been used only to impress potential mates grew aerodynamic enough to allow flight. It's believed that birds' ability to fly may have helped save them from the mass extinction that caused their scaly cousins to die out. Today, while birds are still masters of the skies, they've relinquished the earth to us and other animals, watching over the land that was once theirs.

KITE
BUZZARD
PIGEON
KESTREL
CROW
SWIFT
SWALLOW
DUCK
GOOSE
SEAGULL
HERON

Earn Your Wings

One of the best ways to identify birds is by getting to know their wing and tail shapes. Watch the skies for the different silhouettes.

People often confuse swallows and swifts. An easy way to remember the swallow is that it has a longer forked tail and rounder wings.

A Gift of Robins: Know the Names

Another great thing to learn is the collective nouns for birds (the name for a group of them). Most names have been chosen to mimic a characteristic of the bird, such as the sound it makes, or the way it behaves or acts when in a social group. The names are like small poems in themselves.

Here are just a few:

- A gulp of cormorants
- A siege of cranes
- A murder of crows
- A raft of ducks
- A congress of eagles
- A charm of finches
- A flamboyance of flamingos
- A prayer of godwits
- A bazaar of guillemots
- A screech of gulls
- A glean of herons
- A scold of jays
- A realm of kingfishers
- A deceit of lapwings
- An exaltation of larks
- A mischief of magpies
- A watch of nightingales
- A parliament of owls
- A pandemonium of parrots
- A loft of pigeons
- A conspiracy of ravens
- A gift of robins
- A quarrel of sparrows
- A muster of storks
- A raffle of turkeys
- A committee of vultures
- A descent of woodpeckers

Birdsong

Before Spotify, iPods and even record players, the soundtrack to our everyday lives was birdsong. The warble, whistle and twitter of the birds kept us company as we tilled our fields. Now, with many of us living in towns and cities, birdsong is often drowned out by traffic noise. We've forgotten the simple pleasures of listening to the birds – something many of us rediscovered in the lockdowns during the Covid-19 pandemic, when our streets grew quiet. Learning to identify individual birdsongs and calls will increase your love of nature and improve your well-being (and is sure to impress your friends).

It's tempting to think that birdsong exists entirely for our benefit, to brighten dull grey days, where there would otherwise be nothing to cheer our spirits than a cold wind in the trees. But of course, it has very little to do with us. Birds were singing long before we had walked the earth. It's an evolutionary tool used to attract mates, communicate warnings or other messages, and to claim and mark territory. There has been some debate as to whether birds sing for the pure joy of it, or whether it's simply functional. Some birds, like the robin, continue to sing long into the night, long after their chores appear to be finished.

When out on a walk or in the garden early in the morning, you'll hear a cacophony of birdsong called the dawn chorus. It's like a DJ mash-up of hundreds of different tunes and rhythms playing off each other, and it seems impossible to know which song belongs to which bird. But with some careful listening, you'll soon be able to tell the songs apart – and spot the divas from the prattlers.

Most of the songs you'll hear are sung by male birds, as they try to attract potential mates. Some of the melodies you'll hear seem astonishing – not just in the amount of notes they contain but in the volume of the song. How can such a tiny creature possibly produce such a great deal of noise?

One of the reasons is that birds possess a special bit of kit we don't have, called a syrinx. This comes from the Greek word for 'pan pipes', a type of musical wind instrument. The syrinx is an organ situated in the windpipe of a bird. The sound is produced by air passing through it, causing the wall of the syrinx to vibrate. And that's just the start. Some birds have sacs of air around the syrinx that act as amplifiers too. They also have two sets of vibrating flaps in their larynx that mean they can sing in stereo, and possibly occasionally in harmony with themselves – singing two different notes at the same time. It's an incredible piece of engineering.

Identifying the Birds

Here are some birdsongs to listen out for, along with a brief description of the bird itself.

Blackbird

Meet the back-garden diva. The blackbird's song is a warm, tuneful whistle, with each phrase followed up by a higher pitch phrase to round things off, which almost sounds like it's come from another bird. What a show-off.

Males: black with orange beak. Females: brown with spots, and a brown beak.

Chiffchaff

The helpful thing about a chiffchaff is its name. It loves the sound of its own name and sings this repeatedly as if it could never tire of it.

Males and females look alike: browny-olive upper and pale underparts; pale yellow eye stripe. It wags its tail as it goes from tree to tree.

Dunnock

This bird seems to have an infinite amount of breath in its lungs as it produces a long, evenly paced melodic line packed with high-pitched notes.

Brown/black streaked upper parts, grey underparts, red-brown eyes. The heads of the males are slightly darker than those of females.

Goldfinch

This is famous for its catchphrase 'tickle it', which you'll hear after one of its long, note-packed verses.

Look out for its distinctive red face and bright yellow patch on its black wing feathers. Females are duller in colour than the males.

Greenfinch

The greenfinch is famous for its sneering call, alternating with more percussive repeated sounds.

Greeny-yellow feathers, as the name suggests, with a grey eye patch and pinkish bill. Females are more brown than green.

House Sparrow

The sparrow makes a seemingly random stream of chirps and cheeps; it sounds quite conversational, sometimes cheerful, gossipy or even argumentative. You'll hear pauses then excitable whistles that sound like high-pitched laughter.

Males: black, white and brown. Females: grey and pale brown.

Magpie

An altogether uglier sound. Listen out for the machine-gun rattle, which some have likened to someone shaking a box of matches.

Males and females look alike. At first glance they appear simply black and white. However, you'll notice a purple-blue gleam close up. They also have a long blue-black tail.

Robin

The robin's song is just as sweet as the blackbird's, but in some ways is more fluid and delicate. Listen out for a long note followed by a series of delightful short ones.

Males and females look alike: brown-grey feathers, red-orange bib, large head and eyes, and a short black beak.

BLACKBIRD
CHIFFCHAFF
DUNNOCK
MAGPIE
GREENFINCH
HOUSE SPARROW
SONG THRUSH
WOODPIGEON
WREN
GOLDFINCH
ROBIN

Song Thrush

The song thrush composes bold, tuneful, whistling phrases then likes to repeat them two or three times, just in case you missed it. It then discards this and moves on to a new song.

Males and females look alike: brown backs, cream-coloured underbelly, freckled with black spots, yellow bill, pink legs and feet.

Woodpigeon

The woodpigeon's song is probably the easiest to identify. It's a series of low coos, usually made up of five notes. It's easy to imagine the phrase 'I don't want to go' repeated twice when you hear it.

Males and females look very similar: orange bill, yellow eyes, plump-chested with blue-grey feathers, purple neck and white patches on their side.

Wren

The party trick of the wren is to produce an astonishing stream of super-fast notes in a short burst. It's definitely a case of quantity over quality as our slow ear struggles to pick out the tune.

Males and females look alike, but males have slightly longer bills. Very small, dumpy, short-tailed bird with a brown upper and lighter underpart. Its tail is often cocked upwards.

Keep a Nature Diary

One of the most rewarding things you can do is keep a nature diary or scrapbook. Record the sounds and sights you see – the birds that flit past each morning, the colour of the leaves in the trees, the different flowers and buds, and the light in the sky. If you do this across the year, you'll notice the hundreds of little changes that tell you one season is giving in to the next.

TEN TOP Bird Facts

1 The robin is probably the hardest-working bird. It's one of the first to start singing at dawn, and the last still singing at night. Somehow, it still finds time to feed its own chicks and even the hungry chicks of other birds.

2 One of the blackbird's favourite hobbies is sunbathing. Its dark colours attract the heat, and you'll see it spreading its wings to catch as much sun as possible.

3 As they migrate, swallows can travel up to 200 miles a day.

4 The smallest bird in the world is the bee hummingbird, measuring just 5.5 cm in length.

5 The vorombe titan was the largest bird we know of, weighing 800 kg and standing 3 m tall. It lived in Madagascar, was flightless (not surprising given its enormous weight) and became extinct 1,000 years ago.

6 The wandering albatross has a wingspan of up to 3.7 m, the largest of any bird. The great white pelican is a close second at 3.6 m. This is nothing compared with the pterodactyl, which could have a wingspan of up to 9 m.

7 It's believed that the bassian thrush farts to find its food. This disturbs the leaf litter, causing worms to wriggle and making them easier to find.

8 Pigeons can recognise different people's faces and up to fifty words.

9 A chicken in Japan has a tail measuring 10.5 m long.

10 When a budgie yawns, other budgies start yawning too!

How to

TIE KNOTS

KNOTS ARE AN essential part of Scouting. They help us make everything from bridges and rafts to tables and towers. They're also vital when it comes to securing ropes in mountaineering, sailing, fishing and emergency situations. If you know how to tie just five or six of the most useful knots, you'll be an indispensable member of any team.

If you're going to be a good survivor, and a good adventurer, you need to know how to tie knots. I meet people who think of themselves as practical people, but who don't know how to tie a single knot. Parents often don't pass on these skills to their children as much as they used to. Historically, if you didn't know how to tie knots, you were in a lot of trouble. When people rode on horseback, knot tying was second nature to them. To me, the important thing is knowing how to tie a small number of practical knots. You don't need to know hundreds, or any fancy ones, just the useful ones that you'll use all the time: simple, practical knots that can save your life or someone else's.

There's a reason why there's a knot in the World Membership Badge. It's a symbol of unity – bringing things together – just like Scouting brings people, communities and countries together.

The knot used in it is the square or reef knot, which is used for binding two ends of a rope. It's called the reef knot because it's been used for hundreds of years by sailors to 'reef' their sails. If there's one knot a Scout should know, it's this one. But beware: it's neither the strongest nor the safest knot. It can become unstable if it's jiggled around, so should not be relied on in a life-saving situation. That's why you need a few more knots up your sleeve.

BELIEVE IT OR KNOT

Knots have been used for thousands of years and for all sorts of purposes. In China, they were (and still are today) considered a great art form. Useful and beautiful objects have been created by using intricate and well-tied knots. The friendship knot (see page 268) is an example of a Chinese knot.

Also from China is the extraordinary Pan Chang knot, which resembles a flower or butterfly (which is why it's also known as the butterfly knot). Others call it the mystic knot because it's said to give good luck to those who tie or wear it. The knot is one of the key symbols of the Buddhist religion as it visually expresses the belief that life is a constant cycle.

Knotty Words and Phrases

There's a whole new language to learn when it comes to knots. Here are some of the words you'll need to get to know:

- BEND: A knot for attaching one rope to another.
- BIGHT: Another name for a loop created by twisting the rope back on itself and crossing the standing part.
- CAPSIZED KNOT: This is a knot that's changed shape, perhaps because it was tied incorrectly or too much weight has been put on it.
- HITCH: This is a way to attach a rope to something else, such as a pole or stick. It's not a full knot.
- STANDING END: The bit of the rope you don't use to tie your knot.
- STANDING PART: The bit of the rope between the two ends.
- WORKING END: The bit of the rope you use to tie your knot.

Learning the Ropes: Top Tips Before You Start

- Only tighten a knot once you're sure you want to. Some knots, like the overhand knot, will be almost impossible to undo again.
- Practise each knot two or three times by following the instructions, then two or three times without them. Then do the same two days later. You'll soon find out whether it's lodged in your brain or not.
- Make sure you practise with a rope that's long enough. Lengths of rope around a metre long are ideal.
- Practise on a flat surface, so you can lay the rope down if you need to.

- If someone is showing you how to tie a knot, sit next to them rather than opposite them. It will be easier to copy what they're doing.
- In an emergency, and if in doubt, just tie lots (from the old saying: 'If you don't know knots, tie lots'). Because sometimes, good enough is good enough, and there is no need in survival to be a knot snob.
- As with almost everything in life, when it comes to learning knots, just never give up . . . it will come. Good luck!

Knot Safety

That said, when it comes to managing risk on planned adventures, be careful not to put your (or anyone else's) life at risk while you're still learning. Knots take time to master, and an experienced and qualified instructor should always double check everything first. If you're using a knot while climbing, then a stopper knot should always be used to make sure the rope does not escape from the securing device.

Know Your Knots

Reef Knot

The way most people learn to tie this knot is by following the instructions in the phrase, 'Left over right and under, right over left and under.' Once tied, you should be able to slide the knot forwards and backwards. Remember, don't rely on this knot to secure a rope as it can work loose. It's fine for tying things off or as an emergency belt knot – for example, if your buckle has broken. To make it much more secure, you can add a tight hitch to each loose end, once the reef knot is tied.

Overhand Knot

This is a much stronger knot than the reef knot, but beware, once it's come under load it becomes very hard to undo it again. This is known as a stopper knot – for example, when you need a 'stopper' in a rope to prevent it going through an eyehole in a banner.

Bowline Knot

Pronounced 'bow-lin', this is probably the most useful knot of all. It allows you to create a loop at the end of a rope that means you can secure one object to another. For example, if you wanted to tie the ends of a hammock to a pair of trees, then the bowline is a good

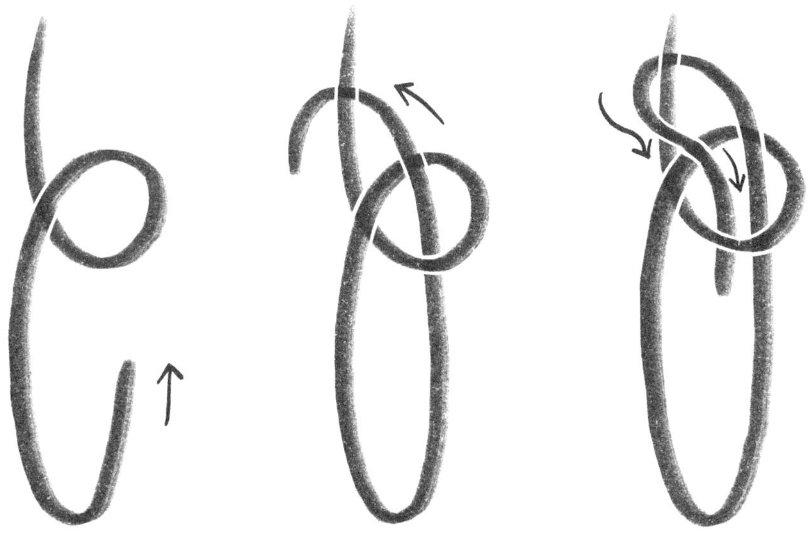

choice. Although it tightens around a load, the big advantage is that it can easily be untied again. It's the knot that bush pilots use to secure their aeroplanes to the ground, and that ocean sailors use to secure their sails to the deck. If it's good enough for them . . .

One easy way to remember how to tie the bowline knot, is to think of the working end of the rope as a rabbit. First create a bight (loop) which represents the rabbit hole. Then follow these actions: 'Up through the rabbit hole, and round the tree; down through the rabbit hole, and off goes he.'

Figure Eight Knot

Like the overhand knot, this is also a stopper knot, used to stop ropes from running out of a securing device.

Sheet Bend

This is perfect for tying together two ropes of different thickness. This is a better choice than the reef knot for tying two ropes together, especially if the ropes are under strain. Remember, it can still come loose if not pulled tight.

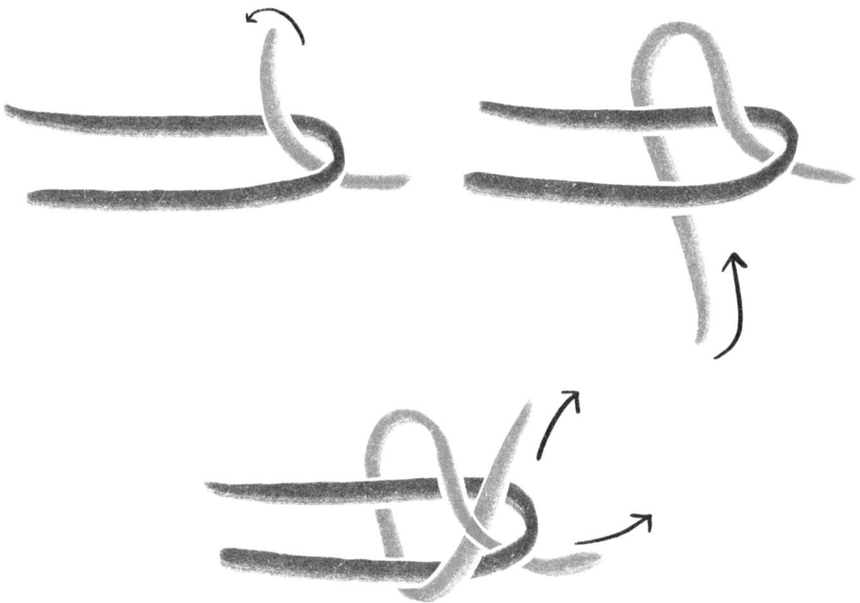

Double Sheet Bend

If there's a heavier load, or you're using less grippy rope, then it's a good idea to use a double sheet bend, which works the same way as the sheet bend, but has an additional turn.

Sheepshank

This knot is used to shorten a length of rope or to get past a stretch of rope that's been damaged, without needing to cut it. A key feature is that you're able to tie this knot in the middle of a rope. But make sure you keep the knot tight, otherwise it may work loose.

Timber Hitch

As the name suggests, this knot is used for attaching a rope to a log or stick, and is often used by people who do forestry work. This will come in handy for diagonal lashing (see page 235).

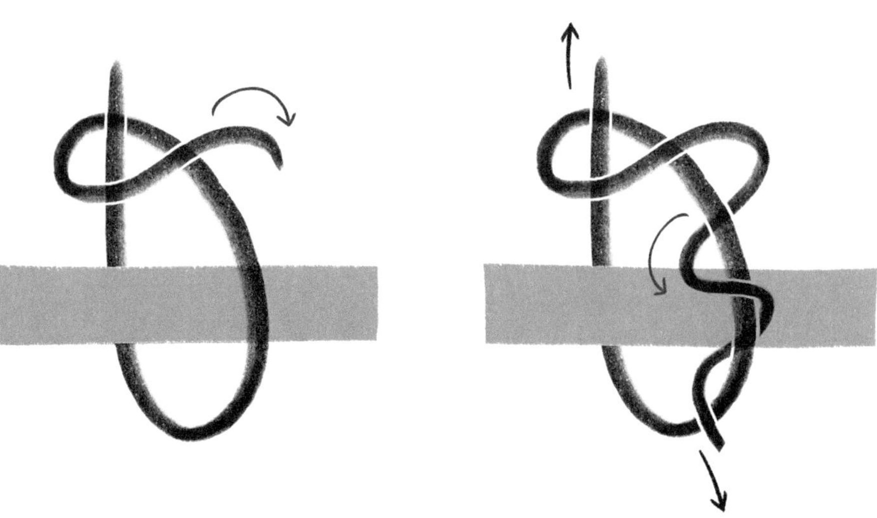

Highwayman's Hitch

One of the most fun knots to tie is the highwayman's hitch. As the name suggests, it was once used by highwaymen – the bandits who rode on horseback around the countryside, robbing unsuspecting travellers with the words, 'Stand and deliver: your money or your life!' Highwaymen were constantly on the run from the law and would often have to make a quick getaway. This quick release knot was perfect for securing their horse, then undoing it in a hurry.

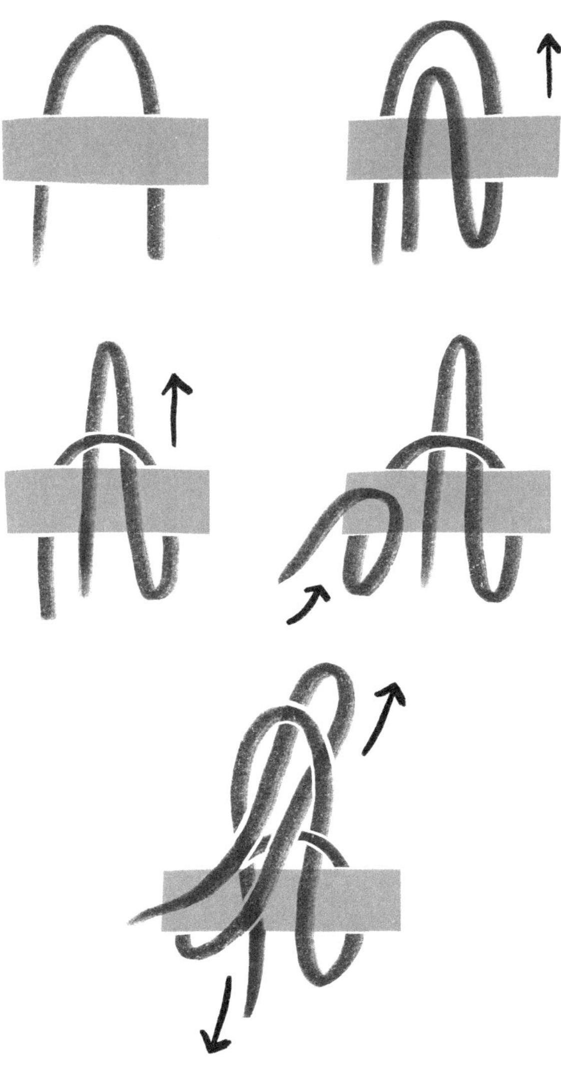

Half Hitch and Two Half Hitches

This is a way to secure a rope to an object. However, it can potentially work loose so shouldn't be relied on. Instead, it's best used on gear and equipment rather than to keep people safe.

Clove Hitch

Use this for tying a rope to a post or stick. It's especially useful if the rope needs to tie onto a pole then continue to tie onto another. Because it's used to bind things together, it's known as a binding knot. This is the knot I probably use the most in Scouting and on adventures. It is truly versatile and will function across many different tasks.

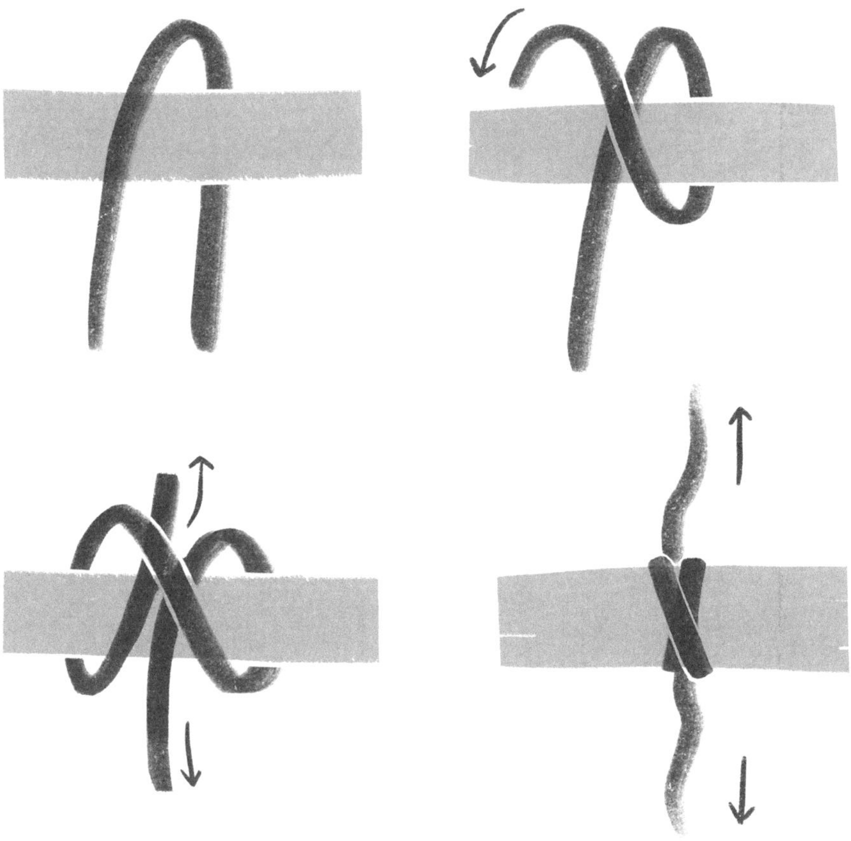

There are hundreds of knots, each with a colourful name, that have been passed down through generations. But learn the key ones and you'll be well prepared.

Lashings

Lashings are a way of joining sticks or poles together to create structures like rafts, stretchers, chairs and bridges. Use them in combination with the knots you've learnt to make sure your structure is secure. Remember, the tighter the lashings, the stronger your structure will be. Raft builders with poor lashing skills usually end up wet, and wet ropes often wriggle loose!

Square Lashing

This is the basic, standard lashing for building projects that are square or rectangular shaped. Start with a clove hitch on the lower pole and pull it tight. When complete, tie two half hitches (see page 232) to make it secure. The most important part of this is the frapping – the turns that go around the middle that tighten the lashing.

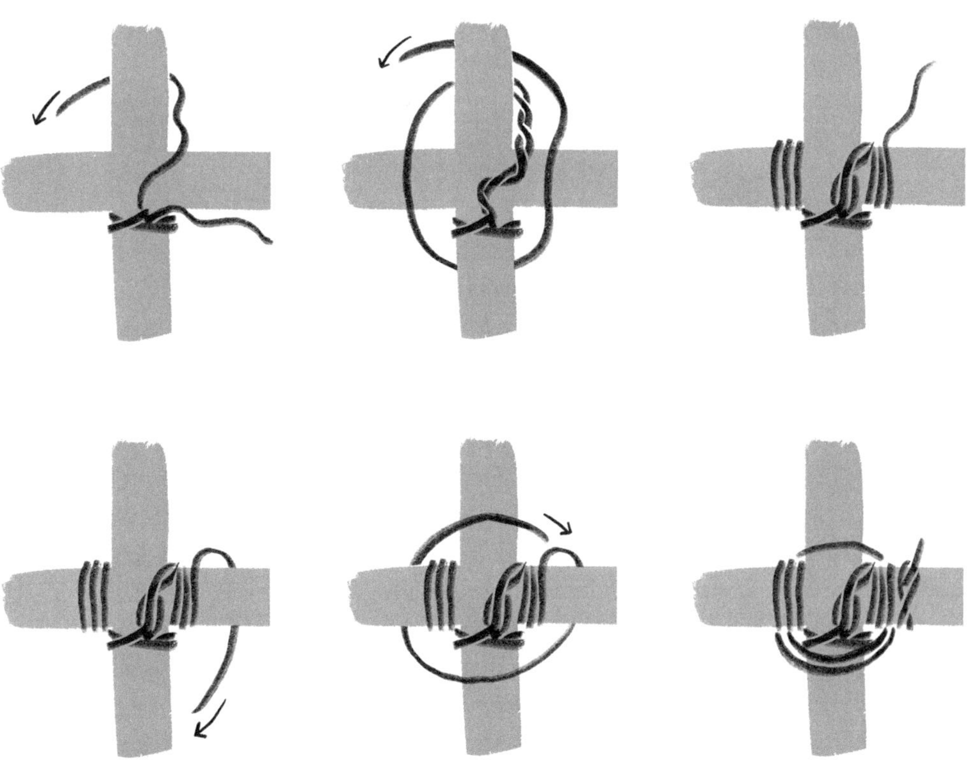

Diagonal Lashing

This type of lashing is also useful for creating rigid structures, and stops two joined poles from yanking apart. It's especially useful for triangular and other non-square structures. Start by tying a timber hitch (see page 230) across the two poles.

A good Scouting tip is to tie the two logs horizontally, next to each other, as tight as you can, then bend them outwards to right angles. This will make the lashing extra tight.

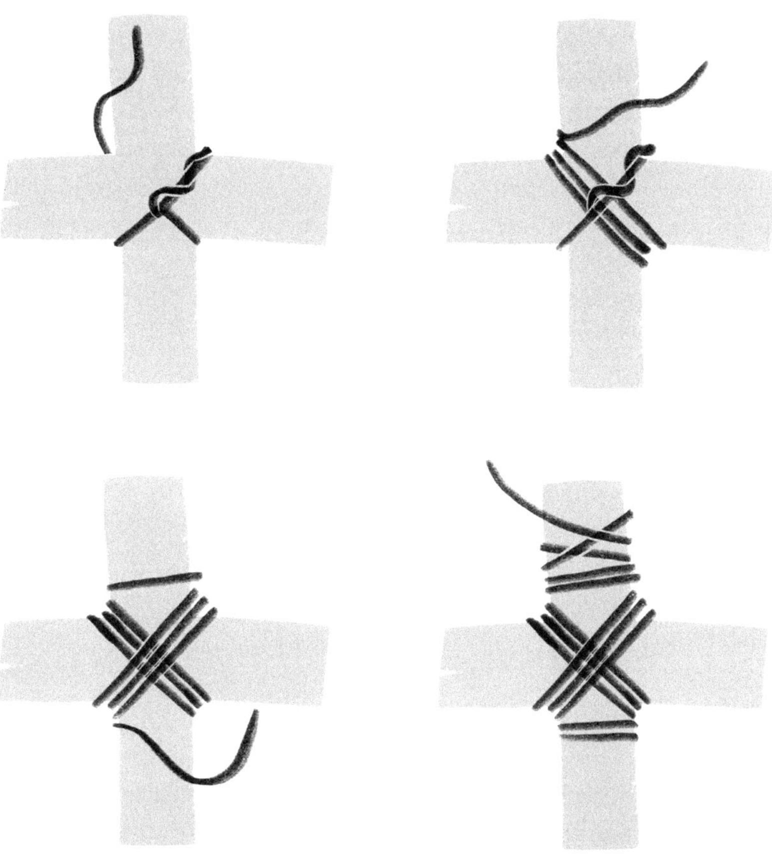

THE KNOT THAT'S NOT A KNOT

Did you know there's a bird called a knot? It's a type of sandpiper which migrates to Britain from the Arctic. It's a wading bird that's often spotted in river estuaries feeding on crabs and snails that it plucks from the mud. As far as we know, it can't tie knots.

However (and quite weirdly), there is a type of fish (hagfish) that can tie itself into an overhand knot, rippling the knot from its head to its tail as a way to get rid of slime from its scales.

THE OTHER KNOT THAT'S NOT A KNOT

The English language is confusing, isn't it? There's yet another meaning for knot. It's a unit of measurement for the speed of aircraft and boats. It's the equivalent of 1.15 mph.

Coiling Rope

When left alone, rope has an amazing ability to tie itself in knots when you're not looking. To stop this happening, coil (or hank) the rope like this before putting it away. Hopefully it will then behave itself.

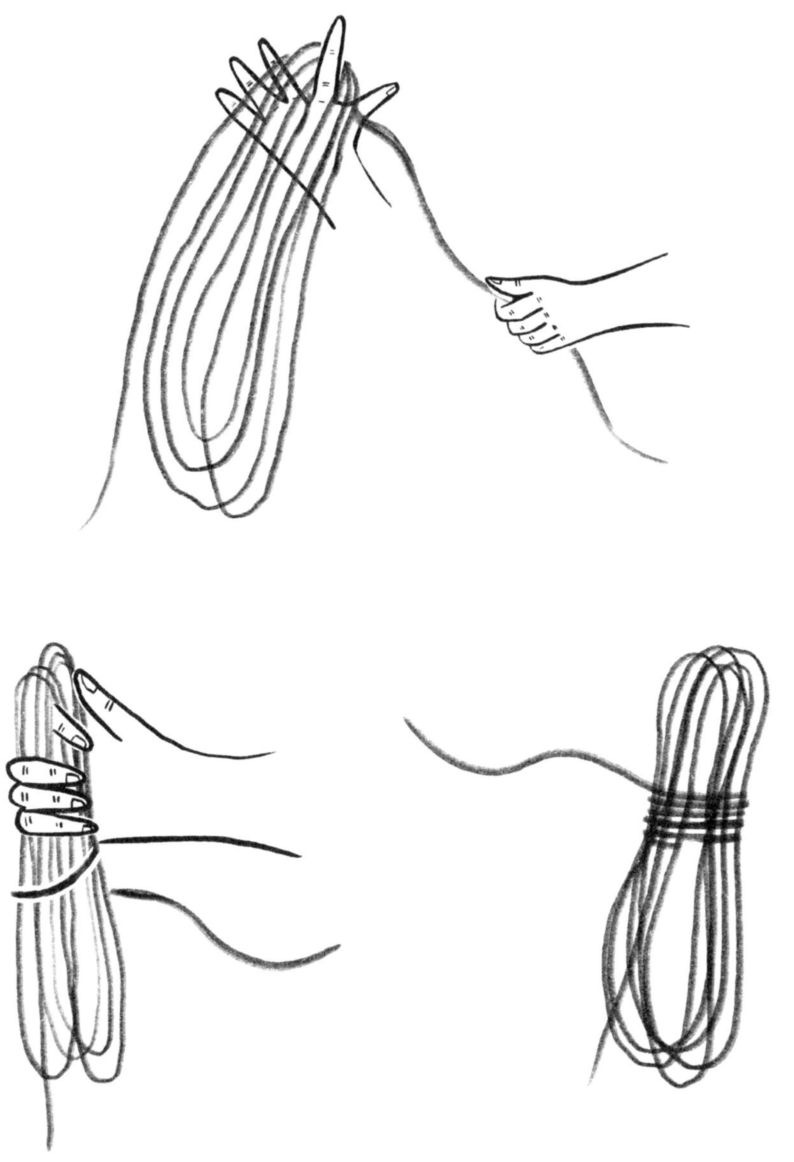

How to be

INSPIRED

THE GREAT ADVENTURERS of the world are also some of our greatest dreamers. But they are dreamers of the day, not the night, because they act upon those dreams to make them happen. These people are the ones who show us the way, always questing, discovering more of the world and more of themselves. Where some of us see barriers, they only see the next horizon.

Adventurers are the optimists, trailblazers and experts in the art of the possible. When most people see a reason to stop, they always see a reason to go. Remember, adventure is a state of mind, it's a choice about how we choose to live our lives. It doesn't necessarily mean we are always on outdoor adventures (although as Scouts we do an awful lot of those!), it is more about having an adventure attitude. To push boundaries, take risks, to pioneer and to never give up.

There are many traditional adventurers still out there though, those people who inspire us all to live our lives with that all-important adventure spirit. While the world is now largely mapped and known, these explorers seem to keep finding something new. From George Mallory, the great English climber who vanished on Everest in 1924, to Nims Purja, the legendary Nepalese mountaineer who climbed all fourteen peaks over 8,000 m in just over half a year, there are many brilliant and adventurous people out there who refuse to know any limits.

They accept danger as part of their lives. But that doesn't mean they don't value life. They live life brightly, experiencing things more intensely than most, and above all, they aren't afraid to fail. Often their greatest successes happen only after many spectacular failures. They seem to cram many lifetimes into one and have so much to teach us about what it is to be truly alive. Like all good Scouts, they dare to go on ahead and to make spectacular things happen.

George Mallory (1886–1924)

Mallory was a brilliant young English climber, who was also a scholar (graduating from Cambridge), a teacher and a soldier. He fought in the battle of the Somme during the First World War, one of the conflict's bloodiest battles. In 1921, he made his first expedition to Everest, the world's highest mountain, which was then still unconquered. The following year, he took part in the first attempt, reaching nearly 8,000 m (26,000 ft). Determined and resilient, he tried again in 1924, this time with a talented young American climber partner, Andrew 'Sandy' Irvine. They were last spotted going strong for the summit, just 244 m (800 ft) from the top.

No trace of them was found for seventy-five years, until 1999, when Mallory's body was discovered in the snow and ice, high up on the mountain. Irvine's body was never found. It was hoped there would be some evidence that they had succeeded in reaching the summit – perhaps from film from a camera – but nothing conclusive was found. To this day, people debate whether the pair reached the summit, a mystery that may never be solved. When asked why he wanted to climb Everest, Mallory famously replied: 'Because it's there.'

Nims Purja (Born 1983)

Nims is one of the world's greatest living mountaineers, having summited Everest an incredible six times. Born in Myagdi district, Nepal, Nims moved nearer to the city of Kathmandu at the age of four. Like his father and three brothers, Nims became a Gurkha soldier. He served in the British Royal Navy's Special Boat Service (SBS) from 2009 to 2018, leaving to focus on his climbing. He summited Everest for the first time in May 2016, returning the following year with a team of Gurkhas to celebrate 200 years of the Gurkhas' proud contribution to the British Army.

In 2019, Nims took on his greatest challenge yet: Project Possible 14/7. His task was to scale the fourteen mountains over 8,000 m (26,000 ft) in just seven months. In fact, it only took him six months and six days.

Nims is not one to sit around. He quickly moved onto a new project, completing the first ever successful winter ascent of K2, the world's second-highest mountain (and without supplemental or bottled oxygen too). A true living legend.

Michael Matthews (1977–99)

In May 1999, Michael became the youngest person ever to reach the summit of Everest, superseding the record that I had set on Everest the year before. At the age of just twenty-two, Michael already had an impressive number of climbs behind him, including Kilimanjaro, before heading to the Himalayas. After reaching the summit, his team faced a powerful storm, with winds as strong as 100 mph. Michael became separated and vanished without a trace. He was the 162nd person to die on Everest. In 2021, his younger brother, Spencer, set out to search for his brother's body with the support of mountaineer Nims Purja. The moving story is told in the documentary film, *Finding Michael.*

Dame Ellen MacArthur (Born 1976)

Despite being born in Britain's most landlocked county (Derbyshire), Dame Ellen went on to become one of the world's most renowned sailors. In 2005, she completed the fastest ever solo circumnavigation of the globe. This was just one of a huge number of achievements from a determined, skilful sailor, having also become the fastest single-handed woman to sail from the UK to the USA in a monohull vessel.

Inspired by the sailor Sophie Burke, and from reading Arthur Ransome's children's classic *Swallows and Amazons*, as a child, Ellen saved her dinner money for three years so she could buy a boat of her own: *Threp'ny Bit*. At seventeen, she bought a Corribee, a type of fast yacht, named it *Iduna* and sailed it single-handed around the coast of Britain. After finishing in second place in the Vendée Globe solo round-the-world race, she was awarded an MBE.

However, her greatest feat was yet to come, beating Frenchman, Francis Joyon, by over a day to win the round-the world-race. It took her seventy-one days. For this, she was made a Dame and Commander of the British Empire.

Matthew Henson (1866–1955)

Born in Maryland, USA, Matthew Henson went on to achieve one of the greatest ever feats of exploration. He became the first person, alongside Robert Peary, to reach the North Pole. Henson met Peary while working in a department store in Washington DC, and Peary hired him to become his personal valet. In time, he became much more than that, acting as navigator, fellow explorer and survival expert.

In total, Henson spent eighteen years in the Arctic, joining Peary on seven voyages to the frozen north. It was on the 1908–9 expedition that Henson planted the Stars and Stripes, the flag of the USA, at the pole. In recognition of his achievements, he was invited to join The Explorers Club in 1937, met presidents, and even had a crater on the moon named in his honour. To this day, however, he's not as well remembered as perhaps he should be, though he is a true inspiration for others that follow in his footsteps.

Reinhold Messner (Born 1944)

The Italian climber Reinhold Messner became the first person (alongside Peter Habeler) to summit Everest without supplemental oxygen, something previously thought impossible. Like Nims Purja, he's also one of the very few to have scaled all fourteen peaks in the world over 8,000 m (26,000 ft). Astonishingly, he climbed them all without supplemental oxygen.

With remarkable natural climbing ability, Messner recorded a slew of 'firsts', finding new ways to climb the world's greatest mountains, often ascending faces thought to be unclimbable, including the direct south face of the Marmolada, the highest mountain in the Dolomites, in the Italian Alps.

Besides his mountaineering accomplishments, Messner has skied across Antarctica, crossed deserts and inspired a new generation of explorers with his many books.

Amelia Earhart (1897–1937?)

Born in Kansas, USA, Earhart was set on a life of adventure from an early age. After crossing the Atlantic in an aircraft as a passenger in 1928 (the first ever air crossing by a woman), she completed a historic solo non-stop transatlantic flight in 1932 in her Lockheed Vega 5B, cementing her place in the record books. She became a major celebrity in the USA and an inspiration to millions, showing that anything was possible given enough determination.

In 1937, she took off on her greatest adventure yet: an attempt to fly around the world. It was to end in tragedy. Along with navigator Fred Noonan, she disappeared in her Lockheed Electra 10E over the Pacific Ocean, close to Howland Island. Searches proved fruitless, and a year and a half later the pair were declared dead. For decades, people have speculated about their fate. While most believed they simply ran out of fuel searching for the islands, others became convinced they landed on a flat reef on the uninhabited Gardner Island, and lived and died there. Whatever her fate, she lived fearlessly and inspired so many.

Ranulph Fiennes (Born 1944)

The son of a decorated army officer, Fiennes has led one of the most astonishing lives of adventure you can possibly imagine. His exploits include summiting Everest (at the age of sixty-five) and reaching both poles. Then there is his trip up the Nile by hovercraft, navigating the Northwest Passage (an almost mythical route over the top of the American continent to join the Atlantic and Pacific Oceans) and an attempt to walk to the North Pole on his own. Severely frostbitten, he eventually amputated his fingertips himself (not something to try at home). Not content with all that, he ran seven marathons, in seven days, on seven continents (just four months after a major heart operation).

He has raised millions for charity, fought for the Sultan of Oman and was once considered for the part of James Bond. Most importantly maybe, he is a humble, kind family man, plus he has been a great friend and encouragement to me on many adventures.

Roald Amundsen (1872–1928?)

Born in Østfold, Norway, Amundsen set his sights on a life of adventure at the age of just fifteen, after reading Sir John Franklin's account of his Arctic exploration. Amundsen's first real adventure of his own came when he was twenty-five, when he headed to Antarctica. He spent a winter on board the ship, frozen in the ice, and learnt a great deal about cold weather survival, particularly the importance of a good diet to prevent illnesses like scurvy.

On his next expedition, he successfully navigated the Northwest Passage, achieving what his hero Franklin couldn't. He managed this in a small manoeuvrable boat called *Gjøa* and became a national hero in Norway.

On 14 December 1911, Amundsen and his team became the first to reach the South Pole. They beat the British explorer, Captain Scott, and his companions by four weeks. Although his original plan was to head to the North Pole, he heard that Henson and Peary had already reached it. He decided to head south instead. Amundsen and four companions set off on their skis and sledges supported by fifty-two dogs.

More expeditions were to follow for the Norwegian, including a three-year trip to the Arctic in *Maud* to explore more of the frozen ocean (where he was attacked and injured by a polar bear). This was followed by airborne adventures, including a successful voyage over the North Pole in the airship *Norge*.

Amundsen eventually perished while on his travels. On a mission to rescue the crew of a crashed airship, Amundsen and his flying boat vanished. Later, some wreckage was recovered, including evidence that he had tried to repair damage to the plane, but nothing further was ever found.

Tenzing Norgay (*c*.1914–86)

The son of a yak herder from Tibet, Tenzing was a true child of the mountains. While the exact date and place of his birth was unknown (even to himself), he was the eleventh of thirteen children and is thought to have been thirty-nine when he helped lead the British Everest expedition – and his climbing partner, Edmund Hillary – to the summit of Everest. Already a veteran of six expeditions to the world's highest mountain, including three previous British attempts and ascents with the Swiss, he used all his skill and experience to eventually guide the 1953 expedition to the top. He forged his partnership with Hillary after saving him from falling into a crevasse with his rope and ice axe.

Tenzing went on to many more adventures and founded a company to help others achieve their dreams too. He will be remembered for all time as the first, along with Hillary, to scale Everest (and there's even a mountain range on Pluto named in his honour).

Edmund Hillary (1919–2008)

Explorer and legendary mountaineer, Edmund Hillary is perhaps New Zealand's most famous son. Alongside the Nepalese Sherpa, Tenzing Norgay, he became the first person to stand on the summit of Mount Everest on 29 May 1953. It was part of a British expedition to Everest led by John Hunt, which helped mark the coronation of HM Queen Elizabeth II and usher in the second Elizabethan age.

Born in Auckland, Hillary grew up tall and strong. He developed a love of the wild while on a school trip to Mount Ruapehu, and later worked in the outdoors too, helping his father and brother with the family bee-keeping business (he was stung up to 100 times a day).

After serving in the Royal New Zealand Air Force in the Second World War, he started climbing more seriously, first scaling Aoraki/ Mount Cook, New Zealand's highest peak, before being invited to join the first of two Everest expeditions. Like Ranulph Fiennes, he also later reached both the North and South Poles.

But perhaps his crowning achievement was campaigning for better education and healthcare for the Sherpa people of Nepal. Scouts help fundraise for this cause, and to this day he is remembered fondly throughout the world and by Scouts everywhere.

Marco Polo (*c*.1254–1324)

Marco Polo remains the most famous traveller the world has ever known. Born in Venice, he became a merchant like his father and followed the Silk Road – a famous trade route – to China. He impressed the great emperor, Kublai Khan, who appointed Polo a foreign emissary, giving him an excuse to travel widely inside China and beyond, to India, Vietnam and Sri Lanka.

When he returned to Venice, nearly twenty-five years later, after many adventures, including being one of the first ever Westerners to see gunpowder used, and guarding a princess on a great journey, he found his home country at war. Polo was captured, and while in prison he told the stories of his travels to an astonished fellow prisoner, Rustichello da Pisa, who wrote them down. After seven years of captivity, Polo regained his freedom and rebuilt his fortune. He married and had three children. Few have travelled so far or taught us so much.

FIVE WAYS to Become an Adventurer

1 **DREAM BIG, BUT START SMALL**
Before heading into the far back of beyond, why not plan an adventure on your doorstep? It could be something as simple as sleeping out beneath a full moon, or a cycling expedition to the next town. Build up slowly and learn by doing before reaching for the stars. A journey of a thousand miles always starts with that first step.

2 **GAIN SOME KEY SKILLS**
Take a first aid course, brush up on your map and compass reading, and learn how to cope in an emergency. These are beginner skills you'll need on any expedition, big or small.

3 **FIND AN ALLY**
Adventures are much more fun with a friend alongside you. Find someone you really trust, who enjoys the outdoors as much as you do, and then plan your adventures together. You'll need to get along well as you could spend many days up a mountain in a small tent together. On Everest, I spent many weeks sharing a small tent with my best buddies, and former SAS soldiers, Mick Crosthwaite and Neil Laughton. We ate over ninety-three meals together in a row. I chose great partners and we are still best friends to this day.

4 **LEARN FROM YOUR SETBACKS**
If you're driven back by the weather or lack of funds, don't worry, this is all part of the learning curve. The important thing is to try again. Accept that fear and failure will be a constant journeyman alongside you. It goes with the job. That's why most don't follow this path. It can be hard and demoralising, but stick with it. Dreams are worth fighting for.

5 **BE INSPIRED**
Read as much as you can about the greatest adventurers. You'll learn so much from their successes, and even more from their failures. And who knows, perhaps one day you'll write a book about your own adventures. I can't wait to read it.

PART THREE

How to be

YOU

How to

ACHIEVE YOUR GOALS

YOU'RE INCREDIBLE. And as a Scout you can truly do anything. You can solve a Rubik's Cube while in freefall. You can do somersaults while singing songs, make chocolate cake while hopping on one leg and play chess while juggling. You can give brand new names to the stars if you want, and no one will stop you.

But here's something that's even more incredible: no one has thought to provide you with an instruction manual. Where's the manual that teaches you how to talk to a huge room of people you've never met before? Or how to make up with a friend you've fallen out with? Or what to do if someone is bullying you?

There isn't one. That's one of the reasons I decided to write this book. Because operating a powerful machine without an instruction manual is a very scary business.

You'll find some of the answers here. But you won't find them all. That's because only you can decide how to be you. You've got a million choices about how to live your life. You've just got to make them wisely.

Here are four key things to know on the road to achieving your goals:

1 **YOU CAN DO MORE THAN YOU THINK YOU CAN**

Your amazing body and mind are the product of countless generations of evolution. The reason you can multiply 12 × 7 in your head is because the human brain has evolved over time to make you one of the smartest creatures on the planet. (The answer's 84, by the way. Multiply the 10s by 7, then times the 2 by 7. Then add them together. If you're still struggling, learn your 12 or 7 times table again. It'll be worth it in the long run, I'm told.)

2 **DON'T LISTEN TO THE 'DREAM-STEALERS'**

These are the people who say it can't be done. They also say things like 'we tried that already', or 'you're wasting your time'. Or maybe simply, 'you can't'. Don't listen to the dream-stealers. Almost anything is possible.

They used to say that it was impossible to walk on the moon. Until we went there. They used to say it was impossible to make a computer smaller than the size of a house. Now people wear them on their wrists. Just remember, people have no wings, yet people learnt how to fly.

As the humanitarian, Pearl S. Buck, once said: 'The young do not know enough to be prudent, and so they attempt the impossible, and achieve it, generation after generation.' That's you, as a Scout.

3 FIND YOUR THING

It can be hard to have self-belief if you feel like you haven't got a purpose. So find one. No matter how big or small. Again, as a first step, start with something achievable and get some progress under your belt. It all starts with starting. It could just be to find out the word for headstand in ten languages. You'll probably be the only person in the world who knows all ten. Or learn the names of the people who walked on the moon, in the right order. Here's a little poem to help you remember them:

Armstrong, Aldrin,
Conrad, Bean,
Shepard, Mitchell,
Scott, Irwin.
All these astronauts did their bit,
Like Young, Duke,
Cernan, Schmitt.

It's really hard in life to get to where you want to get to when you *know* the destination. It's near impossible to get there if you *don't know* where it is that you want to go.

A final word on purpose. Try and make your purpose something that makes other people happier and the world a little bit better. Remember, when we give things away, we actually receive more in return; when we give, we get. That's what your Scout leader will also tell you. It's a part of why they probably love to volunteer. They give a little time and they receive a lot more back in terms of pride and satisfaction.

4 IT'S OK IF SOMETHING GOES WRONG

Remember, fail often, fail more, just keep going!

Let's say your bicycle chain snaps while riding your bike and you fall off. It hurts. You might have torn your best jeans. But think about why it happened. Did you oil the chain? Was it old and rusty? Did you know that it was bound to happen sooner or later because you were putting off fixing it? Whatever happens, you'll be smarter next time. That scar on your knee will remind you to oil your chain.

Believe You Can!

Once you believe you can, anything is possible. The power you'll have is almost beyond imagination. You could choose to walk to school backwards wearing a bow tie, while reciting Spanish poetry. And most importantly, *not care what anyone thinks.* Likewise, you can decide not to scratch a car when someone dares you to. Because you know it's the wrong thing to do. Our life is a product of our many small daily decisions, and those decisions tend to reflect what we choose to believe in.

When we believe in ourselves, and in others, and maybe also in the Almighty above us if that's what we choose to believe, good things often happen. On the other hand, when we lack belief in ourselves and others, we tend to look down and lack courage and purpose. As a Scout, it is important always to try to look up and out. See the good in yourself and in others. Find a faith in something greater than yourself if you can. We all need a little extra help at times in life.

Belief and faith is like an invisible force field around and within you. If anyone asks you what the strongest materials on planet earth are, you can show them this list.

Strongest materials on earth:

1 Belief.
2 Graphene (almost as strong).
3 Bucky paper (carbon nanotube paper, but I like the easier name).
4 Lonsdaleite (formed by meteorites containing graphite hitting the earth. There are some strange things out there in space).
5 Wurtzite boron nitride (formed when volcanoes erupt. That's the kind of oven you need to make it).
6 Diamonds (you know about these).
7 Moissanite.
8 Zylon (sounds like nylon, but loads stronger).

9 Limpet teeth (the teeth of a snail that lives in water. They use them to dig through solid rock to get at their food).

10 Dyneema.

11 Darwin's bark spider silk (yes, you read that right. It can bridge a river 25 m wide and is stronger than Kevlar, which is what they use to make bulletproof vests).

But what can you make with belief? Frying pans? The walls of a space station? We can do much better than that. Here are some things people have done using the power of belief and hard work:

- The swimmer Ellie Simmonds OBE won five Paralympic gold medals and ten world championships.
- The yachtswoman Dame Ellen MacArthur broke the world record for the fastest circumnavigation of the globe. (See page 242.)
- Mother Teresa brought love and hope to thousands of people living in poverty and made the world a better place.

Get Out of Your Comfort Zone (and Grow!)

We all have our own **comfort zone** (or comfort pit, as Scouts call it, because it is something to get out of as quickly as possible!). This zone is where we only do the things we are comfortable doing. People spend years in their comfort pits; sometimes a whole lifetime.

But there's a problem. The author, John Assaraf, said: 'Your comfort zone is a beautiful place, but nothing ever grows there.' It's only when we step out of this place of decay, and put a toe into the fear zone, that we start on a journey towards true growth, happiness and purpose.

That first step outside of this dangerous pit is a big one to take. It could be getting up to speak to a roomful of people for the first time. You'll be scared. You'll feel exposed and afraid to fail. You'll think people will think less of you if you fall flat on your face. 'Why am I doing this?' will be sure to cross your mind. 'Why can't I just go back to my comfort zone, and volunteer or contribute nothing? At least I was safe there.' Wrong. It isn't safe. It's actually dangerous, because we decay.

Alternatively, we can choose to actively enter the **fear zone**. Your stress levels will rise. You'll feel anxious. Your heart may start to race and your palms will sweat. Your body will go into defence mode, sending those warning signals that say 'we're in some danger'. This is all a great sign of positive progress! Embrace it. Make it a habit, to do something difficult every day. Maybe it's making the last thirty seconds of your shower cold water only. Maybe it's talking to your grumpy neighbour and wishing them a great day. Whatever it is, ask yourself two big questions:

1 What have I got to lose?
2 What else good might then happen?

The key is to think of the stress you're feeling as a helpful thing. It's a muscle. And the more we use it and practise living life outside of our comfort pit, and in the fear zone, the better we become at doing it.

This is how we develop what's called a 'growth mindset' – a positive way of thinking about fear. And if there's one piece of advice you need when you're in the fear zone, it's this:

Keep going. It will get easier each time.

It's a bit like walking through a dark wood in the middle of the night. You can't see much, you've been scratched by the thorns and brambles, and can hear the calls of strange, unseen beasts. But if you keep going, then at some point, you'll find yourself on the other side of this wood and in a beautiful clearing lit up by the light of the moon.

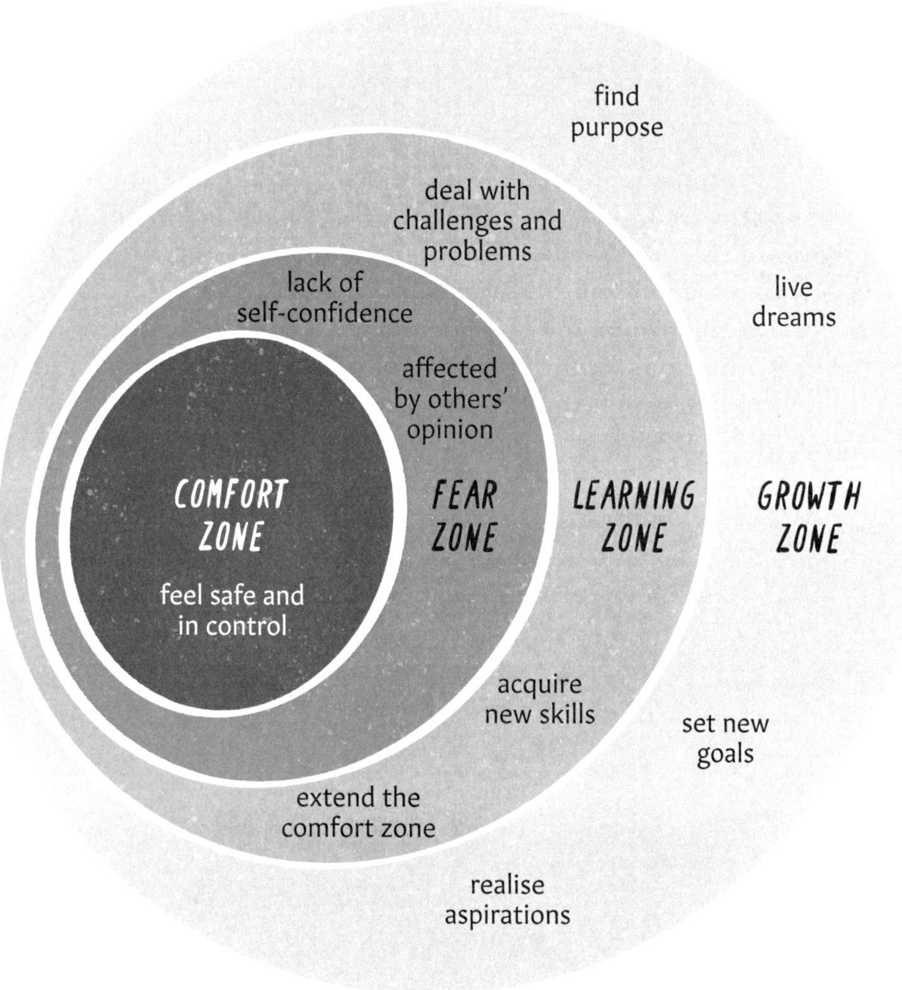

Use this to get through the fear zone, and you'll find yourself in the **learning zone**. This is where the good stuff starts to happen. You find out that you can speak in public after all. You made people laugh. People came up afterwards and told you how good and honest you were. Suddenly, you have a new superpower. And you would never have discovered it if you hadn't left your comfort pit.

Suddenly, all new things feel less scary. Who knows what else you can do now? Now's the time to keep saying yes to opportunities. Lead a team, climb your mountain, whatever it is, take on that challenge. And with your new skills and confidence, you're now ready to step into the best place of all: the **growth zone**.

The growth zone is where you truly become the person you were always destined to be: someone who sees no limits and can achieve anything they set out to do; someone who truly lives their dream. Now that's a positive purpose and a goal to aim for!

The Feeling Good High Five

Scouts is all about being prepared. And one of the best ways to do this is to build up your resilience and develop great well-being. People often say there are five ways to improve your well-being, and you can remember these by the fingers (and thumb) of your hand.

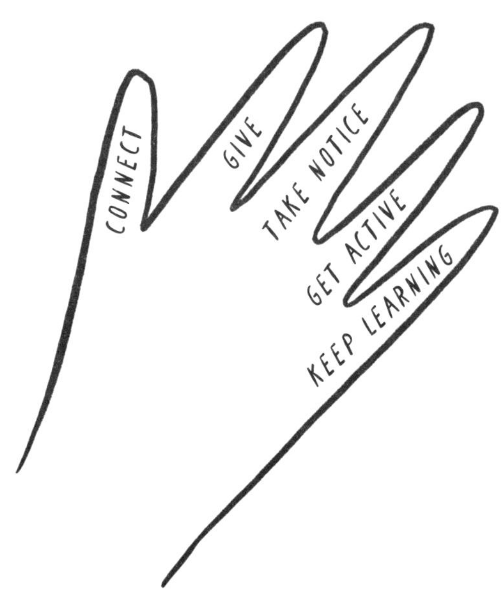

1 CONNECT

It's good to talk. Sharing things with others is one of the best ways to feel good about yourself. Remember, a problem shared is a problem halved. Just by spending time with others, being honest and open with them, and sharing struggles, you'll find it increases your sense of connection and self-worth. That feeling of belonging that we get by being part of a group like Scouts makes us all feel so much better about ourselves too. It also gives us people to fall back on if and when we need them.

2 GIVE

Know that feeling you get when you drop some change into a collecting tin or sponsor a buddy to climb Ben Nevis? It feels good, doesn't it? That's the power of giving. It's good for them and it's good for you. In fact, the founder of Scouting, Baden-Powell, said: 'The real way to gain happiness is to give it to others.' Small acts of kindness every day make us feel better as people. And imagine if we all did it? The world would be a much better place. Remember, you don't have to give money. You could teach someone the guitar or how to tie a bowline. It might save their life (the bowline, I mean, not the guitar bit. Although you never know!).

3 TAKE NOTICE

Sometimes we get so caught up with the big things in life, we forget about the little things. The grass under our feet. The shape of the clouds in the sky. Watching a bird settle on a branch. The feeling of a smooth stone in the palm of your hand. All these things take you back to the here and now, and away from worrying about the future (I sometimes keep a smooth stone in my pocket to help me feel calm before doing a talk in public). They make you appreciate the good things around you and make you feel present. Some people call this mindfulness. Take a moment right now to look out of the window and notice three things.

4 GET ACTIVE
Getting active, especially outdoors, is one of the best things you can do for your body and mind. As humans, we're built to run and be outdoors. It's only in the last 300 years that we've spent so much time indoors. The sun gives us the vitamin D we need, and the chemicals our body releases when we're active make us feel great too.

5 KEEP LEARNING
When you learn something new, you get a real feeling of achievement. It increases your sense of self-esteem, keeps your brain active, makes you feel more confident. Learning how to stand on your head will help you see the world differently too. I do this often!

Reflection

Switch off. Leave the world for another day. Turn off your phone. Walk out into the world. Feel the grass under your feet and the leaves as they brush across your face. Watch how the shadows lengthen. You've grown taller. Grab a handful of soil and let it fall through your fingers. That's the earth you're holding, our only home. See how the sky is changing; how the colours fade. How two birds chase each other across the sky. This day won't ever happen again. Watch the last of the sunlight as it breaks through the trees. See how stars and planets appear one by one as if they're shy about who goes first. As you head back home, see how the world has become quieter, yet how the sounds of nature seem louder, as a bird calls or a twig snaps under your toes. Look up. As you walk, see how the moon peeks through the trees. Breathe. Tomorrow will look after itself.

HOW TO BE YOU

Only you can decide how to be you.
Every mountain is yours to climb.
Every lake is yours to swim.
You can hopscotch through a storm,
Handstand on a hill, sing to the stars,
Or sit very still in a field at midnight.
Some days are for work and helping others,
But some days are for doing nothing
But reading a book or watching the rain.
You can eat chocolate for breakfast
And peaches for tea. And no one will know.
Choose the brightness of your light.
Be a beacon to show others the way
Or a candle that keeps the night at bay.
Tomorrow is a place no one's been.
Your future is a place only you can go.
There are no maps. No charts.
But you don't have to go there alone.
Think carefully about whom you walk with.
Judge them only by the size of their heart
And don't compare their journey with yours.
We're all heading to different places and
the only superpower that counts is your kindness.
So pick your own path. Choose a star
in the sky and call it yours. But most of all be you.

How to be a

FRIEND

LIFE'S A LOT easier and more fun with good friends. But how do you find them? They don't stock them in supermarkets. A true friend is beyond price, because they're the most precious things in the world.

Making a friend is often something that starts naturally. It could be someone at school, a club or Scouts who makes you laugh, is kind and shares adventures with you. You might find yourself spending more time with them than others. There'll be a special spark between you. You know it when you feel it.

Putting the Work In

Once you think you've found a friend, you'll need to put some work in if you're going to be really great friends. Remember, a good friendship is like an electric car. It always needs charging up and looking after. So keep making the effort and you'll have a friend for life. Here are a few tips:

1 LISTEN TO THEM
Make time to get to know them. Ask questions and find out about them and what they think about things. Don't just rabbit on about your favourite band or football team. Ask them about

theirs. What do they like doing? Remember, you don't have to be into the same stuff to be friends. But sharing the same sense of humour really helps.

2 BE KIND

Go out of your way to do something nice for them. Lend them a good book, bake them a cake, stick up for them or help them with their homework. Being kind doesn't have to mean spending money.

3 LOOK OUT FOR THEM

If you see them doing something they shouldn't be doing or isn't good for them, let them know. A true friend will always tell them the truth. They'll thank you for it later. But always do so gently. And lead by example.

4 KEEP YOUR PROMISES

In Scouts, we always keep our promises. That builds trust, and trust is the most important thing in a friendship. Lose it and your friendship will suffer. If you say you're going to do something, or turn up at a certain time, then make sure you do. Great friends are dependable.

5 BE YOURSELF

When you're with a true friend, you should feel able simply to be yourself. You shouldn't have to boast or pretend to be something you're not. Don't be afraid to share things you're worried about or to show weakness. This shows that you trust them, and they'll respect you for it. Remember, vulnerability is where we create connections.

6 STAY IN TOUCH

Life is busy. There's always something to do. But it's important you make time for your good friends. Even if you live far apart, make time to speak to them or message them. Writing a real letter and sending it in the post sounds old-fashioned, but it is special and it shows you truly care – and it's a hundred times more meaningful than a one-line WhatsApp message.

7 BE THERE WHEN THEY NEED YOU
Everyone goes through a tough time at some point. That feeling that it's raining on you and no one else. Don't be afraid to tell your friend if this is happening to you. And remember, there's a great saying that goes: 'A real friend is one who walks in when the rest of the world walks out.' Be that person.

With all these things, make sure it goes both ways. Baden-Powell, the founder of Scouting, said, 'Friendship is like a boomerang: you give out your friendship ... and they give you their friendship in return ... just as the boomerang comes back to its thrower'. If you're the one who is making all the effort, then maybe it's time to look for a kinder friend.

People often say they have loads of so-called friends on social media. But are these really friends? Probably, you only have a handful of true friends. In the words of an Irish proverb: 'A good friend is like a four-leaf clover: hard to find and lucky to have.' You don't need many friends in life; quality wins every time over quantity.

Scouts Is All About Friendship

It's about the shared memories: huddling beneath a tent that's blown down in a storm, the rain hammering on the canvas. Failing to leap that stream, landing face down in the mud (and somehow coming up smiling). Burning your breakfast because you were too busy chatting about the epic fails of the day before. But somehow these were the best moments of all. These are the moments when friendships are made.

New friendships are often made at camp, and especially Jamborees – those huge gatherings of Scouts from all over the world – and those friendships can, and often do, last a lifetime.

The Friendship Knot

Scouts often show their friendships by exchanging badges or neckerchiefs. Another way is with the famous friendship knot. This is a way of tying your neckerchief or scarf without a woggle. The knot itself is Chinese in origin, and forms a satisfying square (which looks especially good if you have a striped neckerchief). It shows the strong bond of trust and friendship between Scouts. It might also be called the friendship knot because it's easiest if a friend ties it for you while you're wearing the scarf!

1
2
3
4
5
6
7
8

GREAT FRIENDSHIPS IN ADVENTURE: SCOTT AND WILSON

Captain Scott, the first Briton to reach the South Pole, had a great friend on his expeditions called Dr Edward Wilson. 'Uncle Bill' (as he was called by the men) was a doctor, an artist and a naturalist. Bill was thoughtful, good-natured as well as being as tough as any of them, and was someone Captain Scott could confide in, especially when he was under pressure.

Wilson joined Scott on his first expedition to the South Pole (the *Discovery* Expedition, 1901–4) and came within 480 miles of the Pole before turning back, frostbitten and exhausted. He was also with Scott on his second expedition in 1910–13 (the *Terra Nova* Expedition). Wilson was involved in some hair-raising adventures – including a winter journey to search for emperor penguin eggs, made in freezing temperatures and constant darkness. At one point, their tent blew away, and they sang hymns in the snowdrifts to keep their spirits up. By amazing luck, they found their tent snagged on some rocks some distance away.

Scott, Wilson and their team set off on their march to the South Pole. The snow tractors they hoped would make things easier broke down almost immediately, and even the ponies struggled in the snow. Eventually, the men simply resorted to 'man-hauling' their equipment on sledges over the uneven ice, which was back-breaking work. In poor shape, the team of friends finally made it, only to find that the Norwegian polar explorer, Roald Amundsen, and his party had beaten them to it. A bitter blow.

Their return journey was horrific. Low on fuel and food, tired and cold to the bone, they struggled for hundreds of miles across the ice. Edgar Evans collapsed and died after a fall in the ice. One of their great friends, Captain Oates, walked gallantly out of the tent to his death, knowing that he was holding them up with his frostbitten feet ('I am just going outside,' he said, 'and may be gone some time'). The three remaining adventurers, Scott, Wilson and the small but strong Henry 'Birdie' Bowers, pushed on, but they were caught in a fierce blizzard, which lasted for days. Forced to camp, they could make no more progress and died in their tent, just eleven miles from One Ton Depot, which would have given them the fuel and food they needed to continue their journey.

The following spring, when a rescue team found their frozen bodies in the tent, Scott's arm was resting across Wilson, a final, tragic symbol of their great friendship. 'Uncle Bill' was a keen supporter of Scouting, and the UK Scouts' Heritage Service now has the copy of *Scouting for Boys* that he took with him on the final expedition to the frozen south.

A Note on Bullying

Bullying is using words or actions intentionally to hurt others. The person doing the bullying often picks on someone they think is weaker than themselves and repeats this hurtful behaviour day after day. They do it try to make themselves feel good. But there's nothing good about bullying. It's a terrible thing to do and can make people upset and confused. It's often the person doing the bullying that has the problem. There's often something happening in their life that makes them act in this way and they probably need support.

Ways to Stop Bullying

- IGNORE THEM. Don't give them the reaction they're looking for. If you ignore them, it can make them look silly in front of the people they're trying to impress.
- TELL THEM TO STOP and hold out the flat of your hand in front of you. Being assertive and telling the person to stop in a confident way will shock and surprise them.
- STICK WITH PEOPLE YOU CAN TRUST. People who bully others are less likely to pick on you when you're with others.
- TELL A TRUSTED ADULT WHO CAN HELP YOU. This can be hard to do, especially if the person doing the bullying threatens you, but often it's the only way. School and clubs have proven ways of dealing with people who bully others, but they can only help if they know about it.

Cyber-Bullying

Bullying happen online too. So called friends can turn into people who bully others especially if they think they can hide behind their phones. Spreading nasty rumours about people, sharing embarrassing images or videos can be just as hurtful as face to face bullying. Here are some of the ways you can stop cyber bullying:

- ASK THEM TO STOP. It sounds obvious, but just tell them that they're hurting your feelings. It might be someone who you thought was a friend. Maybe they think they're being funny and don't know the harm they're causing.
- DON'T RESPOND. If they don't stop, don't keep talking to them online. If they see they're getting a reaction out of you, this might just egg them on.
- BLOCK THEM. Delete them from your social networks, leave the groups they're in and block their contact so they can't message you.
- TAKE SCREENSHOTS. This means you can prove that the bullying took place if they deny all knowledge of it afterwards.

- **TELL SOMEONE YOU TRUST.** Just like any form of bullying, it's important to tell someone you trust who can help you, which could be a parent, carer, teacher or youth leader.
- **REPORT THE BULLYING.** Many platforms have a button to report cyber bullying.

BE THE FRIEND

Be the friend. The kind one. The listener.
The one who asks: 'Is everything OK?'
Be the unexpected thank you.
Be the postcard on a rainy day.
Be the one who'll go round the houses;
Who's there when no one else is.
Be the one at the end of the line,
Be the one who says: 'I'll make the time.'
Be the difference. Be yourself. Be the one
Who knows friends matter above all else.
Be the smile, the one to say: 'I'll sort that out.'
Be there. Be the friend. Be the Scout.

How to

LIVE MORE FREELY

WE DIDN'T ALWAYS live indoors. Our ancestors spent almost all of their lives outdoors in the wild, out in the sun, snow and rain. When it was cold, they huddled together to stay warm. Each day, they spent as much as a hundred times longer in the outdoors than we do today. What if we could rediscover our wild selves and learn to live more freely?

Our ancestors found shelter where they could – in caves, under trees, under rough structures. And never with any closed windows. They definitely didn't have air fryers, streaming subscriptions or games consoles. You get the point.

Being outdoors so much taught them to be in tune with nature. Their senses were honed. They could identity a hundred different kinds of animals just from their scent or sound. They could light a fire with a tiny flint spark, and tell what kind of wood was being burnt from its smoke. They could follow faint tracks in the mud and sand. Now only very few of us have these skills. But they can all be relearnt (and you'll find plenty of them in this book).

Today, the average child spends just four to seven minutes a day playing outside. That's compared with a staggering seven hours each day on their devices or in front of a screen. Whatever way you look at it, that's not healthy. We're missing out on the sunlight we need for a healthy immune system, the sense of joy we get from feeling the sun's heat on our skin. Most importantly, we're missing out on the chance to play and interact with others in the great outdoors. This is where lifelong friendships are made. And that's why Scouts is so important – to give everyone the chance to do this, no matter whether you live in a tower block or a country cottage.

Luckily, there are plenty of things you can do to get back in touch with your wild self. Here are just some of them.

Be Grounded

Take off your shoes and socks. Try it right now. You have an astonishing 7,000 nerve endings on the soles of each of your feet. That's why they're super sensitive. Imagine yourself walking on hot, dry sand or cool, damp grass. Better still, find some real sand or grass and try it for real. Even if you're just imagining it, you probably feel calmer already.

Research has shown that simply walking barefoot on the earth for half an hour each day boosts our red blood cell count, meaning we can better resist disease and illness. This is the true meaning of being grounded. It's so simple, costs nothing and makes you feel great. I try and do this every day. Even in the city, I go and find a park in the morning.

Go and See the World

Life rewards those who dare, those who dream and those who choose adventure. Adventure is not a place; it's a state of mind. A journey into the wild is as much a journey into our soul. When we return, we're a different person.

Whether it's a day trip to a local wood, a hike across the fields or something bigger – like an expedition to the crystal-clear Norwegian

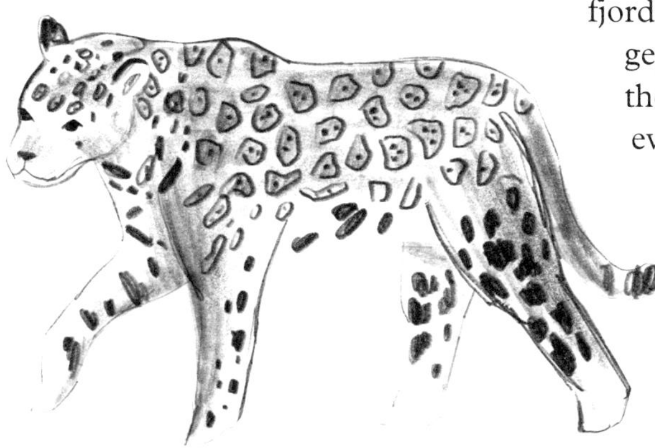

fjords or a trip to Iceland to take in the geysers and stupendous geology – these will expand your horizons in every way. You'll feel more closely connected with nature and appreciate the true wonder of our planet.

Too often, we're thinking ahead or regretting the past. We need to be more present. Live well in the moment. Seize the day and choose adventure.

Out in the jungles of Panama, a jaguar can step out right in front of you. But adventure doesn't need to be as extreme as that. So many special places are just a short hop away. Just get out there and explore. Take a bike on a train. Travel a few stops and you'll be ready to explore a totally new environment, away from your familiar stomping ground.

And the best way to appreciate what we have is to get out there and experience new stuff. Leave early on a Saturday morning and in two or three hours you can be standing on a cliff top, watching guillemots and razorbills swoop and dive around you, or swimming in a lake. Go and discover your country. Research fun things like this that you can do legally and safely near you. You will find lots, I promise.

Be Open to New Adventures

So often our lives run on rails; we cling to our routines, and before you know it, it's Monday morning and school and work again. We can choose to live life more freely – we only have so much time on this planet. Let's fill it with people and memories – not things.

Everyone has the right to an adventure – especially in the outdoors. Life is about grabbing opportunities. Scouts is full of opportunities. Your leaders are always working hard to help you gain new skills and experiences. Always be grateful and always make use of those gifts of time, expertise and experience.

My father used to say that the two most important things in life were following your dreams and looking after your friends along the way. This is what we do in Scouts. It's about loving and doing great adventures and helping others to experience the same.

But it can sometimes be quite hard to get out and experience the outdoors, especially if you're young – it can be quite an intimidating place. And lots of people don't know how to 'get out there'. That's part of why Scouting is so popular, it provides a safe way to explore the outdoors. You're going to have an adventure, but you're going to do it with people you know and trust, and you're going to be looked after.

So never take your place in Scouting for granted. Many wish they could join too. You're one of the lucky ones. (This is why we always need more adult volunteers – to help us reduce the waiting list.)

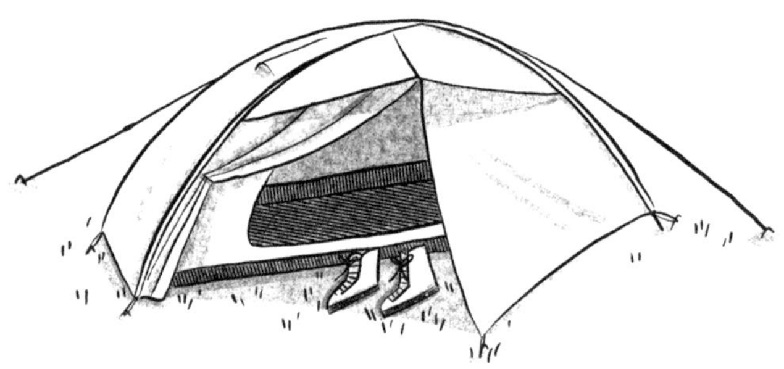

Go Camping

When was the last time you explored the great outdoors? That's *really* explored – where you set out into the unknown with a map and compass, a rucksack, a tent and sleeping bag; the sort of exploring that makes your heart beat faster?

Can you remember the patter of rain on your tent, the sound of owls hooting or the rustling of the wind in the leaves at night? It's a feeling of absolute freedom and belonging – re-establishing our relationship with both ourselves and the earth. Somehow the world looks more hopeful and exciting when you're peering out of a tent flap instead of a front door. It's moments like these that make you feel most alive. A night in the outdoors is also a reminder that not everything that's precious and valuable costs a lot of money.

There's nothing better than spending time with friends in the outdoors. It's among the greatest experiences in life and should be accessible to everyone, no matter where you live, what you look like or how you grew up. Exploring woods and forests, watching foxes and squirrels, playing games, going on nature trails . . . there's a lot to choose from.

Summer is when the world fully comes to life, becoming a sort of adventure playground. When people go away for a weekend's camping in the summer it can sometimes feel much longer. That's because you're spending over fifteen hours a day outside. Summer begins when you can wade through a field of bluebells in May. In June, birds are criss-crossing the skies, foraging for food for their chicks. July and August are the classic summer camping months, joining friends around a crackling fire, enjoying the long nights. The moon seems bigger and the world is full of possibilities again.

Going camping teaches us things about ourselves; it reminds us that we depend on each other to get by and that the most precious things in life are friendships, the natural world and reaching our potential.

I've camped all over the world. I've got great memories of having adventures at home on the Isle of Wight, where I grew up. I remember being up on a cliff top with my dad, looking out at the sea. Those chalk cliffs formed much of the backdrop to my childhood. I think a lot about those cliffs; to me they were like my stepping stones to adventure.

Grow Something

One of the best ways to live more freely is to grow your own flowers or fruit and veg. Not only will you give yourself a free and plentiful supply of produce, gardening is one of the best ways to make you feel good too. Get grounded again!

It feels so natural to be working on the soil, following the seasons and getting to know the cycles of nature. It reminds us we're all part of nature. In the words of Mahatma Gandhi: 'To forget how to dig the earth and tend the soil is to forget ourselves.'

Starting an allotment, a communal space for people to grow and tend their produce, gives you a strong sense of purpose. You'll be doing plenty of manual work, which will tire you out and help you sleep well, and of course, you'll be getting a bucketful of fresh air every day. That's not to mention all the good nutrients and vitamins you'll be getting from the food you grow. Because it's not processed (been through a factory and sat in a fridge for months) it's so much better for you too.

And we haven't even talked about the benefits of making new friends – you'll have neighbours on all sides of you, from all walks of life, many of whom will be happy to share their years of wisdom. (Although some might like to be left alone to get on with their work and enjoy a bit of peace and quiet, so tread carefully!)

A great way to begin is to find a space that's right for you. Most cities, towns and villages have allotments. You'll have your own plot and it's up to you what you grow there and how much work you put in. Find out where your nearest allotment is, then register your interest. There's normally a waiting list, but it'll be worth the wait. You'll then need to pay a fee, but it's usually affordable.

Next, start planning. One of the most fun parts is grabbing a fresh piece of paper and drawing out the different areas, and deciding what to grow. Is there a path or a small shed already there? Would you like to add these? Remember, this is your space (for now at least) and you can do things your way.

Now the hard work begins: preparing your soil. The more work you put in at this stage, the more fruitful your allotment will be. Try and dig up as many weeds as you can, and remove as many loose stones as possible. Turn the soil and enrich it with compost or manure.

It's now time to do your homework. It's important you plant things at the right time to give them the best possible chance. For example, carrots are best planted in autumn.

It's important to keep your allotment well maintained, making sure your plants are well cared for and especially well watered. It might be that there's a central place or water butt in the allotment where you can easily get water. Slugs need to be managed too, as you'll discover!

TOP TEN *Ways to Re-Wild Yourself*

1 Go barefoot (but watch out for glass and splinters).
2 Eat wild (go for fruit instead of crisps and sweets).
3 Stay outdoors and only go in when you need to.
4 Try some forest bathing (see page 203).
5 Start an allotment.
6 Travel to a new outdoor destination near you.
7 Get some morning light on your skin every day.
8 Listen to the dawn chorus (it gets the day off to such an optimistic start).
9 Walk as much as you can.
10 If in doubt, go camping.

IF I WERE PRIME MINISTER ...

What would you do if you were the prime minister or president of your country? Here in the UK, I would be the first prime minister to spend more time outdoors than in 10 Downing Street. I would love to hold Cabinet meetings at the summit of Scafell Pike, Ben Nevis, Slieve Donard and Yr Wyddfa (Snowdon), the highest peaks across the UK. It would keep the meetings focused and remind everyone in positions of power what we are here for: to do good, support the most vulnerable in our society and pass on a healthy world to our children.

On top of this, I'd ensure that every child gets to go camping as part of their time at school. Mountains and the outdoors are great places to build character. The wild doesn't care how you speak or what your ethnic background is. Time and again, I've seen adventures build a genuine pride and confidence in a way that no qualification ever can. Plus, the great outdoors always inspires people to dream big. As Baden-Powell once said: 'A week in the field is worth a year in the classroom!'

How to

COMMUNICATE

SHARING OUR STORIES, thoughts and ideas clearly is one of the most important skills we can learn. It takes time to master, and of course, it's only through practice that we get better. Keep reading, keep writing and make time to have conversations.

Using the Power of Positive Language

In Scouts, we know that how we talk really matters. Using positive language has helped us build a movement that's changed the world. Day to day, it helps us connect with others and influence those around us. What we say, and how we say it, also tells people what we're like as a person.

If we want people to pay attention when we write and talk, then two simple elements contain all the power:

1. Make it about others.
2. Make it positive.

This might sound like obvious advice, but hardly anybody follows it. Most people talk about themselves too much, talk other people down too often and grumble too hard.

Scouts are different. Great Scouts are interested in others. They ask about how you are, they talk kindly and generously about their peers, and their words about life are uplifting, never downbeat. Scouts know: how we speak about others speaks loudest about ourselves.

A good general rule is: if you haven't got something nice to say about someone or something, then leave it out. People will notice and admire you for it – after all, Scouts are there to make the world a better place, remember?

The words we speak and write have power. Our tongue is the smallest muscle in the body but has the most strength. Like the small rudder on a giant ship, our tongue dictates the course of much of our lives. Changing a few words can make a huge difference; there's something special that happens when we use positive language.

Here are a few words to swap in and replace:

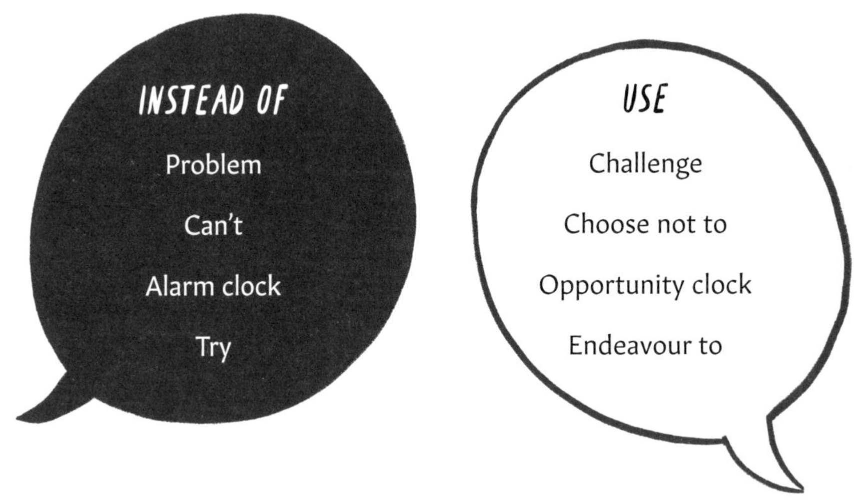

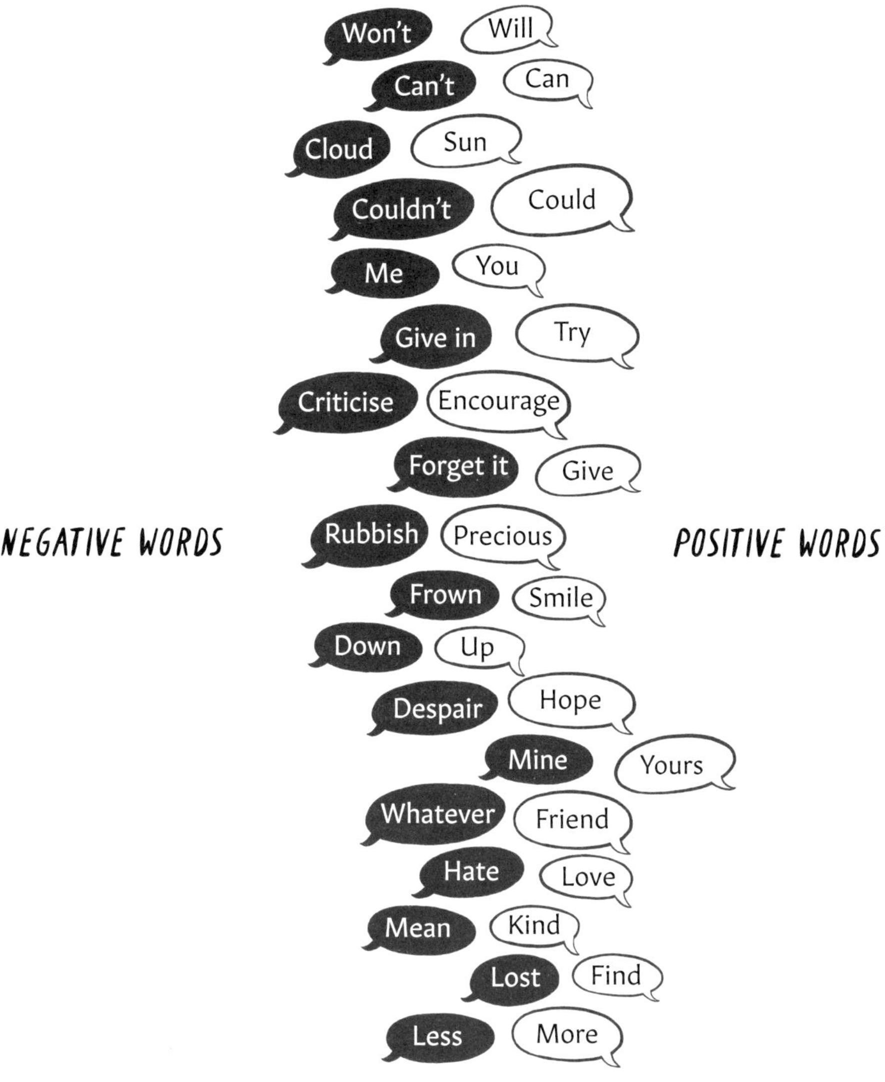

Live your life dominated by the words on the right, and endeavour to reduce the ones on the left, and your life will start to bear 'fruit' that reflects this. When we sow the good stuff, we reap the good stuff. It's the same with negativity. If we think or speak negatively and repeatedly, our lives will reflect that. As a Scout, choose to live in the affirmative. The positive. It's in our DNA.

Always choose words that encourage, empower and inspire. And keep the focus on other people, that way you will rise with the tide.

TEN TOP TIPS When Using Language to Inspire People

1. Use positive, hopeful language. Make your sentence smile.
2. Cut out the negativity. Instead of saying, 'Don't be negative', say, 'Be positive'.
3. Speak from the heart, and relate your experiences to other people.
4. Talk about other people, not yourself. Celebrate and lift them up.
5. Look on the bright side.
6. Tell personal stories – and laugh more at yourself.
7. Make sure everyone feels included.
8. Ask questions.
9. Give people a sense of excitement and discovery – so they want to know what happens next.
10. Tell people what you want them to do. What's your call to action?

Learn Some Positive Body Language

Positive language is not just about the words you use. According to the science boffins, when we're chatting with someone, 55 per cent of their attention is spent reading your body language, 38 per cent is on how you're talking (your tone) and only 7 per cent is on what you're actually saying. So always let it come from your heart. Feel it, rather than just say it.

If you look relaxed, this will relax the person you're talking with. Be as friendly and open with your body language as with the words you use.

- Leaning forward shows you're really listening.
- Smiling and nodding your head shows you agree with someone, or you understand how they feel.
- Keeping eye contact with the person you're chatting with shows they have your full attention. You are allowed to blink occasionally!
- Moving your hands can help you make a point, but don't overdo it (or you might end up hitting someone by accident).
- Folding your arms shows you're not really open to what someone's saying. Keep your arms down or fold your hands together while listening.
- A firm handshake shows good strength of character. But don't crush them. Remember, Scouts shake with their left hand.
- When making initial eye contact, try to notice the colour of a person's eyes. It establishes a winning rapport and subconsciously says, I am really here for you.
- Looking up shows you're present, engaged and listening.
- Examining your fingernails, looking at the ground or checking your phone shows you're not interested.

Think About How You Talk

How you talk matters just as much as what you say. And you can be just as friendly when you write as when you speak.

- Contractions (like 'can't' instead of 'cannot') make you sound friendlier, don't they?
- Make sure you don't use a long or stuffy word when a short or unstuffy one will do (like 'make sure' instead of 'ensure').
- Use questions to chat with your audience. Does that make sense? Thank you.
- Use nice short sentences. Like these ones.
- Use personal language like 'we', 'you' and 'I' to make sure people know you're a real person. Which you are.

Speaking to a Room Full of People

For some people, the idea of speaking in public is truly scary. But if you know what you're talking about, and you take your time and speak from the heart, it shouldn't be any harder than chatting with a friend. That's the key.

Here are some things to consider:

1 PREPARE AND PREPARE AGAIN
Plan what you're going to say carefully in advance. You don't need to write down every word, but having some clear headings will help keep you on track. Speak it out loud on your own beforehand to make sure what you want to say sounds natural and unforced. This helps you make sure that the words reflect what you really mean.

2 TELL STORIES AND SPEAK FROM THE HEART

People will respond best if they see you're speaking from your own personal experience. People remember stories much more than facts and figures.

3 TAKE A MOMENT

Take a look at the room and see how many people there are. This will help you decide how loud or quiet you need to be. You don't have to be too loud – people may pay more attention if you're a little quieter.

4 REMEMBER TO BREATHE

Controlling your breathing is so important. So just speak in your own time and let the audience wait for you. Remember you're in control. Try throwing an imaginary fishing net over your audience – they're now yours!

5 SHORTER IS BETTER

Keep your speech 10 per cent shorter than the time you have been asked to speak for. At least! It's much better to leave your audience wanting more rather than yawning. No one wants to have to look at a room full of tonsils. And you are never as interesting as either silence or lunch!

6 BE HONEST AND A LITTLE VULNERABLE

This is more important than trying to be funny or appearing too smart. When we are sincere and share some things that maybe feel hard to share, it creates a natural rapport with an audience. It takes courage to do this, but people admire it and will engage. Public speakers all too often make the mistake of thinking they have to be amusing, or tell a joke to start things off, when in truth, if they really want to win over their audience, they just have to be humble, sincere and themselves.

The Art of Rhetoric

The Ancient Greeks were masters of the art of rhetoric – using language to influence people and make forceful arguments. They had certain tricks (or 'devices', to give them their proper name) to help them make their points in a memorable way.

Here are ten useful ones to learn:

1 ANTANACLASIS
Reuse the first part of your sentence to change the meaning.

Write well, or you may as well write it off.

2 APOPHASIS
Say that you're not going to do something, then do it.

We won't mention Lucy.

3 APORIA
To express doubt about something.

It might work. It might not. We will see.

4 ASYNDETON
A phrase with the conjunctions taken out (words like 'and', 'but' and 'so') to make things sound punchy.

Rock up, eat up, wash up.

5 CHIASMUS
A phrase flipped on its head.

Wake early, or you'll have an early wake.

6 EPISTROPHE
Repeating a word at the end of a phrase or sentence for emphasis.

We can make it work; we must make it work; we will make it work.

7 **HYPERBATON**
Switching the order of words to create emphasis (like Yoda from *Star Wars*!).

Anger, fear, aggression; the dark side of the Force are they.

8 **OXYMORON**
Wait – you know this one already from your English lessons. It's two opposing words together.

A darkly lit room.

9 **SYLLEPSIS**
One literal meaning followed by one more metaphorical meaning.

For him, reaching the finishing line was reaching the moon.

10 **ZEUGMA**
Using one word to refer to more than one thing.

He managed the team and their expectations.

Telling a Story

We know that people are much more likely to listen and understand something if you tell them a story. People told stories to warn or educate people, and it's still one of the best ways to share or teach something.

Jesus did this all the time to his small group of disciples on the shores of Galilee, 2,000 years ago. We remember stories and their meanings much better than if we are simply being instructed to remember or do something. Instructions go into our heads, but stories with meanings go into our hearts. Always aim for people's hearts.

Here's a story that teaches a simple lesson about the rewards of hard work:

There was once an old farmer with three sons. None of them worked hard and they left their father to look after the land. One day, the farmer fell ill. He called his sons together at his bedside. 'My sons,' he said. 'I will be gone soon. Dig the

top field after my death, and you will find treasure beneath it.' This was enough to get them interested. They dug the field as he had told them, but found nothing. Angry and disappointed, they stared at the dug field. Now they had done the work, they decided they may as well sow some seeds. Sure enough, a rich crop sprung up. They harvested and sold the crops. Only now did they understand the treasure their father spoke of.

TEN TOP TIPS *for Telling a Story*

1. Have a clear message you want to share.
2. Have a beginning, a middle and an end.
3. Watch your audience. If they look like they're getting bored, change your tone, take a dramatic pause, make eye contact with someone, or even ask them what they think will happen next.
4. Add plenty of detail to help them imagine things. Use all the senses, as well as metaphors and similes, comparing one thing to another ('Like an apple falling from a tree, he tumbled out of his hammock').
5. Add some conflict. Like two people disagreeing on a plan. This helps people to relate to the situation better.
6. Leave out the boring bits (or 'side stories'). Keep it all focused on the action.
7. Keep up the pace and keep the story moving forward.
8. Build in some suspense.
9. Show not tell. Reveal the characters by what they do, rather than just telling us what they're like.
10. End with a flourish or a memorable image, then remind people of the message. Or better still, end with a shock or a twist.

Writing and Telling Jokes

Jokes rely on surprise ... and timing. Get both right and you've got a good chance of making someone laugh. One of the best ways to write a joke is to think of a word that has two meanings. For example, 'pause' and 'paws'. Here's a joke based on that:

A bear walks into a shop and says, 'Can I have a . . . lemonade?'
The shopkeeper says, 'Why the big pause?'
'I don't know,' says the bear. 'I was born with them.'

Boom, boom. See if you can come up with a good joke based on this method. What about this:

What flavour crisps do pilots like?
Plain.

Now it's fair to say, some people are naturally funnier than others. Some people have what you might call 'funny bones'. Sometimes they don't even need to say anything to make you laugh. They just have a mischievous twinkle in their eye. These people will often get a bigger laugh from quite a bad joke. And no one really knows why! Don't feel bad if your jokes don't get a big laugh. It's fun simply to try (I mean, endeavour!).

Let's leave you with one more:

How do you tell an alphabet it's missing something?
Send them a letter.

Making a Good Impression

It's tough walking into a room full of new people, isn't it? What will they think of you? Will you have something to say? Yet there are some simple things you can do that will make it a lot easier.

1 MAKE EYE CONTACT
Making positive eye contact with someone for those few seconds is enough to show respect, and is your way of telling them you're interested in who they are and what they have to say. Remember, notice their eye colour!

2 KEEP YOUR BACK STRAIGHT AND SHOULDERS BACK
A good posture will help you breathe more easily and make you look and feel confident. You'll feel like a new person. Imagine you're a racehorse, rather than a donkey.

3 SMILE
People respond immediately to a smile (usually with one of their own). Try it and see what difference it makes. You can literally light up a room. As the old saying goes: 'Smile and the world smiles with you.'

4 ASK QUESTIONS
If you're worried about what to talk about, ask people questions. How was their day? What did they do at the weekend? What do they love to do when they're not at school or working?

5 LISTEN

Remember, if you've asked a question, be polite enough to listen to the answer. Show you're listening by nodding your head, perhaps repeating a word or two of what the other person has just said. If you've got a thought, keep it to yourself for now. You've got one mouth and two ears. Use them in the same proportion. And never look over someone's shoulder. It says you're bored and want to escape (which to be honest is sometimes the case – just don't show it!).

6 COMPLIMENT

Everyone loves a genuine compliment. If someone's wearing nice shoes, let them know. Ask where they got them. But you have to mean it. They have to be really nice shoes!

7 SHOW THE REAL YOU

Don't feel like you need to show off. Share the things that have gone wrong for you as well as the things that have gone right. People will warm to you much more quickly. Above all, try to keep the focus, interest and topic on them, not you.

How to be

ORGANISED

LIFE IS CHAOTIC. Things happen all the time that you can't control. Your phone pings with messages from your friends. Your family wants you to help clean out the garage when you wanted to go out. Meanwhile, your work is piling up and your room is a mess. At times like these, life can seem stressful. Starting even one thing feels like a mountain.

Getting organised is a way of getting back in control of your life. It's about doing the important and urgent things first and spending less time on the unnecessary stuff.

Once you start getting organised, you'll feel less stressed, more accomplished and happier. You'll also get a reputation for being reliable, which comes with its own benefits – people will trust you. If you can manage yourself well, you can probably manage other important things, and people too.

But most of all, being organised will mean you'll have more time for doing the things you love. How many days have ended and you haven't had time to pick up your guitar, make a cake, go for a bike ride or watch a film with a friend? When you get organised, somehow it feels like you have time for the fun stuff, because the boring stuff has magically been accomplished.

It's all about managing your time effectively, having a plan and getting started. Scouts call it discipline, which can be a daunting word, but it's actually the key to so much in life. Get organised with a plan, and have the self-motivation or discipline to work the plan, and suddenly life seems way more manageable – and fun.

Spending Your Time

Life isn't always fair. There are so many inequalities, whether that's money, connections or opportunities. But one thing we all have the same amount of is time.

Along with your health, time is the most precious thing we have. Think of each hour in the day as a gold coin to spend, but with one big catch: if you don't spend it, it disappears.

If you get up late, perhaps at 11 a.m. (because it's the holidays, after all), then you've already lost four or five gold coins. You still have some left, but you'll now have less choice. So now you have to spend them on the things you've *got* to do rather than things you *want* to do.

What a waste of those unspent coins. Think of the things you could have done, the places you could have swum or the mountains you could have climbed.

EAT THE FROG

One of the most famous quotes about getting things done in the morning is from the great American author Mark Twain (who wrote *Huckleberry Finn*). Twain said: 'If it's your job to eat a frog, it's best to do it first thing in the morning.' Huh? What?

Eating the frog first means getting that difficult thing done that you've been putting off. It's likely to be the most fearsome, challenging or unpleasant task you have to do. It could be whitewashing a fence or writing that history essay. But tackling it first thing in the morning is good for all sorts of reasons. Not only do most people have their best energy in the morning, getting it out of the way means you'll feel great for the rest of the day. Some people call this 'slaying the dragon'. Call it what you like, it's a great habit to get into.

Problems tend to get bigger in your head if you don't do anything about them, and most people find that eating the frog first is really not as hard as they thought.

Why It's Good to Get Up Early

Early mornings are quiet. They're good for reading, thinking, planning and dreaming. This is the time when people are less likely to bother you and ask you to do things, which makes it a great time to spend those gold coins well.

The morning is a great time to get ahead and start the day on the front foot. Get the tough and tedious chores or work done early, and then the whole day opens up ahead of you. For the better.

You can work on things with purpose and zest and energy – maybe it's something you're making, some revision for your exams, writing a thank-you letter or tidying your room. These things might sound boring, but they set a pattern that creates the way you live your life. Remember, as Scouts say: 'How we do anything, is how we do everything.'

In other words, how we do the unseen, seemingly trivial stuff, reflects how we tackle the big, important stuff. It sets a pattern and a habit that is positive and empowering. The pattern of the unseen becomes the habit of the seen. You get the idea. Nothing is ever really nothing. Every little deed, habit and word eventually make up our whole life.

Do the simple stuff well, like making your bed (Scouts do this out of respect and wanting to be tidy), and then the rest will follow. As they say: 'Tidy room, tidy mind. Make your bed, success you'll find.'

This sort of approach to life will give you a great feeling of accomplishment for the day. It's a good day before it's even begun. Anything else good that happens is now a bonus.

The morning is also one of the most beautiful times of the day. The hour before sunrise is what photographers call the golden hour. Light from the sun seeps into the dark of the night and you find yourself bathed in a magical golden glow. This makes photographs look good, but it also makes you feel great too. Get up early and get outside. Be reminded how beautiful the world around you is, even in a town or city, before the whistling of blackbirds (or the warbling of the warbler) is drowned out by traffic noise. Out in nature at this special time, you'll find yourself in what feels like a different kingdom. Most people never get to see the morning like this, preferring to hit the snooze button or lie in bed checking their phone. By the time the sun's up, the magic is gone.

Why It's Good to Go to Bed Early

Early mornings are made possible by early nights.

If you end up on your phone late at night, staring at a screen, you will find yourself much more tired – and then getting up early becomes so hard. Plus, too much of the blue light from your phone or screen at night is proven to mess with your ability to sleep well. And as we know, sleep is key to recovery and zest for the next day.

Early nights and early mornings might not sound very fashionable, but Scouts are smart at taking the path less trodden, especially if it means they are then able to get ahead in life. And early nights make that advantage possible. Scouts have always been and always will be pioneers. They do the important things differently.

Why Early Risers Sleep Better

Getting up earlier helps you sleep better. Spending time outside in the morning tells our bodies to wake up and sharpen up naturally. It promotes the release of a chemical called cortisol in our bodies that makes us feel alert for the rest of the day.

Being outside and getting a dose of vitamin D from sunlight also triggers other feel-good hormones. These include serotonin, which keeps you feeling upbeat and in control of things during the day. And if you exercise in the morning, your body releases dopamine – the chemical that makes joggers feel 'run-tastic' when they burst in through the front door feeling smug and sweaty.

Getting up and out early does something else pretty remarkable: it triggers a timer in your nervous system that means you'll sleep better at night. Now your body knows it's morning, it knows when to release another chemical called melatonin, which will help you sleep later.

So people who get up early not only sleep better because they're tired from the day but because their body's alarm clock is set correctly. Your body is a clever thing, isn't it? This is also our reminder that we're part of the natural world – our body responds to the world around us.

I guess you're now seeing why the mornings are the key to so much else. Yet not many people know this secret.

Find Your Routine

It's important you find your own routine. There's no 'one size fits all', but it's certainly interesting to see how different people use their time.

Be More Monk

Monks are an interesting example of people who get up early and benefit from a routine. A thousand years ago (and still in many monasteries today), the day would be dictated by the available sunlight. In summer, the monks would wake at 4.30 a.m., wash, pray, read and do a little work.

Later, there would be a service and then a meeting to discuss the business of the day. Work like gardening, bee-keeping or brewing would happen in the morning before another Mass or spiritual service and then lunch.

Exhausted yet?

Work would then continue into the afternoon, followed by dinner, a little more work, then an early bedtime – as early as 6 p.m. in the summer and 8 p.m. in the winter. They'd then wake again around 3 a.m. to sing and pray, before a little more sleep or quiet time before the day began.

I'm not saying we should all live like this – after all, there are some epic adventures to be had out in the world – but the point is that monks have been historically among the happiest and most productive people on earth. And the clue might be in their structured day and early routines. Just saying . . .

One thing's for certain: going to bed late and waking up late creates a sense of imbalance and disorder that means you'll find it harder to concentrate. It'll make you irritable and you'll be more likely to lose your temper. Even if you don't find a good routine for your own sake, think of those around you! They'll thank you. And me.

TEN TOP TIPS *for Getting Organised*

1 CREATE CLEAR SPACE

When you haven't got piles of random cables, gadgets and papers everywhere to distract you, you can focus in on what really needs to be done. Tidy your room, clear the junk off your desktop and start again with a clean slate. It feels so good.

2 MAKE A LIST

It's the oldest trick in the book, but it still works. Making a list means you have a clear plan for the day. For example, your Sunday list might look something like this:

- Tidy room
- Learn guitar solo
- Twenty-minute workout in garden
- Maths homework
- Ring Gran

When you're making a list, you're using the 'boss' part of your brain to tell the 'worker' part of your brain what to do. Tick the tasks off as you do them and you'll get that great 'win' feeling as your brain rewards you with dopamine.

3 PRIORITISE

Making a list is only half the battle. The key then is to prioritise, which is a way of making your list smarter. It's about using your time most efficiently. Prioritising the right tasks and when to do them is a way of making sure the urgent and important things get done first. This is a good way to manage both your list and your time.

What task is the most tricky? Maybe tackle it first and get it done. (Remember to eat the frog!) What is fun? Maybe make that a reward for after you've done the work part. You decide. But remember, get the tough ones done early.

Make your list and then use this diagram to help you prioritise the things that need doing and in what order. Some tasks you can give to others. They might not actively require you, which allows you to spend your time on more pressing matters. Maybe your brother promised he would pick up your parcel for you on his way back from Scouts. Parcel collection: done (well, I hope, at least!).

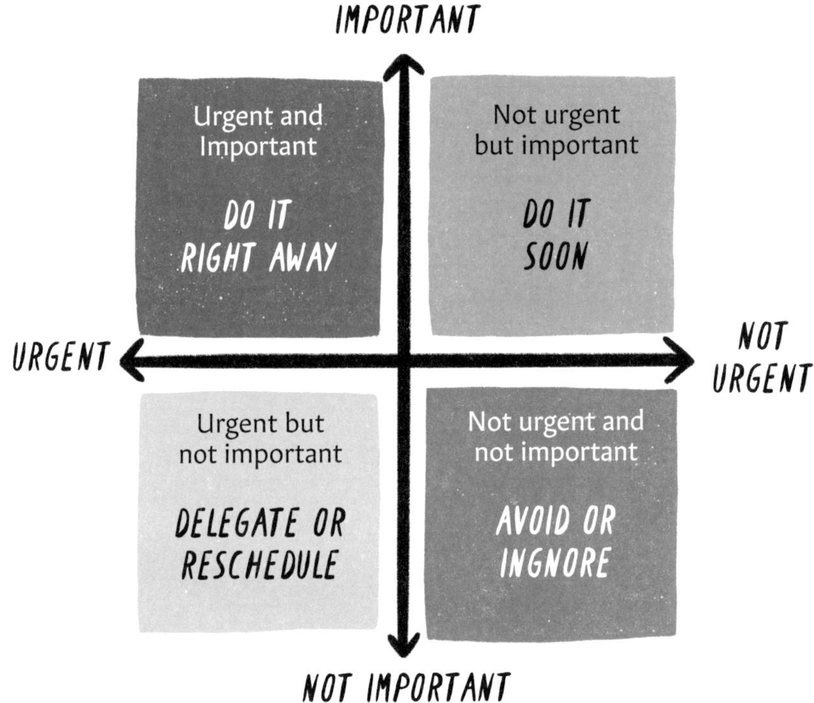

Remember, making time for friendships and your family is important too. Super important. Add it to your list: 'See Tom. Leave Mum a nice note.' Life is about enjoying doing things with the people you love. But as you know, the boring things still need to be done. Prioritising will simply help you make more space in your day for the real stuff.

4 BLOCK OUT YOUR DAY

Remember those precious gold coins? This is all about making the most of your day. There isn't one way of doing this, and different things work for different people. Divide your day into time segments and write down what you're going to do in each one.

One good tip is to use half-hour segments rather than full hours. Often, if you're super-focused, you can do as much in half an hour as you can in an hour. This way, you'll be able to fit more in. The same goes for your leisure time. Why not watch a film over several nights rather than all in one go?

5 CUT OUT THE DEAD TIME

Think of all the time you lose each day scrolling on your phone, wandering around the house, opening and closing the fridge door or looking for lost things. These are classic ways of losing even more of your precious gold coins. Being conscious of time-draining habits like scrolling means you can cut them down. If you enjoy time on social media, make some time for it in your day, but limit yourself. Be your own guardian. Be the guardian of your life and time. Be in charge.

Constant checking on social media will mean you'll be constantly distracted and won't get things done. Get in the habit of catching yourself doing these things and get yourself back on track. Don't let those gold coins spill out of the day, for zero return. That's the danger of scrolling and too much social media. You know the types? They live on their phones and never notice the good stuff around them or outdoors. Scouts live differently. And better.

6 PUT YOUR PHONE TO BED AT NIGHT

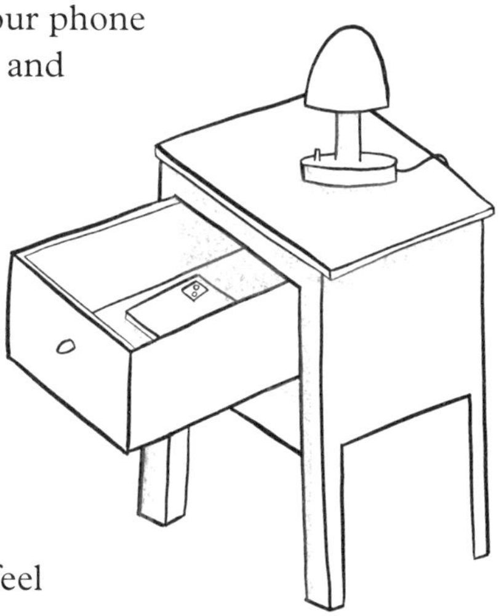

Science tells us that looking at your phone late at night is bad for your sleep and well-being. The bright screen, blue light and constant alerts confuse your brain into thinking it needs to stay alert for daytime activities. It also means that your body won't release that sleepy hormone melatonin you need to help you nod off. The amount and quality of your sleep will be reduced and you'll feel exhausted in the morning. When you go to bed, put your phone to bed too in a drawer or drawstring bag to reduce the temptation to check that one last message. And turn it to airplane mode or sleep focus.

7 FIND A HOME FOR EVERYTHING

The average person spends two and a half days a year looking for things. That's a long time! That's two and a half days lost in your own house or flat. Probably stressed and annoyed. By giving things a home, you'll know where to look. Just like knives, forks and spoons have their own home in the cutlery drawer, make sure you always put things back in the same place. Think what you could do with the time you'll save – that's a whole extra weekend!

8 MAKE DECISIONS AND LEARN TO SAY NO

Without decisions, things quickly start to spiral out of control. Saying yes to everything means your to-do list never gets done. If your friend suddenly invites you to go out shopping or play basketball, that means your maths homework continues to sit there waiting – and your brother probably doesn't want to do that for you. Saying no can be tough sometimes, but you have to learn to do it if you're going to stay organised. No is such a key word to learn to use in life. And remember, you don't always need to explain yourself. Simply saying, 'No I can't today', is fine. Then add: 'But thank you anyway'.

9 SET GOALS AND PLAN AHEAD

Planning your day is important, but you also need a clear sense of where you want to get to in the longer term. One of the best things you can do is look at the week, the month and even the year ahead. This will help you decide what's your priority and what you want to achieve in the months, term or year ahead. Do you want to learn to juggle? Get a better grade in maths?
By setting yourself a clear goal and a deadline, you can plan in the time you need to help you reach it. A goal without a date on it and a plan of how to get there is just a wish. Set goals, not wishes.

10 STAY MOTIVATED

People often have good intentions to get more organised or fitter (particularly around New Year). They'll be disciplined for a few days, then things start to fall apart. They lapse back into their old bad habits. This is why the only thing harder than getting organised is staying organised. It takes hard work and discipline. (See that word again? It's so important. Practise being disciplined and like a muscle, it will get stronger and the tasks will get easier. Trust me.)

And to stick with things, we need to keep reminding ourselves why we're doing it. For example, it might be to achieve better grades or make more time for the things we love. Why not pin some of these targets on the wall to remind you? Because the more reminders of our goals we have around us, the better. So go for it! I can't wait to see what you come up with.

How to be

FIT AND HEALTHY

YOU PROBABLY KNOW that health is more precious than wealth. There are plenty of sick millionaires who would give away every last penny to be healthy again. As the entrepreneur, Jim Rohn, once said: 'Take care of your body. It's the only place you have to live.'

But being healthy goes beyond just keeping your body in good working order. Your mind and your emotional and spiritual welfare are just as important, and they are designed to work together, to make up the brilliant you. Take a look at page 260 to remind yourself about the five things you can do every day to improve your mental well-being.

The best secrets for a healthy mind, body and spirit that I know are a natural diet, regular sun, cold water and exercise, sufficient hydration, breathing through your nose, getting barefoot as much as you can and ensuring you have plenty of sleep. Plus of course, doing something kind for someone else, every single day.

It might all sound simple stuff, but lots of people don't follow any of these life hacks. And then they wonder why they feel sluggish and uninspired. But if the goal is to live an empowered life, making a difference to people around you, changing the world for the better, and achieving all your dreams, then you are going to be busy! And for that you need to do all you possibly can to be fit and healthy, living life on the front foot.

If we fuel up naturally, smile and are kind, then our face will shine. When I meet older people with bright faces and twinkly eyes, I know they are probably living with many of these principles in place.

Sadly, life isn't always like this, and many people suffer illness and disability that makes much of these tasks and principles impossible. But I also want to set a level of aspiration for you as a Scout, to have something positive to aim for, if you possibly can. Obviously, we all have to work according to what we can and can't do, but I do know that you can do so much – often, so much more than you or those around you might believe. If you are one of these Scouts who faces some natural battles, I think you are amazing and I admire you so much. You're incredible. Keep going, and thank you for your example.

So here we go: how to live your best life in terms of health and activity.

The Power of Sleep

It's tempting to think of sleep as the boring bit between days. That's why we often stay up longer than we should, playing *just one more* level of a computer game, watching *just one more* episode of our favourite TV show, or reading *just one more* chapter of our book. We sometimes think of sleep as something that robs us of the time and fun we deserve after a long, hard day at school or work.

In fact, sleep is a vital part of our lives. It's when our body and mind restore and repair themselves, and when we process our thoughts and memories. Incredibly, we'll spend a third of our lives asleep – that's potentially 230,000 hours, 9,600 days or twenty-six years asleep. That's right – *twenty-six years*. Now that's what I call a lie in!

When we get enough sleep, we feel fresh and alert, and make better decisions. We're also likely to be less grouchy and more pleasant to be around. We're happier and healthier. On the other hand, when we get interrupted sleep, or not enough of it, there is a negative knock-on effect to our lives. Without proper rest, recovery and sleep, our brain becomes like a computer with a glitch. We can't think straight; we get confused, grumpy and disorientated. We become erratic and tetchy. Our mental health suffers, meaning we'll feel low or depressed. Life might feel less hopeful and we'll lose our sense of purpose. Even worse than that, our immune system starts to weaken, and we'll be more likely to develop serious illnesses like diabetes, heart disease and strokes.

You might hear some people boasting that they 'get by' on just four or five hours sleep. Or that if you drink three or four cups of coffee it's as good as three or four more hours in bed. It's true that some people do need less sleep than others, but often it turns out that those people are actually suffering from the negative effects of lack of sleep without realising it.

Our bodies are highly tuned in to our planet's cycle of light and dark. We have an inbuilt body clock which works around a twenty-four-hour day – exactly the same time it takes the earth to spin on its axis. The system is called the circadian rhythm, which regulates our sleep. It's triggered by light – so as the light starts to dim, your mind knows that the day is coming to an end and your body needs rest and sleep.

Your brain then releases something called melatonin, which makes you feel sleepy. Likewise, when your brain detects light, it releases cortisol, which makes you feel awake. You have a whole chemistry set inside you that you probably didn't even know about. Super cool.

How Much Sleep Do You Need?

A young person aged between six and thirteen needs eight to eleven hours sleep; a teenager needs around eight to ten hours sleep; an adult needs seven to nine hours. Any fewer than seven hours means your mind and body won't have time to do the 'housekeeping' it needs to do while asleep.

The Stages of Sleep

On the face of it, sleep seems very simple. You close your eyes, you drop off, and lo and behold, it's morning again. But in fact, some quite extraordinary things are going on. There are four different stages of sleep:

1 STAGE 1: LIGHT SLEEP
Your breathing and heart rate start to slow; your muscles are relaxing.

2 STAGE 2: DEEPER SLEEP
Your muscles are even more relaxed; your heart rate slows further still. Your eyes stop moving and your body is cooling down.

3 STAGE 3: DEEP SLEEP
If you've reached this stage, then you're on course for a good night's sleep, because it's in stage 3 that the good things start to happen. Your body is now repairing itself, and your mind is processing all of the chaos of the day into some sort of order. Meanwhile, your body's physical activity is at its lowest.

4 STAGE 4: RAPID EYE MOVEMENT (REM)
Now comes the really interesting part. Something extraordinary happens when you reach this last stage, which lasts around twenty minutes. Your eyes start to move rapidly, and your heart rate and breathing start to quicken again, as if you're waking up. But you're not – this is your dream state. While you're in REM sleep, two parts of the brain – the amygdala and hippocampus – are firing off all sorts of electrical impulses which release a jumble of random memories and images. Because we have rational minds, we try and make sense of these and turn them into a story or narrative that makes better sense. Believe it or not, you're unable to move your limbs during this stage – possibly for your own safety, to stop you doing the things you're dreaming about.

Dreams

We're not quite certain why we dream, but it's likely that it's something to do with processing all the information we've taken on during the day, rather like a computer when it's updating its system. Memories are being filed away in the right places and you are working through your emotions.

Some people are convinced that as we dream, we're expressing our truest feelings. They believe that dreams symbolise things about life; your subconscious mind is telling you a truth that perhaps your conscious mind is not really aware of while you're awake. For example:

- Deserts could symbolise misfortune, emptiness or loss.
- Flying could mean you feel free, optimistic and ready to try anything.
- Floods could mean you're being overwhelmed by something in your life.

Dreaming is like having your own free streaming service running in your brain, delivering stories, films and images. But this isn't just to entertain you during those long, dark hours. It's about making sense of the day so you're ready to start the next one with a clear, focused mind.

Whatever the meaning of our dreams, the key thing to remember is that your subconscious wants to heal and restore you. So generally, there will be a positive purpose to dreams. It's your deep self doing some deep cleaning.

Hydrate, Feel Great

We need water because we're mostly made of the stuff (it accounts for around 60 per cent of our body weight; we really are just bags of fluid). Water is essential to almost every function of our body and without it we'll seize up like a car engine without oil.

Having enough water in our systems means we can digest our food properly, make saliva for our mouths, wash out our waste, get oxygen to all parts of our body, and make sure nutrients are properly absorbed. It also stops us overheating, keeps our joints well lubricated and spongy so they can absorb impact and allow us to move easily, and keeps our skin looking healthy and bright too.

Did you know that not staying properly hydrated can reduce your exercise endurance by nearly a half? Just like getting enough sleep, when we have the right amount of water on board, we feel alert, energetic and ready to take on anything. And as Scouts, we need to be performing at our best.

The best sources of hydration are from liquids that are natural and not laden with processed sugar or caffeine. Aim to drink around two litres of water a day to keep yourself topped up, and more if it's very hot or you're exercising. The best way to do this is little and often. Suddenly remembering at the end of the day that you've forgotten to drink any water and then guzzling two litres isn't a great idea. You'll also end up peeing most of the night.

Signs that you're not getting enough water are a dry mouth, feeling tired and dark urine. If your pee is nearly clear, then you're properly hydrated. If it's yellowish, then it's time to drink a glass of water.

Note that excessive water consumption can be just as bad. It's called water intoxication and can drain your organs of vital nutrients and salts. This will result in fainting, dizziness, weak muscles or worse. So, as with so much in life, listen to your body, and make sure you drink enough but not too much.

Nasal Breathing

This one might surprise you, but nasal breathing is one of the fundamentals of good health. It means breathing through your nose, not just your mouth.

Much research has been done on how breathing through your nose is better for your health. Luckily, kids naturally tend to breathe through their noses.

Your body needs something called nitric oxide to function at its best. And it is the small nasal hairs in your nostrils that enable this gas to be absorbed into your bloodstream. Your body will therefore absorb less nitric oxide when you breathe through your mouth.

So try always to breathe in and out through the nose. If this feels difficult at first, it maybe means you've become a bit of a mouth breather. Persevere and you'll start to be able to do it better. It might take some conscious effort to start with, but soon it will become second nature.

Move It!

One of the best ways to keep fit and healthy is to move. Dance. Play. Jump. Skip. It doesn't matter how you move, just move. We're designed to spring about, not slump in one place. Play to your strength as an evolved human being. You evolved through movement, so keep doing that to stay at your best. If in doubt, or if you're in need of a 'pick me up', simply get up, get outside and go for a quick walk. Even five minutes, especially after meals, can transform how you feel.

It's also so important to endeavour to start the day with movement, fresh air and sunlight if you possibly can. This is the ultimate way to set yourself up for success at the start of a day. It sounds simple, but so few people do it. Maybe get off the bus a stop or two early and walk the last part. Or offer to walk the dog before school three mornings a week. (Maybe you can suggest a little pocket money for this from your parents or guardian!)

Note, if it's summertime and safe to do so, go barefoot. The connection between the earth and your skin is ultimately healing. Try it, close your eyes and feel the earth's energy. I promise I'm not crazy!

Find a Team Sport You Enjoy

One of the best ways to get enough movement into your day is to get involved in a team sport. You might have tried some of these already – football, netball, rugby, cricket, basketball, hockey and so on. Not only will it keep you fit, it'll help you learn to be part of a team. You'll have a particular role or position that's your responsibility. You might not be involved at every moment of the game, but at one point all eyes will be on you – people will rely on you to do your job. Not everyone can be the goal scorer, but it's a great feeling knowing you've played your part.

The best idea is to try lots of different sports and find out which you like the best. You could have the potential to be a world champion volleyball player. But unless you try, you'll never know. Lots of sports and leisure centres offer free taster events, or you could just get something organised with some friends at Scouts.

Keep on Running

Why do so many people love running? You're not usually going anywhere specific, and even if you are, there are many quicker and more efficient ways of getting from A to B. One reason is that it seems to set the mind and body free.

When you run, your body feels like it's doing what it was designed to do – moving your limbs and pumping oxygen. You feel a sense of elation as endorphins are released, and pounding down the pavement or woodland lane, you'll feel like an Olympic hero. As someone said: 'Jogging is life with the volume turned up.'

Running is aerobic exercise, meaning it needs more oxygen than anaerobic exercise, like lifting weights. Aerobic exercise is great for your heart, brain and lungs, which are important bits of kit and well worth looking after. Running will improve your sleep, increase bone strength and give you more energy and stamina during other activities. Running is also a great mood-changer. If you're stuck with a problem, or feel low and can't quite work out why, a winning solution is to go for a run (or a brisk walk). With all that oxygen being fed to the brain, everything starts to feel better. When you get back, it's like you've had a system reboot.

Of course, it's possible to have too much of a good thing, so be careful not to do too much. Maybe don't run every single day, especially to begin with. You need time for your body to recover. Build up to longer distances, and like drinking water, it's better to do it little and often, rather than epic runs that will put excessive stress on your joints.

Be especially careful if you're running on or near roads. Wear high visibility clothing, keep to grass verges and pavements where possible and be especially careful listening to music when you're near traffic – you might not hear cars coming around the bend, for example.

Strength Exercises

It is so important to also do resistance exercise that builds up your strength, rather than just your aerobic fitness. Whoever you are, we all need strength training as part of our overall health. It builds bone density and muscular stability, and we need those elements to be at our best physically.

Here are a few strength exercises to try if you can:

1. **PLANKS**
   Lie on your front and place your hands flat on the floor, underneath your shoulders. Lift your body and spread your weight evenly between your toes and arms. Hold for thirty seconds. Have a break, then go again. You will build up strength and time fast.

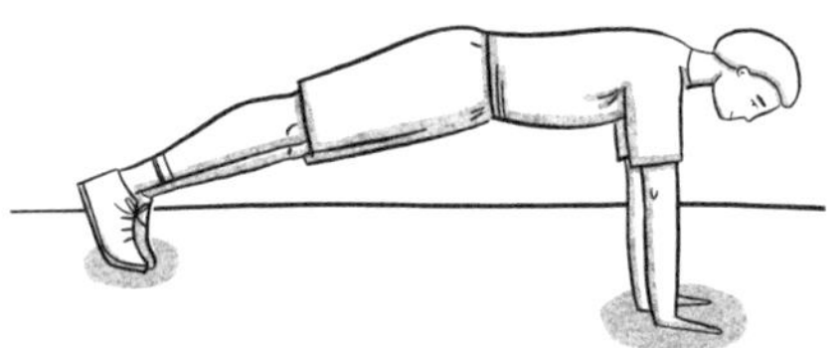

2. **PRESS-UPS**
   Go into the plank position, with your hands at shoulder-width and elbows in, slowly lower your chest to the floor then come back up. Slow and controlled is better than fast and unstable. You are building strength. Aim for ten then increase. If you can eventually do fifty you will be supremely strong!

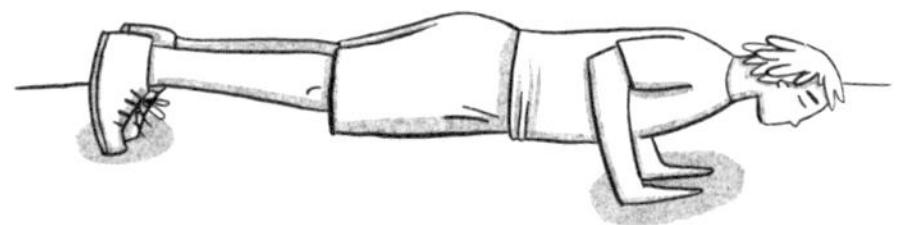

3. **PIKES**
   Lie on your back, with straight legs and straight arms over your head. Raise your legs and arms so that you touch your toes (or as close as you can reach to your toes!) and then return to the flat position. Repeat for one minute. Build to three minutes. Again, slow, steady and controlled.

4 **SQUATS**
Adopt a wide stance with your toes slightly turned out. With arms out to your side, bend your legs to 90° and come back up. Slow and steady. Aim for fifty repetitions.

5 **CRUNCHES**
Lie on your back with your knees bent. Put your hands on the side of your head and lift your chin. Curl your upper body forward, lifting your shoulders, head and neck. Freeze for a moment or two, then slowly lower yourself down.

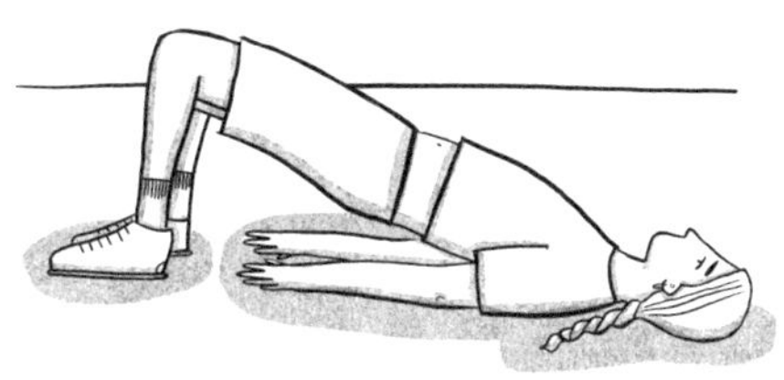

6 **BRIDGES**
Lie on your back with your knees bent and arms by your sides. Lift your hips into the air until your knees, hips and shoulders form a straight line. Then slowly return your back to the floor. Always keep breathing through all your exercises, and ideally through your nose (remember?), not solely through your open mouth.

Eat Natural

It's so important for our health, energy and focus to eat the right kinds of food. Foods that heal, nourish, restore and refuel us. That is why the phrase exists: we become what we eat.

Obviously, research and data will always evolve in the world of nutrition, which is why it's smart to remain open to adapt, learn and ever improve. We're all on our own journeys when it comes to nutrition and health. You've got to listen to your body and do your own research. If you're feeling fit and healthy, then I wouldn't change too much – but it's so important to be aware of how food makes you feel.

Please treat this section as a guide only; it's a reflection as to what I do, rather than what's essential for you. We always need to be respectful of each other's choices and views on food and diet. We should also be mindful that some will have strong moral views, specific health needs, allergies and intolerances, as well as likes and dislikes. All of us have a right to choose our own path.

I like to view nutrition as being about what you do for most of the time. An 80/20 guide of healthy foods, with the occasional treats thrown in, feels a balanced way to approach nutrition. If every now and again you eat some over-sugared, processed stuff, it probably won't affect you much, but get the 80/20 ratio back to front, and there is little doubt our bodies and our health will suffer. Our levels of physicality and mental alertness often reflect what we are fuelling ourselves with.

When it comes to seeking out the best, life-enhancing nutrition, try and develop eating habits that will fuel you naturally. The healthiest foods tend to leave us feeling fuller, faster. The less healthy options tend to make us even more hungry. This means people then tend to eat more, until eventually they just feel bloated and sick. If you're feeling sluggish and lacking in energy, there's a strong possibility you're not eating the right sorts of food for you.

The best sorts of food are natural, whole foods that haven't been processed. The sort of foods you would find in nature. When our foods are processed, not only do our bodies struggle to digest them but many of the natural nutrients are either removed or lost. Maybe consider the types of food that our ancient ancestors would recognise? That way we know that our bodies have evolved to thrive off it.

The Food of Our Ancestors

So what did our ancestors eat, tens of thousands of years ago, before modern farming?

If we go way back, our ancestors lived off the land in a way that was 'evolutionarily optimum'. In other words, what they ate, and how they lived, was how they had evolved best to thrive. That generally involved sufficient sleep, sundown to sunset; morning movement; constant fresh air; physical exertion and struggle, to protect their families and to hunt for food.

Their diet consisted of:

- Animal fat and meat, including organs, which were highly prized, like liver.
- Plenty of fruit (the bright, sweet taste is a clue that fruit is designed to be eaten).
- Eggs, dairy and honey from animals they raised themselves.
- Nuts, roots or leaves as additional sustenance, to keep them going during hunts.

One thing I know for sure, they didn't eat:

- Processed food.
- Fake sugars.
- Highly refined seed oils.
- Gluten-laden products.
- Food from packets with a thousand ingredients that you can't even pronounce.

I'm not saying we all have to live like cave people. After all, a little chocolate is one of the great things in life, especially in a tent by torch-light with friends. And vegetables can bring taste and colour to your plate. But maybe it's also smart to look at how evolution and nature has designed us to sustain ourselves.

Of course, it wasn't all rosy for our early ancestors; many died young from injury and infection. Modern medicine and antibiotics save so many lives nowadays, allowing our life expectancy to be much longer (thank goodness).

But let's remember that up until fifty years ago, humans had never even heard of most of the new food products that people predominantly eat today. And evolution, including our bodies and guts, can't adapt that fast. So if in doubt, copy your ancestors, and see how you feel.

Food grown locally is always the best type to source. And if you are eating eggs, dairy and meat, try to go for grass-fed, pasture-raised. It is better for you and better for the environment.

And remember, don't assume that processed foods are necessarily better for sustainability. Soy and palm oil all has to be grown somewhere, often in rainforests, which then has to be transported, often across continents. So maybe instead: pick local, pick natural.

None of this is rocket science, and it's not new advice either. People have always known that eating well means living well. Hippocrates, the great doctor from Ancient Greece, who lived around 460 BC, said, 'Let food be thy medicine, and medicine be thy food.' He was right.

TEN TOP TIPS *for Eating Well*

1. Eat nutrient-dense food rather than more food.
2. Don't eat out of boredom. Go for a walk, ring a buddy, or open a book (rather than the fridge).
3. Eat more slowly. You'll eat less and enjoy it more.
4. Support local businesses and farms if you can. You'll be proud of every mouthful.
5. Eat simple, natural food rather than products made in a factory. It will always be tastier than processed food.
6. Eat with friends and family. Food should be sociable and a celebration, not just a necessity.
7. Be mindful about the food you eat. Think about where it came from, who grew it and how it got to your plate.
8. Be thankful for the food you eat, and think about those who don't have enough.
9. A great snack is an apple with a little natural cheese. Much better than crisps, which are terrible for our health.
10. Go for a brisk walk after a big lunch and/or dinner to help your digestion.

And finally: if the ingredients list is longer than ten items, think again.

Did you know? You taste with your nose as well as your mouth. If you don't believe me, try holding your nose next time you eat.

HAUTE CUISINE: THE WORLD'S HIGHEST OPEN-AIR DINNER PARTY

Back in 2005, I took part in a record-breaking high-altitude 'dinner party' at the height of 7,395 m (24,262 ft), suspended beneath a huge hot-air balloon. Along with the adventurer Sir David Hempleman-Adams, and several others, we abseiled from the balloon's basket down to a small table, secured by long, thin wires. The temperature was -45°C and we had to breath oxygen through specially adapted high-altitude masks. The Guinness Book of Records told us that if it was to count as an official record, we had to wear formal clothes, have three courses and toast the Queen! We were proud to pull this off, and we never let our standards slip. At the end, we leapt off into the thin air, pulled our parachutes and eventually landed safely. The record was ours and we were proud to have supported (another) exceptional youth charity, the Duke of Edinburgh's Award.

Emergency: WHAT WOULD YOU DO?

NOW'S THE TIME to test your Scouting knowledge. Here are some tricky situations that you and your friends could find yourself in when out in the wild. Take a look and think about everything you've learnt in this book. List some of the things you could do to stay safe, sort things out or call for help.

1 You've been hiking all day through a forest with two friends. Almost everything looks the same, every way you look – just tall, thin trees as far as the eye can see in every direction. One of your friends, who's been navigating, suddenly stops and says he's no longer sure whether you've been heading east after all. The light is fading and you don't have a tent or sleeping bags as you weren't expecting to camp.

What would you do?

2 You're climbing a steep hill when you suddenly hear a cry and shout from below. A rock has fallen and struck your friend on the head. There's blood and your friend is now sitting down, holding their head. You're several miles from help, it's getting dark and you only have a small first aid kit with you.

What would you do?

3 It's midday. You're walking through open fields on a golden summer's day. The sun is beating down on you, and you can feel your arms beginning to burn. You suddenly realise that one of your friends (who you remember wasn't wearing a hat) is nowhere to be seen.

What would you do?

4 You're climbing high up in some hills covered in trees and woodland. Far below you, you can see a town. Suddenly you find yourselves stuck. There doesn't seem to be a safe way either up or down, or either side of you. You only have light clothing and no special equipment with you. To make matters worse, there's no signal on your phones. It's raining and you're getting cold. How do you stay safe, keep warm and call for help?

What would you do?

5 You're alone in a forest on a winter's day, out exploring. For once, you've left your phone at home. Suddenly, almost out of nowhere, it starts to snow heavily. Everything is soon covered in a blanket of white. The path has disappeared and everything looks the same. You wander for hours and shout for help, but it's now getting dark and you're starting to shiver.

What would you do?

6 You're on a night hike. It's a cloudless night and the sky is full of stars. One of your friends tells you that their compass needle has stuck and their phone has no signal. Nor does yours. How do you find the way north again?

What would you do, first, if you were in Scotland, and second, if you were in New Zealand?

7 You're out hiking across an open moor when you hear a rumble of thunder and see a huge, dark cloud gathering in the distance. You see a flash of lightning, then hear more thunder five seconds later. You can see a house about a mile away in the distance and a single tall tree about a quarter of a mile away. Otherwise there's no shelter.

What would you do?

8 You're high up in the Swiss mountains. While waiting for a cable car to return to pick you all up, someone drops their glasses into the concrete docking station. They drop down to get them, then realise that the concrete walls are too smooth to climb back up again. There's a sheer drop on one side, and three walls of concrete four metres high on the others. You can see the cable car coming up the mountain towards the docking bay.

What would you do?

9 You are out for a walk at night while on holiday in France and see a light flashing, high up on a hill. You watch the light and see three short flashes, three long flashes and then three short flashes again. There's no one else around.

What would you do?

10 You're on a hike in your Scout uniform. You come across some thick bramble covered in blackberries. While trying to get to some of the juiciest ones, you fall forward and down into a deep ditch half filled with water. You hear a snapping sound and feel a sharp pain in your left arm.

What would you do?

USEFUL STUFF THAT JUST MIGHT COME IN HANDY

Morse Code

Named after Samuel Morse, an inventor of the telegraph, Morse code allows you to send and receive messages using a series of dots and dashes. These can be made with either sound or flashing light signals of different durations.

I am proud to remember some Morse code from my time in Scouts and in the military. It's pretty fun as a game at night to communicate between tents by whistling Morse or using torches to signal. See the full alphabet below and try it. You never know when it might come in handy!

A	• —	N	— •	1	• — — — —
B	— • • •	O	— — —	2	• • — — —
C	— • — •	P	• — — •	3	• • • — —
D	— • •	Q	— — • —	4	• • • • —
E	•	R	• — •	5	• • • • •
F	• • — •	S	• • •	6	— • • • •
G	— — •	T	—	7	— — • • •
H	• • • •	U	• • —	8	— — — • •
I	• •	V	• • • —	9	— — — — •
J	• — — —	W	• — —	0	— — — — —
K	— • —	X	— • • —		
L	• — • •	Y	— • — —		
M	— —	Z	— — • •		

Flag Semaphore

Flag semaphore is a way of communicating messages over a distance where the sender and receiver are in visual contact. It was used especially at sea between ships, before the invention of radio, and is still sometimes used today in emergencies. At night, illuminated wands can be used instead of flags.

Distance Conversion

Different countries use different units of measurement. Here are some helpful tables to help you work out equivalent distances.

Inches to Centimetres

1 in	2.54 cm
2 in	5.08 cm
3 in	7.62 cm
4 in	10.16 cm
5 in	12.70 cm
6 in	15.24 cm
7 in	17.78 cm
8 in	20.32 cm
9 in	22.86 cm
10 in	25.40 cm
20 in	50.80 cm
30 in	76.20 cm
40 in	101.60 cm
50 in	127.00 cm
60 in	152.40 cm
70 in	177.80 cm
80 in	203.20 cm
90 in	228.60 cm
100 in	254.00 cm

Feet to Metres

1 ft	0.30 m
2 ft	0.61 m
3 ft	0.91 m
4 ft	1.22 m
5 ft	1.52 m
6 ft	1.83 m
7 ft	2.13 m
8 ft	2.44 m
9 ft	2.74 m
10 ft	3.05 m
20 ft	6.10 m
30 ft	9.14 m
40 ft	12.19 m
50 ft	15.24 m
60 ft	18.29 m
70 ft	21.34 m
80 ft	24.38 m
90 ft	27.43 m
100 ft	30.48 m

Yards to Metres

1 yd	0.91 m
2 yd	1.83 m
3 yd	2.74 m
4 yd	3.66 m
5 yd	4.57 m
6 yd	5.49 m
7 yd	6.40 m
8 yd	7.32 m
9 yd	8.23 m
10 yd	9.14 m
20 yd	18.29 m
30 yd	27.43 m
40 yd	36.58 m
50 yd	45.72 m
60 yd	54.86 m
70 yd	64.00 m
80 yd	73.15 m
90 yd	82.30 m
100 yd	91.44 m

Miles to Kilometres

1 mile	1.61 km
2 miles	3.22 km
3 miles	4.83 km
4 miles	6.44 km
5 miles	8.05 km
6 miles	9.66 km
7 miles	11.27 km
8 miles	12.87 km
9 miles	14.48 km
10 miles	16.09 km
20 miles	32.19 km
30 miles	48.28 km
40 miles	64.37 km
50 miles	80.47 km
60 miles	96.56 km
70 miles	112.65 km
80 miles	128.75 km
90 miles	144.84 km
100 miles	160.93 km

Tree Growth Factors

Tree species	Growth factor
Green ash	4.0
White ash	5.0
Aspen	2.0
American beech	6.0
European beech	4.0
Basswood	3.0
European white birch	5.0
River birch	3.5
Paper birch (aka White)	5.0
Yellow buckeye	5.0
Black cherry	5.0
Kentucky coffee tree	3.0
Cottonwood	2.0
Dogwood	7.0
American elm	4.0
Douglas fir	5.0
White fir	7.5
Shagbark hickory	7.5
Common horse chestnut	8.0
Ironwood	7.5
Littleleaf linden	3.0
Black maple	5.0

Tree species	Growth factor
Red maple	4.5
Norway maple	4.5
Silver maple	3.0
Sugar maple	5.5
Pin oak	3.0
Northern red oak	4.0
Scarlet oak	4.0
Shingle oak	6.0
Shumard oak	3.0
White oak	5.0
Bradford pear	3.0
Austrian pine	4.5
Red pine	5.5
Scotch pine	3.5
White pine	5.0
Tulip poplar (tulip tree)	3.0
Redbud	7.0
Colorado blue spruce	4.5
Norway spice	5.0
Sweetgum	4.0
American sycamore	4.0
Black walnut	4.5

For instructions on how to use these, please see page 207.

The World's Top Twenty Highest Mountains

Always got your head in the clouds? While you're up there, take a look at these twenty monster mountains. They're the highest in the world.

Rank	Name	Height in metres (feet)	Range	Summited
1	Mount Everest Sagarmatha Chomolungma	8,848 (29,029)	Mahalangur Himalaya	1953
2	K2	8,611 (28,251)	Baltoro Karakoram	1954
3	Kangchenjunga	8,586 (28,169)	Kangchenjunga Himalaya	1955
4	Lhotse	8,516 (27,940)	Mahalangur Himalaya	1956
5	Makalu	8,485 (27,838)	Mahalangur Himalaya	1955
6	Cho Oyu	8,188 (26,864)	Mahalangur Himalaya	1954
7	Dhaulagiri I	8,167 (26,795)	Dhaulagiri Himalaya	1960
8	Manaslu	8,163 (26,781)	Manaslu Himalaya	1956
9	Nanga Parbat	8,126 (26,660)	Nanga Parbat Himalaya	1953
10	Annapurna I	8,091 (26,545)	Annapurna Himalaya	1950
11	Gasherbrum I Hidden Peak K5	8,080 (26,510)	Baltoro Karakoram	1958
12	Broad Peak	8,051 (26,414)	Baltoro Karakoram	1957

Rank	Name	Height in metres (feet)	Range	Summited
13	Gasherbrum II K4	8,035 (26,362)	Baltoro Karakoram	1956
14	Shishapangma Gosainthan	8,027 (26,335)	Jugal Himalaya	1964
15	Gyachung Kang	7,952 (26,089)	Mahalangur Himalaya	1964
S	Gasherbrum III K3a	7,946 (26,070)	Baltoro Karakoram	1975
16	Annapurna II	7,937 (26,040)	Annapurna Himalaya	1960
17	Gasherbrum IV K3	7,932 (26,024)	Baltoro Karakoram	1958
18	Himalchuli	7,893 (25,896)	Manaslu Himalaya	1960
19	Distaghil Sar	7,884 (25,866)	Hispar Karakoram	1960
20	Ngadi Chuli	7,871 (25,823)	Manaslu Himalaya	1979

World Scout Jamborees

These are large international Scout camps that take place every four years, except in exceptional circumstances, such as during the Second World War (1939–45) and 1979, when the Jamboree was cancelled due to the Iranian Revolution.

Year	Event	Location	Host country	Theme/Name
1920	1st World Scout Jamboree	London	United Kingdom	Develop World Peace
1924	2nd World Scout Jamboree	Ermelunden	Denmark	World Citizenship
1929	3rd World Scout Jamboree	Arrowe Park, Upton, Birkenhead	United Kingdom	Coming of Age
1933	4th World Scout Jamboree	Gödöllő	Hungary	Face New Adventures
1937	5th World Scout Jamboree	Bloemendaal	Netherlands	Lead Happy Lives
1947	6th World Scout Jamboree	Moisson	France	Jamboree of Peace
1951	7th World Scout Jamboree	Bad Ischl	Austria	Jamboree of Simplicity
1955	8th World Scout Jamboree	Niagara-on-the-Lake, Ontario	Canada	New Horizons
1957	9th World Scout Jamboree	Sutton Park, Warwickshire	United Kingdom	50th Anniversary of Scouting
1959	10th World Scout Jamboree	Los Baños, Laguna	Philippines	Building Tomorrow Today
1963	11th World Scout Jamboree	Marathon	Greece	Higher and Wider
1967	12th World Scout Jamboree	Farragut State Park, Idaho	United States	For Friendship

Year	Event	Location	Host country	Theme/Name
1971	13th World Scout Jamboree	Fujinomiya, Shizuoka	Japan	For Understanding
1975	14th World Scout Jamboree	Lillehammer	Norway	Five Fingers, One Hand
1979	(15th World Scout Jamboree)	Nishapur	Iran	Cancelled due to Iranian Revolution
1983	15th World Scout Jamboree	Kananaskis, Alberta	Canada	The Spirit Lives On
1987–1988	16th World Scout Jamboree	Sydney	Australia	Bringing the World Together
1991	17th World Scout Jamboree	Seoraksan National Park	South Korea	Many Lands, One World
1995	18th World Scout Jamboree	Dronten	Netherlands	Future is Now
1998–1999	19th World Scout Jamboree	Picarquín	Chile	Building Peace Together
2002–2003	20th World Scout Jamboree	Sattahip	Thailand	Share our World, Share our Cultures
2007	21st World Scout Jamboree	Chelmsford, Essex	United Kingdom	One World, One Promise Scouting's Centenary
2011	22nd World Scout Jamboree	Kristianstad	Sweden	Simply Scouting
2015	23rd World Scout Jamboree	Kirarahama, Yamaguchi	Japan	A Spirit of Unity
2019	24th World Scout Jamboree	Glen Jean, West Virginia	United States	Unlock a New World
2023	25th World Scout Jamboree	Saemangeum (Buan County)	South Korea	Draw Your Dream
2027	26th World Scout Jamboree	Gdańsk	Poland	Bravely

Emergency postcards

Use these to cheer someone up, let someone know you're safe or ask for help.

The Spare Page

Use this page in case you need to light a fire in an emergency. (Go on, you can tear it if you don't have any scissors, it's an emergency after all!)

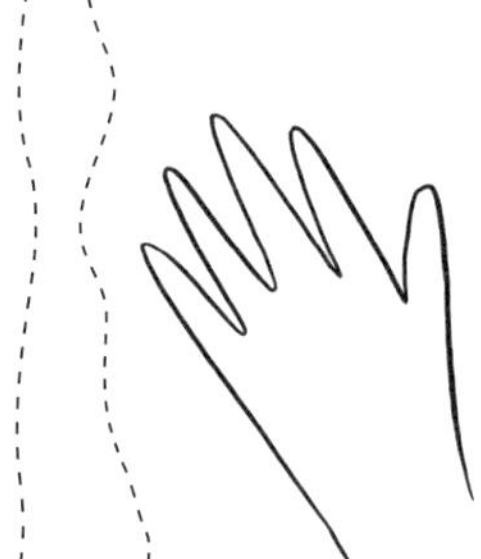

The Other Spare Page

(If you're going to burn the other side, you may as well burn this one too!)

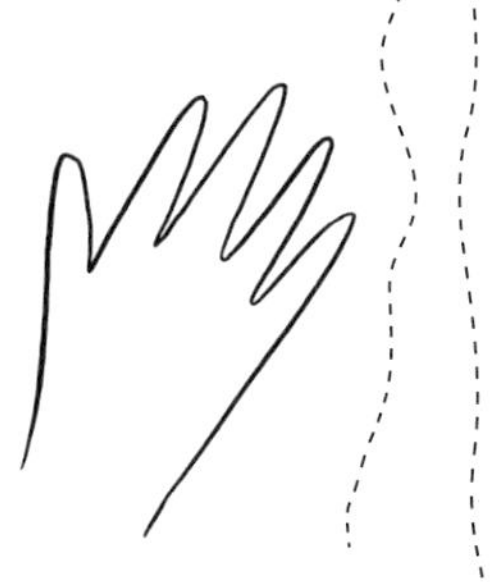

The Final Word

Looking back is all about looking forward.

When I look back on my life, what's made me most proud? I'll give you a clue. It isn't anything to do with Everest, or the Special Forces, or any expedition or TV adventure I've had. All those things come and go and pass. For me, the thing I am most proud of is much bigger, much more important. It was becoming Britain's youngest ever Chief Scout in 2009, and then taking on the global role of Chief Ambassador of World Scouting.

When I took on those challenges, I knew that ahead would be a mountain of a different kind to climb.

Looking ahead, I had a clear goal: to try to serve and be there for the nearly half a million UK Scouts and the many dedicated teams of volunteers who give so much to make life better for young people. And to serve, support and encourage the 57 million Scouts around the globe.

What bigger challenge is there than that?

Scouts is all about potential. Helping young people to grow into their future, equipped and empowered. With the right skills, values and friendships.

When I'm asked what makes a Scout, I say this: Scouts show courage, kindness, resilience, friendship and self-reliance. They live these qualities in all times and in all places. This is what sets Scouts apart. We do our best. We are prepared for life and prepared for adventure. We hold our heads up high and our hearts on our sleeves.

These are the qualities that I value most in life. These are also the qualities that together we call character, which drives success in whatever we choose to do in life.

Scouting is always humbling because every day I get to meet real heroes. Scouts are doing things I never did when I was their age. They are helping flood victims, running food banks and going on expeditions to the South Pole. Their vision and courage is incredible.

I used to think that part of my job as Chief Scout was to inspire them. It turned out they're the ones who all along have been inspiring me. When I see Scouts receiving their many, hard-earned awards, I feel a sense of pride that is hard to quantify.

As a movement, we're about changing lives. There's a world of adventure and opportunity out there, and as a Scout it's yours to live. Because Scouts always believe that anything's possible when we put our heart to it.

When Scouts ask me for advice, I always say this: be grateful, be kind, be determined.

We have so much to be thankful for, not only our precious planet but the people in this great movement of ours.

We have so much we can do. We all have twenty-four hours in each day. But it's how we use them that counts. When we reach the end of our lives and look back, those who've used their time wisely, kindly and resolutely will leave a trail of great friendships, incredible adventures and endless good deeds.

That's our goal as Scouts.

So dream big and walk humbly. We are all on this journey through life together, and as Scouts, let's aim to shine a positive light as we navigate our path.

Which leads me back to what we call the Scouting spirit. The right place to end this book.

Scouting spirit is hard to describe, but you know it when you see it. It's about helping others, sharing skills and seeing the best in people. It's about looking up when others are feeling down. It's a word of encouragement and a hand on a shoulder. It's what has helped teams win gold medals and it's what has put people on the moon.

Take pride in your Scouting spirit. It will accompany you all through your life. It will be a strength at times of struggle and it will be a source of comfort in moments of fear.

Your Scouting spirit, your Scouting light, can never go out.

So let it shine!

Bear Grylls
Chief Ambassador of World Scouting

Acknowledgements

This book truly wouldn't have been possible without an incredible team, and nowhere is teamwork more visible and needed than in the great worldwide family that is found in Scouting.

First up, I want to acknowledge the humble, brilliant, dedicated service and writing of Chris James at UK Scouts. It's his vision, sensitivity and insight that has been such a huge part of putting this book together. He has always put young people at the forefront of every statement and value, target and endeavour, and I couldn't admire him more.

Likewise, Matt Hyde, CEO of UK Scouts, who has guided, steered, persevered and wisely navigated so many complex issues, as well as visionary campaigns. He has been, above all, a true friend beside me on my journey as Chief Scout, and he has always passed the credit on, when in truth it was his to claim. Matt embodies all the courageous qualities of a great leader and has represented the Scouts with huge compassion and care at every turn.

Thank you also to the unstoppable Simon Carter for many years' support, wisdom and insight heading up the external communications for UK Scouts. Not to mention Andrew Thorp and the team for endless good humour and hard work on all Scouts' behalf. And of course, to Caroline Michel, and Andy Lyon at Hodder, for believing in the power of this book.

I'd also like to thank Carl Hankinson, UK Chief Commissioner for his wisdom and leadership, along with the UK leadership team who show so much dedication and service.

A huge thank you also to our Scouts Ambassadors who use their profile and energy to open so many opportunities for our young people. What you give is genuine legacy to those who most need it, and we love and admire you more than you will ever know.

Special thanks and admiration goes to Ahmad Alhendawi, Secretary General of the World Organization of the Scout Movement, for such humble, inspirational and committed leadership. Being front and centre and navigating the politics of a global organisation of some 57 million Scouts is no mean feat, yet you do it with grace and wisdom. Always brilliantly supported by Dave Venn and Annie Weaver, you all make such a formidable team.

Our roles together continue, and as Chief Ambassador of World Scouting, I have a feeling we are only just getting going!

Finally, and perhaps most of all, I'd like to thank every volunteer who shares their time and talents so kindly and freely to support young people in your communities. It's your generosity that makes Scouting possible. You're the great shining lights.

Thank you all. This truly is your book. Our book. Together.